D0651790

They Lived to Tell the Tale

The Explorers Club Classics Series

Volume I: *As Told at The Explorers Club: More Than Fifty Gripping Tales of Adventure* edited by George Plimpton

Volume II: *The Worst Journey in the World: Antarctic 1910–1913* by Apsley Cherry-Garrard, with an introduction by Paul Theroux

Volume III: *Famous First Flights That Changed History: Sixteen Dramatic Adventures* by Lowell Thomas and Lowell Thomas Jr., with a foreword by Buzz Aldrin

Explorers Club Books

Some Like It Cold: Arctic and Antarctic Expeditions by Neville Shulman

Arctic Sun on My Path: The True Story of America's Last Great Polar Explorer by Willie Knutsen and Will C. Knutsen

House of Tears: Westerners' Adventures in Islamic Lands by Dr. John Hughes

The Moonshine Mule: A 2,700-Mile Walk from Mexico to Manhattan by Tom Fremantle

They Lived to Tell the Tale

TRUE STORIES OF MODERN ADVENTURE FROM THE LEGENDARY EXPLORERS CLUB

Edited and with an Introduction by Jan Jarboe Russell

THE LYONS PRESS
Guilford, Connecticut
AN IMPRINT OF THE GLOBE PEQUOT PRESS

The Lyons Press is an imprint of The Globe Pequot Press

10 9 8 7 6 5 4 3 2 1

Printed in the United States of America

ISBN 978-1-59228-991-2
Library of Congress Cataloging-in-Publication Data is available on file.

Some spot images courtesy Photos.com
Part openers credit by Casey Shain

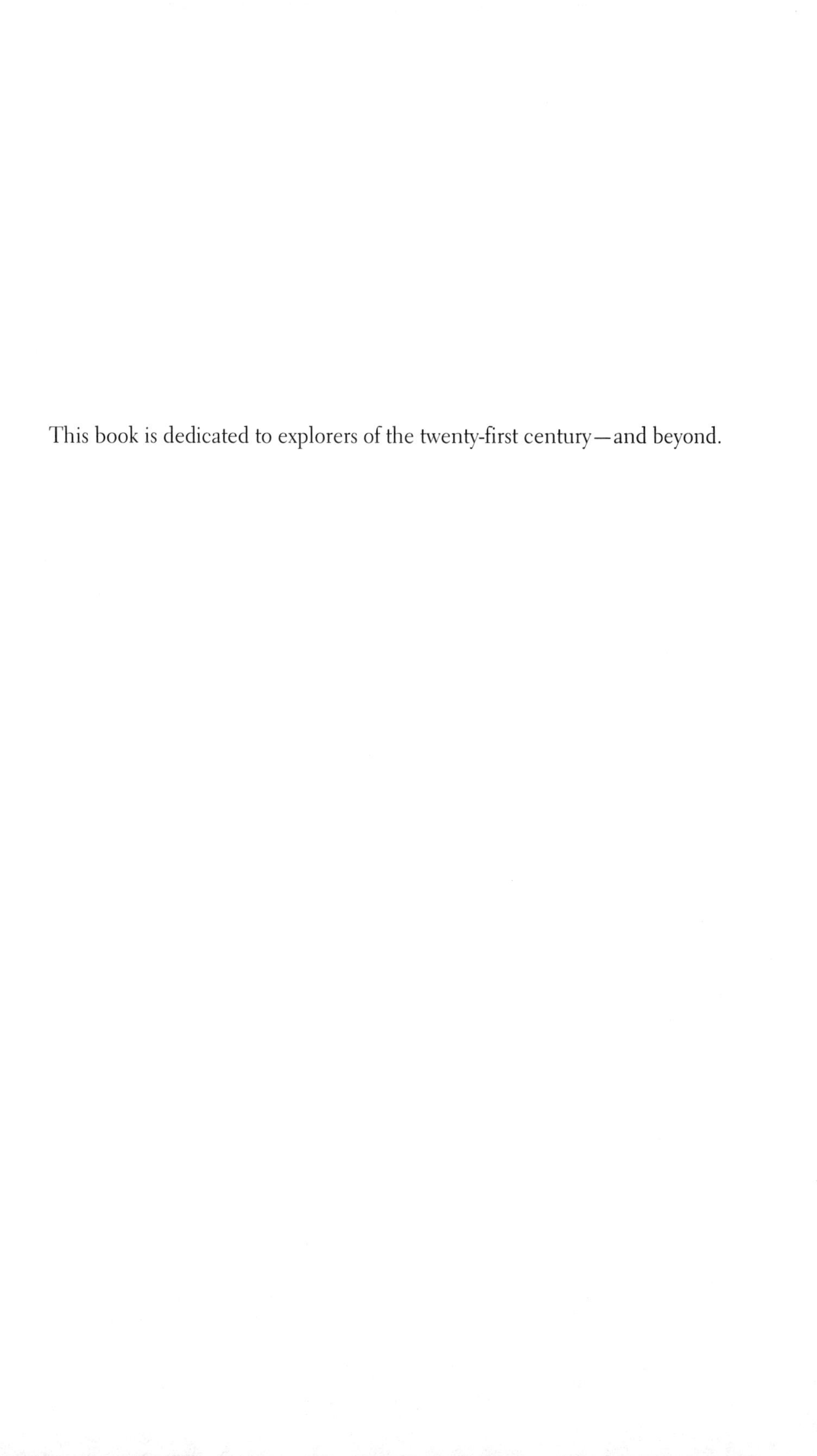

This book is dedicated to explorers of the twenty-first century—and beyond.

Contents

Acknowledgments

They Lived to Tell the Tale is the fourth book published under The Explorers Club imprint. It logically follows *As Told at The Explorers Club* (2003), edited by George Plimpton. Our vision of a book of tales by our current members is now a reality.

Gathering and editing stories from a worldwide membership might have been a colossal undertaking had it not been for the dedication of Explorers Club President Daniel Bennett, Club Secretary Catherine N. Cooke, editor Jan Jarboe Russell, and former Club President Richard Wiese.

The Explorers Club staff provided invaluable help and pitched in graciously. Thanks go to Clare Flemming, Curator of Research Collections, and Jeff Stolzer, Club Manager. At any given time, tracking down a member could mean he or she is in outer space, on an ocean floor, on top of a mountain, or at a pole. But the EC staff never gave up.

We continue to enjoy a rewarding collaboration with our publisher, The Lyons Press. Editor Holly Rubino, whose idea it was for The Explorers Club to publish this collection of tales, is to be thanked for her guidance and her patience.

Most of all, our membership is to be thanked for enthusiastically sharing their tales of risk, comradeship, and discovery. They have also shown that to go forth into the world is to ultimately find oneself. This book is an outstanding reflection of all the diverse personalities and extraordinary experiences of the members of The Explorers Club.

Lindley Kirksey Young
Chairman of the Book Committee
April 23, 2007
New York, New York

Catherine Nixon Cooke
Gary Hermalyn
Daniel Kobal
Milbry Polk
Ronald Rosner

Introduction

Inside the venerable headquarters of The Explorers Club, located at 46 East 70th Street in New York, lives a fat black-and-white cat named Shredder, which arrived at the club in 2003. He was brought in by an eagle-eyed caterer who noticed that the old, storied building was infested with mice in the basement. By day and by night, the fortunate cat roams the six-story, wood-paneled mansion, which houses, since 1904, the club of the major explorers in the world. Originally, Shredder was named "Sir Ed" in honor of Sir Edmund Hillary, the first mountaineer to reach the summit of Mount Everest. Over time the cat's grand name was shortened to "Shred." Then, after members of the club noticed how well the cat earned his keep as a fierce hunter, the name evolved to Shredder.

As Shredder silently stalks the nooks and crannies of the club, passing by the stuffed polar bear on his way to the library on the second floor, or curling up under the Long Table in the lecture hall near an imposing pair of elephant tusks, he no doubt eavesdrops on the tales of glory and adventure passed on by the members. But Shredder wisely holds his tongue. Fortunately, the forty-one members of the Explorers Club whose true-life stories of exploration appear in this book have not held theirs.

This is the latest volume in a series of Explorers Club books. The first volume of collected stories, *Told at The Explorers Club*, was published in 1931. A second, *Explorers Club Tales*, appeared four years later, and a third in 1941 was published under the spirited title *Through Hell and High Water*. The fourth volume, *As Told at The Explorers Club*, edited by George Plimpton, founder of *The Paris Review*, was published in 2003 in honor of the club's centennial celebration.

The present volume considers the present and future state of exploration, in contrast to other volumes that have drawn heavily from notable expeditions of the past. The book is titled *They Lived to Tell the Tale* because all the authors, twenty-first-century explorers and still living, did just that. In

1904, when The Explorers Club was founded, Theodore Roosevelt, the rugged, adventurous embodiment of Western exploration, was in the White House, a few explorers were determined to reach the North Pole, and many places on the Earth were still undiscovered. When Shredder's namesake, Sir Hillary, reached the top of Mount Everest in 1953, the New Zealand mountaineer was hailed as a conquering hero. Fast-forward to now. In a world where the globe itself has been reduced to an accessible sphere, and treks to Everest are unremarkable, what new stories capture the spirit of exploration?

What follows, the forty–one stories in this volume—nine of them by women explorers—express the complexity and challenges of exploration in the twenty-first century. Ours is a cynical age. Many people think there are few places left to explore, nothing new under the sun, no mysteries to solve. Yet the stories by these writers lead us to the opposite conclusion: today, 97 percent of the planet, much of it the ocean, is unexplored. These stories describe a new age of exploration, where advances in field research, scientific exploration, and the many uses of technology may help discover knowledge that will help sustain life on our planet. For instance, Margaret Lowman, a canopy biologist who climbs trees for a living, writes about all that we don't know about rain forests. "We do not know the commonest tree in South America," she says, "nor do we have any idea how many creatures live in a cubic feet of foliage." By discovering the secrets of the rain forests—one tree at a time—she and others are documenting critical connections in the planet's ecosystem.

In these stories, we are reminded of the grave risks of modern-day exploration. In his cautionary tale about what it was like to be the only physician on Mount Everest in 1996 when thirteen climbers lost their lives in a brutal snowstorm, Kenneth Kamler begins: "Huge, steep, cold, and windy, Mount Everest is the highest mountain in the world—and entirely indifferent to the fate of those who try to climb it."

There are tales of harrowing trouble in jungles, such as "Escape from Darien" by Cameron McPherson Smith and "How Not to Take a Jungle Bath" by James H. Powell; and thrilling sea adventures, such as "Seven

Miles Down" by Don Walsh and "Finding the *Oxford*" by Barry Clifford. The present volume contains no shortage of animal stories, some scientific, such as Jim Fowler's tagging of the condors in Peru, and others that describe Holy Grail adventures, such as Bobby Harrison's remarkable sighting of the ivory-billed woodpecker in an Arkansas bayou. In addition, there are sublime stories about the transpersonal dimension of exploration, such as "The Running of the Boundaries" by Wade Davies" and "The Elixir of the Spirit" by Robert "Rio" Hahn.

Often as I read the manuscripts, I wondered about the writer's motivations. What would entice a person such as Ranulph Fiennes to circumnavigate the polar axis of the Earth? The nineteenth-century answer—"Because it's there"—no longer satisfies, although it still exists. Fiennes expresses it in the opening line of his chapter, "Dictator or Democrat": "Nobody knows what lies ahead because nobody has been here before." Ambition then is part of it, but ambition alone is not enough to sustain the cause of exploration. As I made my way through stories from all corners of the globe—the deepest parts of the ocean and the heights of space—I discovered there are as many motivations as there are explorers. Some are motivated by the desire for knowledge, others by altruism. Some have traveled far in order to find themselves. For others, exploration is their livelihood; many, however, thrive on risk and are never more alive than when face-to-face with death.

However, in the end, I concluded that the writers whose work appears in this volume are a lot like Shredder, their mascot. They are motivated primarily by instinct—bred and born for exploration—and could no more stop doing it than Shredder could stop his daily hunt for mice. It's as if they had an exploration gene, an inbred propensity to reach for the unreachable and to search for scientific answers to the Earth's many mysteries. Who knows, someday some researcher might isolate the particular gene that drives explorers onward. For now, stories such as these will have to suffice as documentation of their deeds.

Storytelling is a vital part of everyday life of The Explorers Club. At the house in New York, members from all over the world gather among the relics of glorious expeditions of the past—the sledge used by Robert E. Peary's expedition to the North Pole in 1908–1909, flags carried on Thor Heyerdahl's voyage on the Kon-Tiki in 1947, a wax cylinder recording of Amelia Earhart, many animal trophies—and tell their own modern-day tales, thereby extending the cause of exploration and pondering the philosophical meaning behind it.

The original founders of the club stated their mission as follows: "Promote exploration by all possible means." At the end of this volume, Daniel Bennett, the current president, and two past presidents discuss why that mission is important for the future. In the past, exploration was in large part a mythical journey—individual heroes ventured forth into the unknown, carrying victorious flags into uncharted lands. In the future, voyages to places not yet fully known may yield scientific discoveries that help us understand—and protect—our collective life on this planet. The flags explorers carry into the future are for our common survival.

Jan Jarboe Russell
April 3, 2007
San Antonio, Texas

PART ONE

Chapter 1

On the Edge

ALISON M. JONES

On the African continent, I breathe deeply, stand tall, sweat profusely, and let winds tumbling down the escarpments blow my worries off into the sunset. For twenty years I've photographed and explored issues surrounding Africa's endangered species, cultures, and ecosystems. I believe these issues are inseparable. I've resisted narrowing my focus, instead concentrating on creating images with empathy, authenticity, and as much insight as possible.

While on assignment for nonprofit organizations, I've witnessed market-driven approaches successfully address rural poverty. Documenting species from lions to lion ants and from leopards to leopard tortoises, I've seen through the lens of my cameras the overlapping land needs of wildlife and exploding human populations.

Along the way, I've had plenty of adventures. I've feasted on roast oxen at a male circumcision ceremony where I was welcomed, because, as a white American, the Africans believed that I didn't count as a woman. I've climbed Kilimanjaro for conservation fund-raising, and with a strong push from a Masai friend, made that one agonizing stretch on Barranco Wall. I copiloted a Cessna round-trip from Nairobi to Cape Town for two months, and I photographed forests and waterways across nine countries. My takeoffs and flying were fine, but luckily I never had to land on any short dirt strip with elephants crossing.

Once in Kenya, while asking uncomfortable questions of a public official, scaly pattern of browns passed by my feet. The puff adder then slithered along the edge of the rock where I was photographing. I watched that dose of instant poison disappear and shakily downed a Tusker, although I hate beer. Others beasts have showed up from time to time. One night under netting on a dry riverbed, I awoke smelling cat urine. Drowsily opening my eyes, I watched a leopard circle me, leaving tracks, moon shadows, and me behind. In Ghana, two-legged beasts tracked me and menacingly kept phoning my hotel room.

As a conservation photographer, I've learned that successful journalism demands participation and often requires facing the twin edges of disaster and creativity. When on those edges, whether dangerous or philosophical, I've found unexpected reserves. Edges can be exclamations of existence. Without edges, there are no images. It is framing the images around edges that translate moments into permanence. Photographer Lisl Dennis claims that worthwhile photographs resemble sandwiches where the peanut butter and jelly are spread out to the very edge. Photographer Niall Benvie notes the lure of nature's edges, such as where water meets land. Edges evoke that vulnerability that we feel at the point of change. On the edge, our hearts beat loudest.

Africa is full of edges that push me to new purposes. In a middle channel of the Zambezi River, six of us were led out to the lip of Victoria Falls to an unimaginably still pocket of water. We realized that this could never happen in the litigious United States. There were no ropes or life vests to hold anyone who slipped. Shoulder-deep in warm water, less than two feet from plunging waters, I peered over the edge into a rainbow. From the edge, it was quiet. The thunder was below. The Zambezi's tumultuous waters, literally inches away, grabbed my spirit and seduced my soul. Momentarily, I felt pulled to tumble into its force.

Instead, I started thinking about how many of my photographs involved water: nongovernmental organizations drilling village wells, wildebeest migrating to rain-soaked plains, and girls with fistulas, stunted and crippled from having collected heavy buckets of water. Will Durant wrote, "Civilization is a stream with banks. The stream is sometimes filled with blood from people killing, stealing, shouting and doing the things historians usually record—while, on the banks, unnoticed, people build homes, make love, raise children, sing songs, write poetry, whittle statues." Perched on the edge of Victoria Falls, I decided to consciously focus on photographing the importance of water as a way to tell the story from both sides of the banks: the side recorded by historians and the side where people live their ordinary lives, unnoticed.

In search of this story, I enticed five friends to travel with me to Ethiopia. Less than a third of Ethiopia's sixty-seven million people have access to clean water. While Ethiopia's highlands are the water tower of Africa, feeding twelve major river systems and countless streams and lakes, recurrent droughts in Ethiopia's deserts affect millions. A country of beauty, danger, history, isolation, and mystery, Ethiopia is not quite of Africa, nor of Asia. Never colonized and perhaps now the least advanced African nation. Ethiopia is a country with its face turned inward. Despite the sheen of past glories reflected in a camel's eye and caught in shifting caftans, Ethiopia is mistrustful of outsiders. It was the perfect landscape to explore the importance of each drop of water.

Planning our five-week "Waters of Ethiopia" trip was like an easy jigsaw puzzle, but the trip itself got off to a rocky start. When I arrived at the airport in New York, I realized that I'd forgotten my cash, credit cards, checks, and plane ticket. Panic set in. How could I be responsible for others on the safari if I couldn't remember my own wallet? With only a passport, I convinced airport officials that I had paid for a ticket and even gained a sympathetic upgrade to business class. I quickly borrowed a phone and arranged to have my wallet FedExed to a safari mate who was traveling to Ethiopia five days later.

I arrived in Nairobi one day late; my luggage arrived three days after that. Penniless and wearing dirty clothes, I took refuge in the Mara Conservancy, where in 1921 Martin and Osa Johnson took famous photographs of the Mara's migration of wildebeest. In the conservancy, I camped in a tent surrounded by dusty clouds of wildebeest wandering to water. Each night I wakened to the bleating of wildebeest herds. Their bulk was bigger than my tent.

I traveled to Addis, where I met up with my safari mates, my luggage, and my wallet. Our trip seemed on track. However, problems immediately surfaced. The Hilton Hotel in Addis had no rooms for us. I was insistent that we needed rooms, and the hotel clerk took mercy on us and gave us no less than the Presidential Suite, which had nice beds and a dining room with seating for eighteen. That night, we counted our Ethiopian currency. Two birr equaled twenty-five cents, the cost of one photo, so we each had procured a one-hundred-cubic-inch block of single birr notes.

The next morning, we headed to Bale National Park in two shabby Toyota 4x4 vans. The Bale Mountains, kickoff to our water study, include twenty-five volcanic peaks over fourteen thousand feet punctuating an eleven-thousand-foot plateau the size of Britain. The potential of this catchment for 1.23 billion cubic feet of annual rain is immense, but mismanagement is creating disastrous water shortages in arid lowlands. After a visually dramatic, but wet, eleven-hour drive, we saw that early rains had washed out the road to our campsite. It was dark, cold, and raining. We were tired and had no backup lodging. Our drivers disappeared into the fog with soup ingredients to build a fire.

I went looking for a nearby home that occasionally served backpackers. I found a deserted house that had a metal fireplace and cots clustered five to a room. My friends and I slept tucked into our cots under moldy wool blankets. The next morning the sun burned through the mist as Menelik's bushbuck passed our balcony. Revitalized, we pony-trekked across the wet valley among herds of nyalas, tawny eagles, and wildflowers. Donkeys bearing firewood cut from the national park reminded us of the reality of Ethiopia's ecology. These villagers were desperate for warmth and fuel, but how long could they tap this resource? What are the effects of such deforestation? Similarly, water usage is growing twice as fast as Africa's populations, but there is no corresponding increase in water supplies. Who should control essential resources? Such questions fueled lively discussions that evening.

We left the next morning to travel across the Sanetti Plateau to photograph giant lobelia and russet-coated Simien wolves and visit the mossy Harenna

Forest. Finally, the trip felt on track. Assefa, our guide, was well schooled in Ethiopian and world history. Siyeum, our driver, was a knowledgeable birder. These were important elements of our safari, as Ethiopia's rotten roads took hours longer to negotiate than maps suggested.

However, a couple of days later, I noticed that our usually ebullient driver, Siyeum, seemed fatigued and had an offensive body odor. He complained of headaches and devoured my supply of Advil. He determinedly kept going, but when he removed his shirt and unzipped his pants to cool off, I became worried. I insisted he see a doctor, knowing Angola alone had 125,000 cases of malaria that year, resulting in over 11,000 deaths. The next morning Assefa assured me Siyeum had proper tablets and was better. I put myself in the front seat of Siyeum's car. He looked fresher and apologized for being sick.

We cheerfully set out, noting migratory birds cruising flyways over Rift Valley lakes. We were shocked to see more livestock than wildlife. Birds seem immune to Africa's struggle for land. From village to village, Siyeum drove carefully around sharp, newly paved curves, a relief from previous drives down Nech Sar National Park's muddy escarpment roads. In Konso, our last stop, residents mobbed us, shouting "Farenji, birr!" (Foreigners, money!) They were so aggressive that we couldn't see the village, examine its unique totems, or photograph the people. Quickly escaping, we headed to Jinka, where we would bid adieu to our drivers and begin our boat trip down the Omo River into Lake Turkana.

As Siyeum quietly drove on, I focused on photographic challenges. Could I avoid exploitative portraits of villagers? Could my images evoke empathy for such distant peoples? Then there were specific problems, unique to each village. For instance, could I document traditional bull jumping among the Hamar-Koke people without dismissing the difficulties they face today? Would the patterns of Karo body painting conceal today's alcoholism in their communities?

Suddenly, the car veered across the road. A large fig tree loomed. I looked at Siyeum and my heart stopped. He was in a coma. The car sped to the edge of an embankment. A split second later, the car skidded twenty feet down, yet somehow stayed upright. None of us were injured, but Siyeum appeared to be dying. His eyes rolled back into his head, he was vomiting green bile. He had yellow fever, a disease spread by mosquitoes that breed in standing water. Diseases from unsanitary water kill five million to twelve million people yearly. This indirect cause of our accident was an unanticipated aspect of our water study. Siyeum hung on the edge of death for another week but ultimately survived. Later, Assefa quietly confessed that during our trip, Siyeum never saw a doctor. To maintain an appearance of health, he took homeopathic tablets that he bought on the roadside.

On the edge of that road, I reconsidered gripping adventure tales. African snakes, floods, a leopard, and thieves had provided adrenaline-charged stories. But our Ethiopia accident was more than a moment of chance or a "mark of incompetence." Africa is a continent of dire issues.

Our Omo River excursion presented additional water concerns. Maize fields replaced Cape mahogany trees that had stabilized steep riverbanks. Illegal fishermen poached Nile perch. AIDS, alcohol, and AK-47s were also problems. People and entire villages are dying. Ethiopia's withering, ancient cultural roots, anchored by some of the world's largest lakes and longest rivers, carry the message that there is not enough clean, freshwater to quench Africa's thirst.

Many water images are still magical. Sunshine still spills over the edge of the Ngorongoro Crater rim after it bathes Kilimanjaro in light. Water still tumbles over the edge of Victoria Falls. But glaciers melt. Deforestation erodes topsoil, and the silt from rivers kills lakes. Three hundred million Africans live in water-scarce environments. Nairobi slum dwellers tap into wastewater mains. Paraphrasing Humphrey Bogart's comment from *Casablanca*, one thing is obvious: our peril on the edge of that road in Ethiopia doesn't amount to a hill of beans compared to the daily struggles of millions of Africans.

• • •

Alison M. Jones is a conservation photographer currently documenting watersheds of Africa and North American for her nonprofit project "No

Water No Life." Focusing on the connections between wildlife, culture, and ecosystems, she uses her photography to publicize environmental issues raised by data from scientists and watershed stakeholders. With an honorary masters degree in photography from Brooks Institute, she is a fellow of the International League of Conservation Photographers; a member of The Explorers Club, the North American Nature Photography Association, the American Society of Media Photographers and TechnoServe; and a founding supporter of Kenya's Mara Conservancy. Her images, published in numerous books, magazines, and other media and widely exhibited, can be viewed at www.alisonjonesphoto.com.

Chapter 2

Retracing Alexander's Footsteps

MILBRY C. POLK

The sandy plain stretched forever under an ominous sky. I strained my eyes for signs of a trail—a stray hoofprint, ashes of a campfire—but I could see nothing. We had lost our way. My camel trudged on, casting frequent glances at my guide stick. Pulling my woolen shawl tighter against the wind, I turned in my saddle to look behind us. What I saw chilled me even further. Out on the Egyptian desert, we were about to be engulfed by a sandstorm.

The sky darkened. A tidal wave of sand rushed toward us. "Ride for the mound ahead!" our guide yelled. Before we could make it, the wall enveloped us.

Sand filled my nose and mouth, stung my eyes, and burned my skin. We rode. No mound materialized. Shouting above the wind, the guide ordered us to stop. We forced our camels down, tying their knees together and looping the ropes around their necks to keep them couched. If they wandered away now, we might never find them.

The guide pulled out a sheet of plastic, spread it on the ground, ringed the edge with stones, propped up the front with his camel stick and crawled inside. At the entrance, he hollowed out a deep pit. My cousin and I fought the wind to reach the camels and fetch the tea tin, sugar, kettle, cups, brushwood, and a jerrican of water. It had been six days since the last well. Our camels, going waterless, showed signs of distress. One young male had to be unloaded completely, forcing us to abandon gear.

The well we had hoped to find from our maps had sanded in years ago. Because we had lost the trail, we were several days from another probable water site. But how far we had wandered and in which direction was still unknown. Fighting my way back to the plastic shelter, I saw my companions huddled in tight balls against the wind. Our guide was clapping his hands and singing, "Praise God. We will be with Him soon."

This confrontation with nature occurred eighteen days out on a twenty-five-day camel safari from Siwa Oasis in western Egypt through the desert, along the ridge of the Qattara Depression, across the plains, and finally arriving at a monastery in Wadi el-Natroun in the Nile Valley—a harsh journey of seven hundred kilometers. We were tracing the route of Alexander the Great, who in 331 BC probably took the same course from Siwa along the Qattara trail to the pharaonic capital of Memphis, near Cairo. Alexander had made the pilgrimage to free himself of debts from the past and accept his fate. He asked the priests if he had avenged the murder of his father, Philip. They answered that his father could never die as Alexander was the son of the god Zeus Ammon, but they also told him that Alexander had avenged Philip. Freed by the oracles' pronouncements, Alexander was then deemed a god and allowed to accept the crown of the Egyptian pharaohs in Memphis. Retracing his footsteps was the inspiration of our journey.

To see the past, we must live it. And doing that meant traveling by camel; sleeping in ancient camps; losing gear, which fell alongside Roman water jars; stepping lightly through the active minefields of an old war; eating with a forgotten people whose speech and mannerisms brought to life brittle museum parchments; and learning, finally, to look at the world through ancient eyes.

My interest in this part of the world began while I was writing a college thesis on symbolic design in Egyptian architecture. Although I had traveled extensively in Egypt, I had missed Siwa—an oasis that captured my imagination and continued to haunt me. In January 1979, I resolved to go there.

Our group consisted of my cousin, Margaret Lorenz, and her husband, Douglas Griffes, whom I invited for their compatibility, as well as for Margaret's familiarity with medicine and Douglas's with navigation. The others were Ibrahim el Shayeb, an Egyptian architect; Ibrahim Helmi, field supervisor for the U.S. Naval Medical Research Unit 3 in Cairo (who spent the journey collecting ticks for research); and three Bedouin: Belhaq, our guide, who was a dead ringer for Anthony Quinn; his friend Meshayt; and Mohammad, who was fascinated by our tape recorder and gaped open-mouthed at the novelty of Western women.

After eight months of cooling my heels in Cairo, where the formidable bureaucracy thwarted my every turn, I finally received permission for our group to travel through the politically tense Western Desert (relations with Libya were strained). But at least the delay gave us a better traveling month: December's rains would bring more greens for the camels to eat.

For the last several years, Siwa has been a trading center for caravans traversing the North African desert. Siwa's language, like its people, is a mixture of Bedouin, Berber, black African, and southern European. Squeezed between the sea to the north and the Qattara Depression to the south, Siwa was regarded as a prize during World War II. The British and Germans fought a desperate war in that area, the most famous battle of which was El Alamein. Siwa's strategic importance is clear today as well, given its proximity to both Israel and Libya.

The Western Desert is harsh. Only those with a specific purpose go there: geologists looking for oil and minerals, the military, police, and a few nomadic inhabitants. Because borders are closed, Siwa is empty of traders. It is a shame that archaeologists have rarely worked in Siwa. Valuable information is lost there under the picks of grave robbers and the casual destruction of temples by house builders.

Siwa is a depression where many springs surface. Each spring inspires a pocket of green palms around it—some springs are large enough to support small villages. Beyond Siwa stretch endless vistas of hard-packed gravel plains. To the south lie treacherous sand seas whose windstorms have swallowed whole caravans. The hapless Army of Cambyses fell to such a fate in 525 BC on its way to conquer Siwa.

When we purchased our gear in Cairo, we dismissed most modern necessities since the trip was, in part, a re-creation of the past. All of us wanted to experience a way of life that is over in Egypt—and all for different reasons. For the Americans, the trip was a history lesson and the ultimate in outdoor rigors. For the Bedouin, it meant stepping back into the tales of their grandfathers. The Egyptians viewed the trip as a way to come to grips with the split in their culture between living in a modern world but being surrounded by the desert and the past.

A camel snorted. A pan knocked against a stone. Someone swore. Predawn. Instantly awake, I slowly unzipped my sleeping bag and shivered against the tide of chilled air. I sat up and pulled a second robe over my shoulders. I had brought only the clothing of the desert: two ankle-length cotton robes, two pairs of cotton riding pants that tapered to a tight-fitting ankle, a sweater, and head scarves to protect against heat and sand.

In the faint light, I made out the shapes of couched camels, our packs and saddles strewn over the sand. Near the food packs, a figure snapped apart twigs that had been scrounged the day before for the morning fire. I wanted to linger in my sleeping bag and wait for the morning tea. But remembering the chaos of the previous morning, I roused myself to organize my gear.

The day was soon full upon us. Saddling the beasts, hauling water and heavy packs to the camels, tying them on, cooking and eating breakfast, roping fallen packs, and gathering the odds and ends of camp life took three hours. Finally the camels were loaded, standing unhobbled and waiting for the lead bull to start walking. Taking one last look around, we smelled a powerful sweet odor, like that of a rotting animal. The source was Umak, our second bull. His neck was infested with hundreds of fat, wriggling maggots. The ropes that held Umak down in the truck had cut his skin, flies in Siwa had laid eggs, and now Umak bore the horrible results.

"Ibrahim, get some soapy water. Mohammad, hold Umak's head so he doesn't bite me," yelled Margaret. My cousin unpacked the medical kit and took command. While we held the camel, she flushed out the maggots and cut away the putrefying skin. Such challenges soon put everyone's special talents to use.

Camels can survive in an environment where no other domesticated animal can. They have the capability to use about 95 percent of the water they drink. Humans only use about 12 percent. A camel will keep moving until it is ready to die—an asset that I am sure has saved many travelers' lives. Finally, camels cross terrains that still daunt the mechanized traveler. Without camels, crossing the sebkha floor of the Qattara would have been impossible.

Sebkha is a salty, dried-mud crust of varying thickness that covers a pockmarked earth. Heavy vehicles are particularly susceptible to breaking through it. In World War II, Rommel's army tried to make a dash for Cairo across the Qattara but was stopped by a fatal combination of sebkha and Allied bombs. For us, too, the danger was real. A camel could plunge through the crust into a hole, possibly breaking its leg. Since our food and water were carefully distributed among our ten camels, losing even one of them would have been disastrous.

Back in Cairo, we made our own saddles with the help of an eighty-year-old carpenter who specialized in traditional Islamic furniture. We turned coils of fire hose into girths, muzzles, and strappings. In a slaughterhouse, we bought fresh goatskin to sheathe the sharp nubs of the saddles. But in the desert, every step of my camel rocked the wooden saddle pommel against the inside of my chronically raw leg. The animal's constant swaying made my lower back ache. Even the pillows we had made to soften the ride were soon worn thin against the unyielding wood of the saddle frame.

The trail was full of useful treasures, notably the thirty-six-year-old debris of the Desert War. An old German water bottle became a rolling pin on bread-baking days. A slab of airplane fuselage was our grill. The petrified wood of an ancient forest and the sand dollars of an ancient sea lined our fire pits. We, too, added to the litter of the trail. I particularly regretted losing the stump of an English telephone pole that had taken a lot of effort to dig up for firewood.

One serious problem was our lack of accurate information about the trail. Our maps were pre–World War II. Anything more recent was classified and unavailable to us. Supposedly reliable sources assured us that certain wells contained sweet water, but most of those turned out to have been dry since Roman times. Luckily, we found one new spring inside the Qattara. It was the only water available to us in a thirteen-day stretch.

Days passed. My face became the color of sand and my lips cracked under the relentless winds. Camp was determined by the presence of greens so the camels could graze, and every night was a struggle to get the camels couched and unloaded. Often I failed to tie my camel down tight enough; with a gurgle she would clamber to her feet and lurch toward the greens. I had to grab my stick and beat her down again, holding off the angry jaws as I wound the rope around her knobby knees. As soon as her packs and saddle hit the sand, I raised her and hobbled her two forefeet, allowing her to hop away to graze. Then I set up my camp. The saddle served as a windbreak, while a cushion or two under the sleeping back provided some relief from the gravel plain.

Before the trip, I had repacked my bag at least ten times, eliminated unnecessary items. When I left Siwa I thought I had the bare minimum for a month in the desert. But three weeks out I realized that over half of the gear, such as extra T-shirts and socks, remained untouched in my bag. Other items, like the thermometer, had broken early on, or like my hair clips, were lost and only briefly missed. The demands of the trail quickly erased trivial worries. The great lesson of the desert is that the most important things are those you carry inside you: knowledge of your surroundings, of yourself, and of your strengths and limits—and how to make do on nothing.

At home in New York I had known the loneliness of the crowd. But one of the attractions of the desert was to experience real solitude and face its awesome solemnity. In reading earlier desert accounts, I had been impressed by the intensity of relationships on the trail. We, too, experienced a similar intensity. Seemingly trivial incidents could give rise to murderous anger, such as when one companion decided to become attuned to the environment by watching the sunset while the rest of us struggled to set up camp. But we had to rely on each other for the day-to-day tasks of lifting and hauling, and the sharing and dependency provided a deep current of unspoken understanding between us all. Because of the deprivation, the desert imposes the necessity of leaning heavily on other people. Life in the city, on the other hand, demands isolation.

This understanding did not always come easily. We had to overcome not only individual personality barriers, but cultural ones as well. Since none of us had traveled the route before, and some of us were unfamiliar with the demands of camel travel, our patience and understanding were stretched to the limit. This was apparent during our discussions over our route. The Bedouin resorted to memory to guide us—a memory expressed through songs. Music, then, was a kind of map. Listening to Meshayt sing of the Bedouin families killed on raids in the past century in these places conjured up their ghosts. An inaccurate song, however, could be fatal.

The second day out we took our first "shortcut." After days of roaming the high plateaus, Belhaq admitted he was lost. Clearly we needed more than memory to guide us. When we became desperate, a military helicopter appeared on the horizon. It buzzed us several times in a hostile manner and finally landed in a swirl of sand, disgorging paratroopers. In seconds we were surrounded and found ourselves looking down the barrels of submachine guns. We'd been mistaken for a band of terrorists. Some fast-talking Egyptians saved us from being blown away by a diligent army. The commander angrily told us we were far off the trail. Before leaving, however, he pointed out our direction and wished us better luck.

Doug, who had learned navigation in the navy, decided we could not rely on folklore to guide us. When we reached the second oasis of Qara, he got a fix and started to use his compass. The Bedouin regarded his methods with suspicion. After all, they thought of him as American and soft, not a person of the desert. The Egyptians were torn: they wanted to believe in the technology, but they also wanted to prove the superiority of inborn ability. Decisions were usually made in the midst of a crisis: the trail divides, but in which direction should we go? As distrustful as we were of mythical navigation and as distrustful as they were of the compass, we struggled to find solutions. Not everyone spoke English or Arabic. In the heat of the argument, tempers flared and usually did not cool off until the following morning.

In addition to getting lost and facing sandstorms and squabbles, we also landed in a labyrinth of old minefields. On the ridge of the Qattara

Depression, our trail skirted lethal bomb craters, more treacherous than quicksand, left over from World War II. We hugged old tank and camel tracks to guide us through the deadly fields. "War is good," our guide, Belhaq said, enigmatically. "Before the Europeans fought, we had nothing." But after the war, it was a different story—a gold mine. Guns and ammunition were there for the taking. The women found jerricans, tent pegs, and strips of metal for domestic use. Everyone was clothed in the muddy and often bloodstained greens and browns of the army.

But it was a gold mine with a price. To get to the prize, the Bedouin had to cross battlefields. Mines had been laid, indiscriminately, in the millions on both sides. Belhaq said he had lost relatives and friends in the minefield. In any gathering of Bedouin it was not uncommon to see a number of them with missing limbs—lost reaching for the gifts of war.

The last week of our journey was marked by fierce sandstorms and rainstorms. We had left the ridge and were crossing a flat, sandy plain dotted with green that led into Wadi el-Natroun—our destination. We were headed toward the Monastery of Baramus, standing in the desert like an anchored ship at sea.

I watched the last morning's sunrise through a filter of sand. The branches of the protective palm whipped around in the wind like bird feathers. In twenty-five days the jerricans had been refilled four times, no serious injuries had befallen us, the camels were all alive, if a bit straggly and humpless because they had drained their stores of water, and our food could easily last another week—another week of rice, beans, dried soup, wormy dates, tomato paste, and onions. Still I wanted to stay, to draw out the little time left. Every fiber of my body was in tune with the desert, the camels, and my companions. Rebellions of earlier days were one. Instead of racing to my book in odd moments, I wandered off from the camp to sit alone. I took delight in finding gazelle tracks, picking up strange stones, and laboriously embroidering my robe. This was it. I was content. Not even a hot shower could lure me away. But the Bedouin, perhaps more attuned to practical matters, drove us on. We had nearly run out of sugar. For them we carried two luxuries: cases of sugar lumps and cartons of cigarettes. As long as the sugar and cigarettes lasted, the Bedouin would go anywhere in any kind of weather.

We made a final quick breakfast of sandy brown beans and gritty tea. Bowing into the wind, we made our way to load the camels and walked out of our protective hollow into the full force of the storm. As we walked in single file, I tried to keep the bulk of the camel between me and the wind.

After several hours, Doug, consulting his compass, signaled that we were headed in the wrong direction. Everyone pulled up beside Belhaq for a route discussion. Mohammad, pulling two camels, dropped the ropes and ran to us. "No good ahead. Bad for camels. Must go that way," he yelled, jabbing his finger to the left. But Doug said the monastery was dead ahead. Helmi suggested that Mohammad was heading us toward a bad salt swamp. Outnumbered six to two, Mohammad sulkily pulled behind the train, occasionally trying to push up to the left. Finally a lull in the wind settled the sand, exposing the bulk of the monastery a few kilometers ahead.

The closer we got to the monastery, the farther Mohammad hung back. We called to him to come, but he angrily shook his head. Stumbling in exhaustion, we finally reached our destination. Beside the door a rope pull, connected to a bell, swung in the wind. Ibrahim grabbed the rope and pulled it several times. The wind carried off the peals. We took turns beating on the massive wooden doors. Half an hour later, the door opened a crack. A hooded figure peered out and promptly slammed the door. I heard a large bolt slide into the catch on the other side.

Slowly we realized how we looked—like filthy nomads, with our camels screaming and tossing behind us. The poor monk probably thought he had seen ghosts of desert pirates who once preyed on the monasteries. I looked up to the hole in the arch over the door, half expecting a ration of bread and water to be lowered in a bucket, as happened in ancient times. Turning around, I saw Mohammad; he was quaking as if he, too, had seen a ghost. I then understood why he had tried to take us off the path—he was frightened of the monks. Superstitions come easily and die hard in the desert.

At last the door opened, revealing several bearded, black-robed monks. They apologized for the rude welcome and ushered us into the guest room. A hot meal was brought in. But even fish and fresh tomatoes could not entice Mohammad in from the sandstorm. He took the camels two kilometers away to wait for us.

After gorging ourselves on the fresh vegetables, meat, and sweets, we bade farewell to the monks. Grasping the lead ropes, we pulled our camels along the last leg of our journey, toward a nearby village. For a brief moment I felt like the nomads of long ago who stopped on the outskirts of town to trade rather than enter and become tainted by city life. As our small group rode into Wadi el-Natroun, I could see in the eyes of the settled Bedouin the same look of wonder, trepidation, and reserve with which the city merchants had once greeted the desert traders. For one moment, as we had planned, we had all merged with the past.

• • •

Milbry C. Polk, a graduate of Harvard College, worked in several museums including the American Museum of Natural History with Margaret Mead, founded several film festivals, and is a photojournalist and an explorer, primarily in the Middle East and Asia. She is a fellow of the Royal Geographical Society and The Explorers Club. Polk is the author of nine books including *Egyptian Mummies* (Dutton Children's Books, 1977); coauthor of *Women of Discovery* (Clarkson Potter, 2001), which recounts the accomplishments of women explorers during the past two thousand years; and *The Looting of the Iraq Museum, Baghdad* (Harry N. Abrams, 2005).

Chapter 3

How Not to Take a Jungle Bath

JAMES H. POWELL

To most, pygmies are the "little people." To me, one will always be very big. He probably saved my life.

It had been an exceptionally grueling day in the great Likouala Swamp of northern Congo, five thousand square miles of the most unexplored real estate left in Africa. There were eight of us. Besides myself, there was Roy Mackal of the University of Chicago; Rev. Eugene Thomas, a Protestant missionary based at Impfondo on the Ubangi River; Ehoula Boubakar, our Congolese security guard; Ikole Marien, head pygmy porter; and three additional pygmy porters. It was February 1980, and Roy and I had come to Congo to investigate what, if any, reality lay behind the legends of the Mokele-mbembe, a mysterious creature said to still lurk in the everlasting green night of these swamps.

For sheer physical hardship, our slog through these swamps—often in muck up to our waists and plastered with insects—dwarfed anything I had experienced. And then there was the thirst. In the Selva Lacandona, a jungle in the state of Chiapas, Mexico, the ubiquitous liana, a climber vine that starts at the ground level and climbs trees up to the canopy of the forest, were a reservoir of potable water. All one had to do was to slash a liana and obtain a cool, refreshing drink whose slightly woody flavor only enhanced it. But not in the Likouala, the swamp. Here the lianas yielded only an acrid juice. One could not "drink off the land." As for the swamp water, even the pygmies wouldn't touch it. "Water, water everywhere, not a drop to drink" was our situation. The water supply in our canteens was as exhausted as we were. In our dehydrated bodies it wasn't much better.

Next came the hassle over the leopard. There was a pygmy village on a small island in that part of the swamp that we had to reach before nightfall, as spending the night in the swamp itself was unthinkable. On firm, if soggy, ground at last, we knew we had reached the island, and had picked up a trail that could only lead to the village. We were strung out along this trail when one of the pygmies came up to say that a leopard was stalking us.

Although the leopard (*Panthera pardus*) was officially listed by the International Union for Conservation of Nature and Natural Resources (IUCN) as a threatened species, at that time the Likouala region was crawling with leopards. Even in Impfondo it was dangerous to go out at night, as leopards came into the town and roamed its streets like stray dogs.

Was a leopard really escorting us? I never saw it, but that meant little. Children of the rain forest, the pygmies "know" things we do not and cannot, and are seldom wrong. Was the big cat hunting or merely curious? More likely it was the latter. Leopards normally hunt at night, especially right after dusk and just before dawn. Still, I urged that we tighten up the column. No leopard will jump a party of eight. The only danger would be to a lone straggler, out of sight around a bend in the trail.

I've forgotten the reverend's exact response, but it exuded the piety inherent in his being. I admired Gene, a man whose courage was forged from the same steel as his faith. I also respected his beliefs, though this didn't always keep his fundamentalism and my liberalism from clashing. After the ordeal of the day, tempers were frayed all around; it was with effort that I held mine. I wasn't in the mood for a Sunday school lesson. This wasn't a point of theology, simply a common-sense precaution.

Even by Likouala standards, it was a harrowing day. It was about to climax. Unexpectedly, we came upon a pool beside the trail. It wasn't the popular image of a jungle pool, limpid and overhung with tropical blossoms, but muddy, foul, and fetid. Still, it was cleaner than I was. I stripped down and plunged in, intent on making it still cruddier with the accumulated dirt from my body.

Suddenly I felt a hand on my shoulder, urgent in its grip. One of the pygmies was frantically pulling me out of the pool, to the accompaniment of an equally frantic diatribe in Lingala.

Free of the water, I looked back and understood. One of the inert chunks of rotting vegetation choking the pool was not quite inert but had been languidly drifting toward me. It was not a floating branch, but a huge Gaboon viper, the biggest I had ever seen.

While the king cobra (*Ophiophagus hannah*) of southeast Asia and the East Indies is the longest poisonous snake, the Gaboon viper (*Bitis gabonica*) of equatorial Africa is the heaviest, with nearly two-inch fangs that can penetrate a jungle boot. It is not normally aggressive. But in one of nature's most perfect camouflages, its markings, gaudy when viewed in a zoo exhibit, blend imperceptibly with the litter of the rain forest floor. It is this that makes trekking in these jungles ticklish. You don't see a Gaboon viper until you step on it. And once you've stepped on it . . .

Death from a Gaboon viper bite is agonizing. While serving as curator of reptiles at the St. Louis Zoo the great herpetologist, R. Marlin Perkins, was bitten by a captive specimen. A massive transfusion of blood, amounting to replacement, eventually saved his life. Meanwhile, the press carried lurid accounts of his sufferings.

Still dirty but still alive, I watched spellbound as the great snake hauled its massive and hideously beautiful body onto the bank, to become instantly invisible amid the litter of the forest.

We reached the village that evening. Roy, an older man than I, collapsed to the ground, unable to rise.

The drums took over. What they say about the "jungle telegraph" is true. Within hours, the news had been drummed to Impfondo that a white man was lying incapacitated on the island in the swamp.

Gene had a history of heart surgery, and his wife, Sandy, had been frightened concerning his ability to withstand the rigors of our venture (he held up better than Roy or I did!) When the drummed message reached her, she assumed it referred to her husband and became very ill. It was only after we reached Epena on the Likouala-aux-herbes River and were able to make radio contact with Impfondo and clarify the matter that she began to recover.

* * *

James H. Powell has been awarded the flag of The Explorers Club four times. From 1965 to 1975 he worked with the IUCN conducting field surveys of endangered species of crocodiles in Mexico, Central America, the Florida Everglades, Africa, and the islands of the southwest Pacific. A mountaineer, he has climbed fifty-six peaks throughout the world, and was one of the six featured speakers at the 2002 Centennial Celebration of the American Alpine Club.

PART TWO

Polar

Chapter 4

North Greenland by Dog Team

LONNIE DUPRE WITH KARIN REDMOND

In December 1999, sunset skirted the horizon as I stepped carefully down the gravel path to the shoreline. It was midday in Qaanaaq, Greenland, and stars flickered overhead. I pulled my anorak tight and bristled against the minus-eighteen-degree breeze. Looking south far across the Bredning Fjord, where the sun should rise in another two months, the sky was less dark than directly overhead.

A ten-by-sixteen-foot shack with peeling red paint stood by the water's edge, and an empty meat rack slouched between the house and the beach. Qaavianguaq Qissuk, a tiny gentleman in his late seventies, stepped out of the shack into the dim winter light. His tattered clothing was dirty and shiny with seal fat. I introduced myself with the name the hunters gave me, Miksoq Americamiut, meaning "Little American." Qaavianguaq greeted me warmly and, with a leathery handshake, invited me inside.

The one-window shack housed a bare mattress, a miniature oil stove, and candles for light. Rusting rifles, harpoons, and an old fishing net rested under the bed, and sealskin kamiks sat at the foot. There was no room for chairs so we sat on the edge of the bed, and Qaavianguaq poured me some tea. He said that as he grew older he was unable to handle a dog team anymore. The younger men in the village didn't like to have him come along hunting, afraid he might get hurt. I was there to buy his team, but my heart sank into my stomach as we negotiated the sale. I regretted taking his dogs, though he seemed to need the money. When the transaction was complete, we walked outside to where his four dogs were tethered. He handed me the traces.

Two months later, on February 12, we set out for the second leg of our Greenland circumnavigation. Our goal was to circumnavigate the entirety of Greenland, which had never been done. I wanted to live, learn, and travel with the polar Inuit, and I believed this ambitious journey was the best way to do it. During the first stage of the trip, we covered 3,200 miles of coastline by kayak and dog sledge. On the second leg of the trip we would journey 1,800 miles north and northwest to the island. The final leg would involve an additional 1,475 miles around the island. It was an ambitious quest. Greenland has dangerous shifting sea ice, marauding polar bears, and stormy seas. We faced extreme weather, physical hardships, and navigational challenges.

After a couple of days of travel toward Thule Air Base, the official launching point, my partner, Australian John Hoelscher, and I saw the sun for the first time in four months. Though we were bitterly cold to the bone, the sight warmed our hearts. For a short time, the golden orb rode the snow-frosted horizon from right to left and illuminated the flurries billowing around our feet. It was as if we were walking on clouds.

We planned to rest every sixth day, but on day five we woke to a blizzard so intense that we had to yell over the deafening racket caused by gusts ripping across our nylon tent walls. John hollered, “It’s definitely a storm day.” We stayed in our sleeping bags to conserve fuel, but after fifteen hours our sore backs and stiff joints forced us out of the tent to stretch, check on the dogs, and shovel heavy snow away from the walls of the tent.

The temperatures dropped the next day, which offered a break in the storm. Ahead, we could see that recent windstorms off the water drove sea ice into the shore, creating pressured sea ice and frozen, misshapen masses nearly impossible to traverse. The only alternative to our planned route was over impassable mountains. Inch by inch, the fifteen dogs labored and strained to pull our half-ton sledge, packed full with two months’ worth of supplies, over random blocks of ice and snowdrifts as tall as trees. Early in the day, with a biting wind assaulting our face and causing our eyes to water freely, the lashings of one of the sledge’s runners gave way with a thud on squeaky snow. The runner collapsed under the load, crippling our progress in the midst of a growing storm. We began unloading the sledge to make repairs.

For three hours we took turns, bare-handed in minus twenty degrees and thirty-five-mile-per-hour winds, working the new nylon lashings and running in place to stay warm. Our hands, cold from the whirling snow, were numb to the blisters we got from pulling the lashings tight. Too exhausted to relash the other runner, we hoped it would hold up for a while. But it was not to be, and two days later it collapsed as well. Disheartened, we made camp. The next morning we huddled under a flapping tarp to protect us from the searing winds, and with raw, swollen hands made repairs to the second runner. Coming off the sea in gusts of 50 mph, the wind parted the dogs' dense fur, cutting through the layers to the skin. With their backs to the wind they whined from the discomfort. The wind pushed them to bed for another night and forced us into our tent.

I passed the hours through the night studying the sounds of the storm and the blowing snow that collided with our tent. Lying on my back I looked up toward the ceiling at a rising column of my breath's frozen crystals. After more than sixteen hours I ventured outside to check on the dogs. They were fine. Inuit sled dogs are hardier than polar bears. They can live in sustained temperatures up to minus seventy degrees Fahrenheit. Famed explorer Robert E. Peary took this breed with him to the North Pole in 1909. Our own dogs were just as reliable. However, we had missed the brief day and already the sun was setting into a magenta horizon behind sphere-shaped clouds.

By the third day of the storm, the sledge was covered in snow to within an inch of the tops of the thirty-eight-inch upstanders. I had slept the night before with my sleeping bag pulled over my head to drown out the constant roar of the wind. I awoke in a panic, gasping for air, ripping at zippers and toggles to break free. The ordeal left me with a migraine headache and the vision of my epitaph: THE GORE-TEX BREATHED, BUT LONNIE DIDN'T.

To conserve heat while weathering a storm, many of the dogs lay still, curled up in one place to allow the snow to create an insulating cover over them. As time went on, they developed hardened snowballs in their fur. We were glad to escape the torment of our tent to rub down the dogs, break their snowballs free, and fluff up their fur.

After a brief break in the tent to warm up we went back outside to free the sledge and move it to higher ground. Snow filled in almost as fast as we could shovel; it took us three exhausting hours just to unbury our gear. Less than a month into our journey, we had only two more storm day's rations left before we would have to break into our travel day's rations. Shifting into polar-travel survival mode, we decided that any leftovers would be allowed to freeze in the pot to be mixed in with the next meal.

Once ready to resume our journey, we checked outside and found that our tent was almost completely buried in snow. Two pairs of ski tips poked out of the snow like tiny bird beaks. The only evidence of the dogs was fifteen snow-covered mounds scattered across the ground, like miniature moguls on a flat ski slope.

We made one of our three-per-week scheduled radio contacts to a remote weather station in south Greenland and got a positive forecast for the next day. Encouraged by the news, John and I remained good-natured about our predicament. The forecast was right. For nearly three weeks after this initial storm we enjoyed three hundred miles of ideal conditions for Arctic travel: cold temperatures, firm footing, and favorable winds. We were on our way to our supply depot at Danmarkshavn, a remote, six-man weather station that is located in the Northeast Greenland National Park in the Danish territory of Greenland. The weather station is the northernmost location on the east coast of Greenland that nonicebreaking vessels can get to and serves as a supply station in the wilderness. Three-foot-tall hares scurried between a half dozen buildings and large rocks on the mountainous landscape. Few spots on Earth are as remote as this.

To escape a growing crosswind that bullied our dogs and sledge sideways, we decided to break route and take a four-mile overland crossing to the protective lee on the east side of Store Koldewey Island. Our new path passed between two palisades, colorful cliffs of red, rust, and dark brown fading into a snowy base. Two miles into our trip we descended onto a frozen lake so smooth and deep that its surface was like a polished blue-black lens. There were thousands of light blue fractures at the surface that our eyes could follow down eight feet or more, giving the lake's flatness an eerie three-dimensional appearance.

Just three and a half hours' travel from Danmarkshavn, we were stopped by a storm and forced to set up camp in blowing snow and the dark. By the time we ducked into our tent we couldn't see beyond ten meters. Around 2:00 a.m., with the gale blowing 40 mph, John woke me and blurted, "There's water under our tent!"

In our haste to camp we had unknowingly staked our tent on a tide crack: the point where sea ice meets the land and develops a hinge from the constant rise and fall of the tide. At high tide, seawater pushes up through the crack and develops slush pools on the ice. We decided that if we tried to move the tent in the storm, we could lose hold of it and be completely without shelter—even a wet shelter—in a matter of seconds. Worse, the moon was a double threat. Though full, the clouds of the storm shrouded any possible beam of light to see by, and because the moon was full, it would produce a very high tide.

We tried to hold off until daylight, but the rising tide overcame the eight-inch-high sidewalls of our waterproof floor and began soaking through the seams and spilling to the floor. Our sleeping bags began to soak up the flood, and we had no choice but to make our move in the dark. We secured our saturated sleeping bags and pads under the weight of a dog food box outside, and then parked the stove and personal bags on top. Snow and slush were built up twelve inches high on the outside of our tent, and we got thoroughly soaked while clearing it away. We raised the tent from its soggy hole and staked it on higher ground. Two inches of standing water sloshed around inside. We shoveled a foot-high pile of dry snow in through the door to soak it up.

Our sledge was in similar straits, but after three hours of digging and prying it came loose like a boot suctioned in mud. We moved it to higher ground and spent the rest of the day using precious fuel, trying in vain to dry our kit in the apex of our tent. The dogs, tethered on long lines, were able to move to a high ledge of snow above the tide crack and aside from needing their fur freed from hardened snow, were no worse for the wear.

Finally, we were able to resume our travels. After three hours and fifteen miles through a brisk ground blizzard, we arrived at Danmarkshavn to pick up our depot and take a two-day break. We were able to enjoy a change of diet and a short wash. I was shocked at the sight of my skinny frame. John and I each had lost eighteen pounds in forty-one days.

After our break, we navigated down a riverbed that would lead us to the Arctic Ocean. Because of a navigation error we were forced to camp on a glacier at the end of the valley, exposed to high winds and colder temperatures. We had been on the move for more than eleven hours, and our energy reserves were low. Our steadily freezing fingers held a death grip on the tent as we fought to set it up in the wind. The wind blew fine powdered snow that filled every void—pockets, mittens, the tent, our stove, around our necks and cuffs. Our energy was fading fast. My hands were critically close to losing some fingers. Waxy-yellow spots of frostbite had developed on the raised features of our faces. We heaved the sledge horizontal to the wind to serve as a windbreak for the tent as well as a structure for tying it down. I jumped and ran in circles to bring my core temperature back up, and waved my arms like a lunatic trying to pump blood to my throbbing fingers. The pain was excruciating as they thawed. It was the most dangerous camp we'd made, the type of situation that kills less-experienced adventurers. The dogs lay down immediately upon arrival with backs to the wind, foregoing their regular meal.

Years of formal expedition travel and informal backcountry hiking have made me wise to the old snoring tent-mate trick. You're sure to drift off to sleep while your companion sits rapt; listening for the bear you've convinced him you heard prowling just outside the tent as a ruse to keep him from snoring. So I was doubtful when John shook me in the wee hours at our camp at Cape John Flagler, telling me that he thought he heard a bear.

I quickly ruled out the possibility of a prank, however, when I heard the unusual yip from our dogs outside. We peered out the tent door and saw four wolves within twenty yards of our teams, with two of them just two feet away from our lead dog, Knud. They approached Knud low, hunkered down with their tails tucked between their legs. It was a submission trick, an effort to get

Knud to allow them to get closer. Knud stood his ground, kicking snow like a bull preparing to charge. We held our breath.

The wolves were scruffy and white, with little meat on their bony frames. A long white-and-gray streak of longer fur ran down their spines, culminating in a low, bushy tail. Intense, cunning, and methodical with every move, they waited out the standoff. Accustomed to bringing down musk oxen as big as seven hundred pounds, these wolves could dispatch any number of our dogs with little effort. Luckily, one of Knud's gang was holding position close by, and the nearest pair of wolves slowly backed away. They settled for some leftover dog food. As John and I emerged from the tent and stood outside in plain view, they walked away slowly, in their own time.

With wind chills of minus sixty degrees on April 30, we reached Kaffeklubben Island (Coffee Club Island), the northernmost piece of land in the world, aside from a tiny gravel bar a half mile farther south. Despite the name it's no place to stand around and have a cup of coffee. We pushed on directly over Robert Peary's hundred-year-old tracks toward our depot at Hall Land, just one week's travel away.

The warmer temperatures of late spring and the accompanying soft ground cover forced us to switch to nighttime travel, when the sledge runners wouldn't be slowed by the sloppy surface. While we rested just one day out from Hall Land, I left the tent to fetch our map case and confirm our position before that night's travel. I pulled the segment that showed our current location and our Hall Land destination, but before I could get a fix on it, the blustery 40 mph winds snatched the map and swept it out of sight.

I was frozen in shock before a wave of panic hit me. Shod only in loose-fitting, thinly soled camp socks, I ran after the map. John, still resting in the tent, was completely unaware of what had happened. Although it was daytime, visibility was reduced to fifty feet by the blowing snow. My slippery socks caused me to stumble and fall frequently. With bruised and cold feet, I searched for the map in every crack and divot I could find. It was like trying to find a tiny white speck of paint on an endless white canvas. Soon I was some two hundred yards from camp. I realized I could die out there.

Turning back into the wind toward the tent, my sore feet and the bitter wind stinging my eyes brought me back to the seriousness of our situation.

It was critical that we have detailed map information about the terrain in order to avoid impassable rocks and gorges during our upcoming crossing of Washington Land to reach the inland ice cap and then on to Qaanaaq. It was even more critical that I reach the tent quickly. I had no traction in my camp socks, and the wind was steadily fighting my every step. I propelled myself forward using elevated slabs of pack ice and in what seemed like an hour I spotted a ski, then a dog. Soon the camp came into view and I stumbled through the tent door.

"John," I gasped. "I made a mistake—a big one. The wind took the map, and I couldn't catch it." John's face went into a blank stare. "We have that military ONC [Operational Navigational Chart] map, only it's got lousy definition. We're in trouble," I said. I waited for him to comprehend the gravity of our situation.

John's frown slowly graduated to a smile. "Not to worry, little buddy," said John. "I entered all the critical waypoints of our route in the GPS [global positioning system] two days ago!"

If he had been my wife or girlfriend, I would have kissed him. We double-checked the GPS and John was right. I was never much for busying myself with those electronic gizmos, but John's attention to detail saved the day.

After a gradual twenty-mile ascent of an unnamed glacier we called "the Ramp," we reached the plateau of the inland ice just east of Kane Basin. The empty white expanse of the plateau was like a punishment to our eyes. The only thing that kept us from daydreaming into a trance was the occasional crevasse we would spot out of the corners of our eyes. Often, we saw the far ledge of a crevasse first, our eyes following down the polished aqua blue walls as we peered over the lip. Soon, a crevasse some forty feet wide and running four miles in length, large enough to swallow a tractor, came into view.

John took off on skis and found a snow bridge only ten yards away. When he reached the other side, the dogs bolted. I threw myself onto the bouncing sledge and struggled to get the rope brake in place. Just as I was considering jumping from the sledge to save myself, I managed to slip the rope brake over the runner. The sledge slowed and I raced ahead of the team, cracking the whip and stopping the dogs just a few feet from the edge of the crevasse. Several deep breaths later I crossed the sledge and team over to the other side.

After three months on the trail our wind shell pants and anoraks were dirty and waxy from camp chores and dog food. They resembled tattered turn-of-the-century oilskins worn as waterproofs by old sea dog explorers. We wondered if the clothes couldn't make it all by themselves the rest of the way to Qaanaaq.

About twenty days after our depot stop in Hall Land we could see the faint outline of mountains across Kane Basin from the inland ice cutting the western horizon only fifty miles away. It was Ellesmere Island, Canada. Three days later we reached the far side of the inland ice, and though unseen through the fog, we knew the Bowdoin Fjord was below, our route home. Our greatest craving other than the company of others was a change in our diet. I was plenty sick of stale oatmeal and chocolate. Fresh veggies were at the top of my list, and a cold beer was a close second. John dreamed of fresh mangoes off the tree in his backyard.

Before we began our expedition, we could find no one who had any details of the Tugto Glacier, but our map made it look like the best route into Qaanaaq. A third of the way down the middle of the Tugto Glacier, the moraine across our path separated in a confluence of bottomless crevasses. The hair on the back of my neck tingled as I peered over the edge into the black abyss. The moraine, an accumulation of earth deposited by a glacier, was only a thin layer of frosting on the cake.

We backtracked, and John skied down a possible route through a shallow, snow-filled contour. He returned an hour later and reported there was steep, polished ice at the bottom, impossible to get a stable footing for the dogs or us. We had no choice but to pursue crossing the battalion of snow-filled crevasses. I probed along the way for black voids.

We continued on and made it to where the western edge of the glacier dipped one hundred feet into a corridor at the base of a nunatak, the Inuit name given for a mountain top coming up through the inland ice. The gully was crevasse-free and filled with loose snow, though there were plenty of large boulders to navigate around.

The slope down to the corridor was too steep to descend with even a lightweight sledge as it could easily overtake the dogs. I unhitched the team and handed the traces to John. I grabbed the sledge and, slipping a rope brake over the nose of each runner, edged it over the lip. John and I discussed the possibility that if for some reason there was an unseen roadblock down the corridor we may not be able to return up this slope to find another route.

While considering the consequences of my planned maneuver, I spotted a large boulder at the base. My heart raced as I imagined crushing the sledge into it with an explosion of flying wood. John clutched the traces to keep the dogs from following me, and with my heels dug into the snow I eased the sledge over the fulcrum and down the slope. It felt like being shot from a gun. Snow piled up in front of my legs as I dug in to try to guide and slow the descent. With a shift of my weight and a heave to the right, I missed the boulder by the thickness of a candy wrapper. John coaxed the dogs to the edge. I called calmly from the bottom, and they began to pussyfoot near the edge, looking down at me, testing their footing. John sat down and scooted over the edge with the traces in hand. The dogs followed his lead, all landing safely at my feet in a pile of snow and fur, seeming to enjoy this new style of getting around.

We followed the corridor in hopes that it would intersect with a strip of moraine where we could cross back over to the eastern side of the glacier and follow a hillside corridor that we believed would get us safely to the bottom. A mile down the passage we encountered a complete separation where a small spur glacier intersected the main glacier. The underside of the glacier was exposed far below. Melt water at the bottom rushed around huge boulders and gravel. It was as if a flood of melt had, in a single catastrophe, eroded away the glacier, creating a cavity in the tooth of ice. Our jaws swung open in the cool breeze as we viewed the chasm blocking our route.

"It's a canyon," I whispered, as John climbed the loose rock of the nunatak to get a better view.

"Our only recourse is to climb back out of this corridor here and skirt the chasm along that slope!" John yelled from one hundred feet above.

"You sure there's no other way?" I pleaded.

"I'm positive," he replied.

We pushed the sledge from behind while barking at the dogs to pull. Slowly we inched back up onto the side of the glacier and arrived at the top completely soaked with sweat. I steered the sledge gingerly, using a rope brake to keep it from sliding, and dragged the whole works over the ice cliff. It was a slow twelve hours, laboring our way down nine miles of slick ice, crevasses, and rocks to the glacier's base. Now at sea level, the sweltering thirty-two-degree temperature supported a small lake and series of streams thinly veiled by ice. The streams presented a three-mile-long obstacle course between us and Bowdoin Fjord, the route to Qaanaaq. Once we arrived at the fjord the dogs would instinctively pull us the remaining twenty miles to Qaanaaq without the need of commands.

Since this was the first thaw of spring, I wasn't feeling optimistic about our chances for a dry passage. Sure enough, suddenly thin ice gave way with a crashing sound like broken glass. The sledge and dogs went for a swim. John and I remained dry, perched atop the teetering sledge trying to keep it balanced while the dogs pulled it through the water over their backs, resembling harnessed beavers. After a few tense minutes of debating whether to grab my camera equipment and abandon ship, the dogs reached a spit of gravel footing and dragged the sledge onto solid ground.

We followed the edge of the icy stream in front of Tugto's ice face, past a one-hundred-foot palisade for three miles and to Bowdoin Fjord where we soon spotted our friends camping with their two dog teams along the far western shore. We had called them by radio from our last camp on the inland ice to plan a connection. With sweat pouring down our backs, we forced our legs through the deep snow maneuvering the sledge across the fjord. When we finally arrived, Oodaaq, our Inuit friend, commented on how good the dogs looked, and John mentioned jokingly that we tried to bathe them regularly. We rested in the twenty-four-hour sun, filling our bellies with Danish rye bread and pastries, cheese, and coffee. After the break we shaved our runners smooth and drove all three teams down the west bank of the fjord, running and laughing like children.

As Qaanaaq, our final destination, came into view, the dogs adjusted course and, like horses running for the barn, they headed directly to the tethering spot from where we had trained them, near the old folks home. In the few short months, their former owner, Qaavianguaq, had moved into the home and was sporting thick tape-repaired glasses as he emerged to greet us. Still longing for the independence of handling a dog team, Qaavianguaq helped us with unhooking the dogs. He took the traces of his former four dogs, and giving them each a caress and pat on the head, tethered them down with the rest of the team. I could see through his thick glasses a young hunter again, proud of his dogs.

* * *

During the past twenty years, *Lonnie Dupre* has traveled more than fourteen hundred miles throughout the polar regions by dog team, ski, and kayak. In 1991, he organized and led the Northwest Passage Expedition, making a three-thousand-mile west to east transit of the Canadian Arctic route by dog sledge. In 1999, he successfully circumnavigated Greenland. Dupre lives in northern Minnesota and is the author of *Greenland Expedition: Where Ice Is Born* (NorthWood Press, 2000). By 2006, Dupre completed the first summer expedition to the North Pole, pulling canoes over six hundred miles, which brought the attention of millions of people worldwide to the problem of global warming. Karin Redmond is the former executive editor of *Sea Kayaker Magazine*.

Chapter 5

Exit Strategy

LORIE KARNATH

The magic and wonder of Antarctica, even when capped by the adventure of reaching the South Pole, dims when you find yourself imprisoned by the weather within the confines of your tent. There, you are corralled by raging winds that swirl the blinding snow, hurtling ice chunks into the spiral mixture, which ravage the tent's thin shell. At the mercy of nature's vicissitudes, thoughts on how one might extricate oneself from such a predicament gradually begin to take precedence over any veneration for Antarctica's pristine magnificence. This is the story of one such escape.

The South Pole has always been a place of intrigue, representing one of the most sought-after quests for exploration. When compared to the hurdles faced by early Arctic explorers, numerous technical advances have facilitated access to this distant, frozen landscape. However, modern devices cannot overcome the extremely volatile nature of the environment. Antarctica is still one of the remotest areas on Earth. Logistical problems remain substantial, and the pole is particularly capricious and elusive. Notwithstanding the region's renowned inhospitable nature, the advent of the millennium only conjured up another milestone that renewed people's fascination in the pursuit of the pole.

And so it was that in early January 2000, I, along with several others who were all ready to embark and disclose Antarctica's mysteries, found myself in a tedious holding pattern in dank and dreary Punta Arenas, the world's southernmost city, located on the Strait of Magellan in Chile. These circumstances were not unfamiliar nor completely unexpected. A successful foray that I had organized to the North Pole two years earlier, which retraced and commemorated the ninetieth anniversary of Frederick A. Cook's original voyage, prompted all those who took part in this expedition to turn their sights in a southwardly direction. Planning for our South Pole journey began in earnest, and by the following year, along with the majority of participants from the North Pole quest, I sat out the weather in Punta Arenas. After several early morning drills preparing for the LC-130 Hercules flight to Antarctica, each time aborted as the mercurial weather conditions shifted, our time constraints tightened. Numerous such attempts failed, forcing us to pull out for the season. The weather got the best of us.

By the following year enthusiasm for the venture had dwindled, and only two others from my original North Pole group, Max Gallimore and my husband, Robert Roethenmund, accompanied me for another assay. Our experiences the year before had us hopeful for better weather. Despite this, the days in Punta Arenas seemed insufferably long and the evenings even longer. Rattling around the city, we soon mapped out its three best restaurants, where we would often run into other explorers also waiting for the journey south. At last Mother Nature cooperated and the cloud cover broke. It appeared that the right combination of wind and visibility had materialized to load up the Hercules. Although reaching the actual South Pole offers one of the Earth's greatest challenges, oftentimes attaining the Antarctic Continent provides an even greater one.

The requirements to attempt a LC-130 landing on the approximately six-thousand-foot-long blue-ice strip thirty-three hundred feet above sea level at the base of Patriot Hills (our intended campsite) include winds under fifteen knots, visibility of more than 6.2 miles, and a minimum cloud cover just under seventy-eight hundred feet. Some wind is required to keep the haze from building and the runway clear of snow, providing a better contrast between the deep blue of the ice strip and the frozen whiteness of its borders. However, crosswinds exceeding fifteen knots can set the LC-130 spinning toward the mountain range upon landing.

These ice landings are particularly tenuous because the Hercules lands on wheels. We were told that only Hercules LC-130s on official government missions are allowed to land on skis. The military, which developed the technology for ski landings, does not share that technology with civilians—like us. Consequently, our situation was precarious. Once the Hercules's tires hit the ice, the engines are thrust into reverse, causing the plane to slide across the bumpy ice terrain. Without the stability of skis it becomes exposed to wind gusts and other potential hazards before it gradually settles and cleaves to a stop. In the best-case scenario, this is a typical landing with wheels on ice.

Despite the promising weather conditions on takeoff, after six hours' flying time across an unsettled Drake Passage followed by an even more turbulent sub-Antarctic Peninsula region, we reached the Ellsworth mountain range. Arriving within a few hundred feet of this landing site, it became obvious that the window provided early that morning by the breach in cloud cover had disappeared. The invading clouds made it impossible to discern the landing strip from the horizon line. The fuel capacity of the Hercules does not much exceed what is needed to reach the landing site, circle for a short period, and fly back. Therefore, the dismal visibility and projected outlook for continued bad weather forced us to turn around and begin the journey back.

As we endured the waiting game in Punta Arenas, we were reminded of the importance of patience as a key component to a successful expedition. Patience finally prevailed. Early one morning we were mustered to bundle up in arctic gear and board the cramped confines of the Hercules. This time the weather held and after the lengthy crossing of just over six hours, we found ourselves careening across the rutted ice strip. Mercifully the plane eventually shuddered to a stop. We unfolded ourselves from our compact quarters and tumbled out through the door hatch toward our first acquaintance with this icy continent.

In moments like these, we know exactly why we explore. When I first stepped out of the plane and onto the ice, I was overcome with awe for the otherworldly beauty before me. Ripples of glistening frozen water stretched endlessly toward the Earth's vanishing point. The pale sky vibrated with the sparkle of floating ice crystals, as if an infinite number of diamonds had been flung into the air. Everything from crust to the heavens was cloaked in pristine white. Apart from the engines of the Hercules and a faint brush of the wind, there was no sound, no infringements of any sort to stain the scintillating, ethereal backdrop.

Over time our eyes adjusted to our surroundings, and the original impression of ubiquitous whiteness, like the palette of a Whistler painting, took on hue and color. The introduction of color broke the spell and led to more pragmatic contemplations. Days of being pent up by pounding winds and plummeting temperatures that could cause frostbite can do this even faster, and the initial enthrallment begins to wear thin very quickly. However, this is not to say that the first observations—moments where time and space seem suspended—are not preserved forever. They are. These are memories that are vividly brought forth later in the safety of home, by the warmth of a fireplace.

At the Patriot Hill base camp, the exploration and research teams had completed the work they had set out to do, including reaching the South Pole, conducting meteorite and extreme life-form studies. The research work mainly involved gathering samples that would later be tested. All through this process, the weather was the decisive factor, as it determined when and how we could gather samples. Ultimately, our expedition was a success, but now the inclement weather threatened to delay our departure. February was soon upon us, leaving not much room to maneuver before March, when Antarctica is wreathed in darkness, the beginning of its eight-month winter. It was time to think about getting out.

Our choices were slim. It was clear that the bad weather would not allow the LC-130 Hercules to land in Punta Arenas anytime soon. We'd heard rumors, however, that a group of Russians camped nearby would be picked up by an Ilyushin jet, a Russian military aircraft. This created a dilemma: if the rumors were true, the Russian aircraft would be flying in conditions deemed unsafe. On the other hand, Antarctica's encroaching months of darkness loomed large. We decided to take the Russian exit strategy—if we could.

On a day when the winds took a moderate turn, a few of us tentatively ventured outside our frozen confinement. It was not long before we saw a magnificent site: a polished glint in the sky soaring like a giant bird. The Ilyushin pilots did not hesitate and in fluid motion dove toward the narrow ice strip. We held our breath, as this was only the second time that an Ilyushin had reportedly ever landed in Antarctica. The first plane had deposited the Russian explorers a few weeks earlier. The weather conditions were difficult, and the pilot and crew virtually untried in the unpredictable nature of a Patriot Hills landing. As the plane swooped past the mountain range, huge cracking noises accompanied its descent. Enormous billows of snow rose skyward blocking out the aircraft and mountains. Its speed and thrust had unleashed a series of avalanches throughout the mountain range. It took a few minutes before we were even able to ascertain that the plane had landed intact.

Once on the ground, the cargo hold opened and military personnel in camouflage, allegedly former members of the KGB, began loading the hull. Cigarettes were passed around. The Ilyushin was soon packed to its gills. Nonetheless, the Russians agreed to take a few of us out with them. I was relieved to see that fellow camp members, astronauts Jim Lovell and Owen Garriott, had also decided to board the Ilyushin. Owen's Skylab mission and Jim's experience as commander of Apollo 13 might come in handy. Also several of the Russian team kept insisting that we stay on the flight all the way to Moscow. I hoped having the astronauts on board would keep that from happening.

Outside, icicles formed along the wings and underbelly of the Ilyushin, which added to the tremendous weight of the burdened hull. Inside the plane were only the bare bones of the shell. By comparison, the Hercules seemed luxurious. No windows, seats, or oxygen accompanied the flight. Every corner of the plane was crammed with people, supplies, and cargo; we were literally on top of one another.

Before takeoff, I climbed to the pilot's cabin with the two astronauts and Max Gallimore, who is also a pilot. We had been reassured by the Russian team that we were under the command of one of Russia's top pilots. He certainly looked the part. Despite the confusing assortment of cables, sundry food products, and sleeping crew members that draped the cabin, the pilot appeared immune to the fray. With his chiseled features and swept-back salt-and-pepper hair, he looked right out of central casting. I reminded him that mountain ranges lay ahead. He told us not to be concerned.

In the cabin below the navigator was suppose to be monitoring the situation. However, when we descended to the cabin, we found the navigator napping, which did little to improve my concerns. Garriott sat at the navigator's seat for a moment, tapped on the frozen gauges, and announced serenely that the plane probably dated from the 1970s.

Back in the main hold we squeezed between a tumble of bodies, many of these in varying states of sobriety. Several bottles of vodka, chocolate, and raw bacon were already making the rounds. One of the crew members noticed that each time that I received a vodka bottle, I passed it on. He assumed that I was reluctant to drink directly from the bottle and procured a tin cup of dubious provenance. Even the cup did not convince me, but to this day I keep a bar of the chocolate intact, in its red wrapper with its golden wreath and yellow-and-black-striped ribbon insignia, in my refrigerator as a reminder that no matter the situation there is usually a way out. The Russian exit strategy worked.

• • •

Lorie Karnath is an international member, board member, and Western European Chapter and United Nations Committee chair of The Explorers Club. Formerly Karnath worked in the field of investment banking, but currently she dedicates her efforts toward the fields of science and education. She has sat on numerous international scientific and educational boards.

Chapter 6

Living Opposite the Bear

KRISTIN LARSON

Time in Antarctica is measured as "ice time," and I had accumulated more than sixty months of it as I stood on the fantail of the MV *Green Wave* gazing at McMurdo for the last time. Emotions crowded in, among them relief and profound fatigue. It was late February and at last I was leaving. This had been a tough year, and I was toast, "deeply burnt toast," as the saying goes in McMurdo.

Melancholy and longing also stalked me. The Transantarctic Mountains, just starting to be tinged in pink and butterscotch, hinted at the coming winter. I knew those long Antarctic winters and I actually liked them. The camaraderie, the luxury of time, the crystalline night skies that showed more white from stars than black from the universe beyond, and oh, the dreadful ferocity unleashed in this place during its winter isolation. Quite simply, it terrifies and captivates all who experience it.

I also felt fear and anticipation. What would I do next? What would be my post-Ice identity? How could I weave the skills and experiences gained in this wild place into the next phase of my life? What if the old Antarctic maxim proved true: the first time you go for adventure, the second time for the money, the third time because you no longer fit into the rest of the world. This was my eighth year. Was I destined to be a "lifer?" An end-of-the-roader? Was that really the reason people came back to Antarctica time after time: because they no longer fit in? I suspected the answer was something more profound than that simple explanation.

The *Green Wave* pulled away from Winter Quarters Bay and made its traditional farewell lap in front of "Mactown," belching a plaintive yowl from its claxon that reverberated off the snowy hills. The five-hundred-foot cargo ship then clocked around into a northern heading. So began my prolonged leave-taking of this place. Starting out from Ross Island at nearly eighty degrees south latitude, we had twenty-five hundred miles and a week of sailing ahead of us before disembarking at Lyttelton Harbour, New Zealand. All my previous trips to and from the continent had been by military airlift—a trip that took less than eight hours. Thus, this gradual recession northward was especially poignant not only as a passage but one following in the tentative sea tracks of earlier explorers.

Leaning against the starboard rail, I watched as familiar landmarks slid by: Arrival Heights, Danger Slopes, Castle Rock, and Hutton Cliffs; all names given during British explorer Robert Falcon Scott's 1901–1904 Discovery Expedition to the Ross Sea. Soon the Erebus Ice Tongue came into view. This five-mile-long, fingerlike projection of floating ice is formed by the rapid flow of glaciers off Mount Erebus, the southernmost active volcano. Besides being a geographical oddity, the ice tongue's many cracks and crevasses transform into labyrinthine ice caves decorated with delicate ice chandeliers and chiseled walls when sea ice forms a floor beneath them. But now, staring down into the viscous, inky water from the deck of the *Green Wave*, I thought about a time just seven months earlier in the dead of the polar winter when I had been flying gleefully over this same surface by snowmobile on an outing that nearly took my life.

There is nothing, and I mean *nothing*, like a winter visit to the historic huts of Scott and Ernest Shackleton. The lingering circumstance of these hastily departed huts affects all who visit, even in the middle of summer. In the dark, with only the moon and a cold-soaked headlamp for light, the experience is especially disconcerting. Equipment and personal belongings from another era litter the huts abandoned midtask—rumpled bedding and sweethearts' pictures, a mummified dog still tethered by rusting chains, pony feed and snowdrifts commingled in lonely mangers. A wraithy presence pervades these places.

Ray Tien, one of a few scientists who winter in Antarctica, was completing doctoral research on antifreeze proteins in Antarctic fishes that year. It was midwinter, and temperatures had been hovering at minus thirty degrees Fahrenheit for more than a month when we decided it was time to visit the icy crypts of our Antarctic forebearers. The new ice in front of McMurdo was already two feet thick, and we figured that northward along the twenty-mile coastline toward Cape Evans it would be thick enough for safe travel by snowmobile.

However, this wouldn't be just any garden-variety winter boondoggle. In addition to visiting the historic huts, we had two important missions to accomplish. One was to confirm that a large portion of the Erebus Ice Tongue had actually calved off earlier in the winter. Such an event only occurs every five years or so and we wanted to be the first to know. More important, we needed to locate good fishing spots because Ray's stock of live specimens was running low. One morning, the two of us hopped on our snowmobiles at the land-ice transition in front of town.

"Two souls departing for the sea ice around Turtle Rock," we radioed to Mac-Relay, "and, if possible, to Big and Little Razorback Islands. Expected time of return, 1600 hours." "Do you copy?"

"Charlie, Charlie, loud and clear," came the reply.

We were off. It was the extreme depth of winter, and a full moon shone brightly. The feeling of freedom was exhilarating. Accelerating across the featureless sea ice on a fast machine seemed like unbelievable good fortune after months of confinement in McMurdo. We yipped and high-fived the air despite the bone-crushing chill. Our plan was to head north, taking ice-thickness measurements as we went, and to set out flags in promising fishing locations. We would return later with larger vehicles and a drill capable of making wider holes in the ice so we could collect *Dissostichus mawsoni*, a close relative of the so-called Chilean sea bass.

We sped along, leaving a wake of diamond dust in the air, and casting lapis-colored shadows across the smooth ice surface. Every twenty minutes or so, we stopped to warm up and to measure the ice using a Kovacs auger. This is a handheld drill with a steel bit that is approximately four centimeters in diameter and a meter long. The new ice was cold and hard, and drilling it required the full weight of my body in order to gain purchase.

North of Hut Point, the ice was averaging fifteen inches, and we proceeded with confidence, inspecting tidal cracks and skirting the jagged, wind-blown sastrugi formations as we made our way north. At one crack I nearly jumped out of my boots when the silence was abruptly broken by a violent *whoooshing,* accompanied by a bloom of vapor from a nearby crack. A Weddell seal had come up for air at a hole barely big enough for its snout. It seemed both inconceivable and comforting to know that we were not the only living creatures in this forbidding lunar landscape, as though we had somehow conspired against nature by surviving out here. With a bit of envy, I imagined the seal was much more comfortable than Ray and I. At twenty-eight degrees Fahrenheit the super-cooled seawater was nearly sixty degrees warmer than the air.

We continued north on our snowmobiles, spurred on by the faintly gleaming remains of the ice tongue in the distance. "Its true," I thought, "It did calve off, but how much?" We stopped for another ice check. To this day, I'm not sure what prompted us to stop just then. There had been no discernible change in the texture of the ice, but as I bore down on the auger it pierced the ice easily and kept going all the way up to its handle, toppling me forward to my knees.

The ice was spongy and soft. I looked up at Ray, and though he wore goggles, I saw that his eyes, normally calm and almond shaped, were as wide and round as those of a freshly hooked tuna. Motion was suspended as neurons fired furiously. Walk? Crawl? Slither? Where was land? How far back did the ice change?

Simultaneously and without a word, we gingerly turned our machines and accelerated out of there. My heart and stomach were not even in my mouth, they had flown out ahead of me, so certain was I that the ice would momentarily open up beneath me like an elevator shaft. The chance of surviving a swim in such conditions was nil.

We simply held on and flew back the way we had come, ignoring the wooden numbness of our hands and feet; not letting up until we were well within the halo of light cast by McMurdo. Back at the transition, we shakily dismounted, nodded, even grinned a little, and never spoke of the incident again.

But now, from the deck of the *Green Wave*, I saw only tiny remnants of last year's sea ice in the sheltered bays and bights around the ice tongue. The tracks we had made and routes we had flagged were melted, simply blown away.

I wondered if this quality—perpetual renewal—could be a key to Antarctica's attraction. The intense activities of each new summer are erased by the shifting sugar-fine snow, by the annual disintegration of the vast sea ice, or borne away on ceaseless winds. With a few exceptions like the "permanent stations" (a term that seems to acknowledge the transitory nature of man's toehold in Antarctica), everything else disappears, whether it be the business of raising seal pups, establishing ski-ways for thousands of pounds of cargo, or man-hauling sledges to the South Pole.

Antarcticans are not distracted by the footprints of their predecessors. Rather each sojourner is presented with an untrodden path, a pristine campsite, and a trackless horizon. And is it not true that the quest to be first and our strong affinity for unspoiled places are the very things that drive us to explore?

I continued in these musings as I made my way to the *Green Wave*'s galley for my first shipboard meal. Similar to McMurdo's early days, the military tradition of segregating officers and seamen in separate mess halls was de rigueur on the *Green Wave*. Our small cadre of shipboard guests was expected to dine with the officers. The atmosphere was relaxed and convivial. For us, the work of the season was complete, and for the ship's officers the challenges of a Southern Ocean crossing were still out on the horizon. We spoke of favorite port calls, of the "freshies" we would consume upon arrival back in civilization. We debated the significance of formerly landfast ice shelves breaking loose; some drifting northward never to return and others remaining captive to the circumpolar flow. We also talked about our plans for returning to the ice. It was a marvelous evening, though I could not help wondering what subjects were discussed in the other mess hall that night.

Most forms of military hierarchy had been relaxed by the time I arrived in Antarctica in the late 1980s, especially for civilians. We were generally free to chum around with the entire rank and file. That was all well and good, but no matter how hard we tried to cultivate a semblance of normalcy, the fact remained that the overall population of women still hovered at little more than 20 percent, and our presence was akin to putting lipstick on a wolverine. Besides, even in those days the single-mindedness of the scientific mission was so pervasive that social norms were pushed aside anyway—often to memorable effect.

One such occasion occurred on a midsummer evening. I had stayed late at the lab to oversee the transfer of hundreds of ice cores, just arrived from the deep field, into temperature-controlled environmental rooms where they could be analyzed. Despite the late hour, sunlight filtered in through the scratchy, smudged Plexiglas windows of the Erebus Club where I had stopped on my way to the dorms. The bar's patrons were mostly indistinguishable, as all were dressed in some form of standard issue garb. The revelers at the unfinished plywood table where I sat down were no exception. I grabbed a semifrozen can of beer and was soon engrossed in their lively discussion. By the end of the evening, we were all best friends. One could hardly imagine a more unlikely fellowship: a congressional staffer from Washington, DC; a heavy-equipment operator from Salmon, Idaho; a world-famous atmospheric scientist; a general laborer from Cordova, Alaska; a Canadian pilot; and me, a peripatetic lab manager. I know of few other places on Earth where one may so freely consort with others of such diverse backgrounds on such a level playing field.

Maybe this too was one of the keys to Antarctica's attraction. It's a place to shed extraneous social inhibitions and focus instead on the common drive that brings us together at the ends of the Earth. Could it be that we all harbor an intrinsic desire to participate in an untamed brand of social congress? Certainly this was a source of gratification among the people of Antarctica's early expeditions. It was true for me as well.

Meanwhile, it was our second day of sailing on the *Green Wave*, and we were about to leave Ross Sea. The northern fringes of Victoria Land would soon fall away and we would enter the circumpolar Southern Ocean at approximately seventy degrees of latitude. From there we would proceed into the "screaming sixties," the "furious fifties," and the "roaring forties"—so called by earlier mariners who ventured into these high latitudes without the benefit of powerful engines and satellite weather maps.

Earlier in the day, we had passed Coulman Island, a place where I had spent an idyllic week camping in the company of one hundred thousand emperor penguins. Jerry Kooyman, a forty-year veteran of Antarctica and renowned for his research on the diving physiology of penguins, had asked me to accompany him and his son, Tory, to Coulman where I assisted in tagging and censusing the birds. In November, when we arrived via Twin Otter from McMurdo, the chicks had already moved from the individual care of their parents into groups of large, gray downy masses, known as crèches, attended to by many adult birds encircling them in a protective barrier. This communal arrangement freed up the parents to forage at sea, where they would spend several days, diving to depths of four hundred meters in pursuit of fish, crustaceans, and squid before returning to regurgitate a nutritious goo for their chicks. Lines of penguins more than a mile long could be seen both leaving and returning to the vast colony, like pilgrims moving across the landscape with single-minded intent. When walking, emperors have an unmistakably regal bearing, upright and stoic. And even when tobogganing along by belly, their ochre-colored neck feathers throw off a reflection on the snow, preceding them like a golden aura.

Having evolved in the absence of land-based predators, emperors closely inspect any new object in their midst, whether it's a helicopter, a person, or an open-air outhouse. By contrast, they have a healthy fear of their marine predators: leopard seals and orcas, which patrol the ice edges waiting for a plump, warm meal to plop in. Leopard seals frighten me too, with their shifty eyes and serpentlike heads, not only because they lack fear of humans, but because they are known to actually pursue us as quarry. Antarctic orcas, on the other hand, have no such evil reputation, and seem to differentiate between humans and their favorite foods. So says my navy pilot friend "Beez," who touched one once while waiting for scientists with his helicopter near a lead in the sea ice. "It felt like a damp watermelon," he confided.

The closest I ever got to orcas was on my very first day in Antarctica. Fresh off the long LC-130 Hercules flight from Christchurch, New Zealand, and exhilarated by my first views of the continent, I was in no mood to go to the crowded, windowless mess hall, so I wandered down to a point of land adjacent to Scott's Discovery hut. It was January and there was open water in front of the station. A pod of orcas cruised into view less than twenty feet off the point.

In a few moments, the water was churning and the whales were frenzied. I saw that one of the larger whales had a seal in its mouth and was whipping it back and forth violently, presumably to tenderize it a bit before the feast. I was mesmerized. "Where is everybody else?" I wondered. "Was such a marvelous spectacle so commonplace in Antarctica that no one bothered to watch?"

Soon, skuas, fiercely aggressive Antarctica avians, were dive-bombing the scene picking off stray bits of flesh. I *really* wanted to capture this on film, but my camera was still in my unpacked bags in the Quonset hut. Should I stay and watch, or risk missing some of the action by retrieving my camera fifteen minutes away? Finally, I took off at a run up the rough lava slope. McMurdoites might not be impressed by Antarctica's *Wild Kingdom*, but my friends back home would be.

During the thirty minutes it took me to snag my camera and return to the point, a huge crowd of people had gathered, including some Kiwis who had driven over from the nearby New Zealand base. My unimpeded view was no longer available. "Of course this is *not* commonplace!" someone assured me in a condescending tone. "You must be newly arrived." I nodded and smiled, suddenly realizing that Antarctica had given me something remarkable. I was dazzled. Only later did I learn how remarkable a gift it truly was. What I witnessed all alone on that point has never been observed, before or since. In those first few hours the seed for my lifelong attachment to Antarctica had taken root.

It was day four on the *Green Wave*, and I was on the ship's bridge looking for icebergs. Having passed over the Antarctic Circle, we were now in the midst of the furious fifties and would soon leave ice-bearing waters behind. Up ahead, thick fog heralded our imminent entry into the band of ocean surrounding the continent where cold Antarctic waters meet the relatively warmer waters of the Atlantic, Pacific, and Indian oceans. This zone is known as the Antarctic Convergence, or Polar Front, and is marked by an abrupt change in surface temperatures. Like the tree line in boreal regions, the convergence forms a natural boundary between different ecosystems, and few species cross over it.

The Antarctic Convergence served as a formidable barrier to people as well. In the sixty thousand years since we began our migration out of Africa, humans have colonized all other parts of the Earth, from the far north to the tiniest midocean islands. Yet throughout time Antarctica remained as remote and untouched as the moon. It wasn't until 1773 that James Cook first breached the convergence, and it was another fifty years before the lands of Antarctica were finally touched by human hands. This is an extraordinary fact, considering how long Antarctica has resided in our imaginations. Even the Ancient Greeks sensed its presence and gave it a name. The north polar region they named for the constellation that rode above it: the Great Bear, or *Arktos*, and, in accordance with their symmetrical view of the Earth, they named the south polar region *Anti-arktos*, or Opposite the Bear. Antarctica is indeed opposite the Arctic in many ways. One is an ocean surrounded by land and the other a land surrounded by ocean; one has been inhabited for thousands of years whereas the other remains largely untouched.

The ship's captain showed me satellite weather maps downloaded directly to the *Green Wave*'s bridge. I noticed a ring of dark smudges encircling the continent at roughly the same latitude as the ship. He explained that the dark spots, which he called "thumbprints" because of their dense isobars, were cyclonic storms that tracked along the circumpolar flow. Looking at the map, I imagined a demonic circle dance of whirling dervishes. The trick, Captain Peter explained, was to transit between the smudges, or at worst, to ride out the trailing edge of one, all the while giving wide berth to icebergs and their submerged progeny known as "growlers."

Unlike modern navigation on the Southern Ocean, travel in the interior of Antarctica remains almost as risky now as it was a hundred years ago, especially for those not prepared for the worst conditions. Polar-orbiting satellites and autonomous weather stations scattered around the continent have improved forecasting in Antarctica. However, given the vast emptiness of the continent, which is bigger than the United States and Mexico combined, it is still a formidable challenge to predict local weather other than by direct experience. The more benign storms come from the north carrying moisture off the open water and generating rare snowfall around McMurdo Sound. However, Antarctic snowstorms are not what make an impression. That honor is reserved for the "Herbie," a navy term derived from formal meteorology: Hurricane Force Blizzard, or Hurr B, a storm that is utterly mind bending in its power and fury. Herbies come out of the south and create frigid, whiteout conditions with astonishing speed. Their winds, often in excess of one hundred knots, pick up fine granular snow and move it horizontally with the force and effect of a locomotive. It is rare for anyone who is caught unprepared by a Herbie to survive, and it is for Herbies that elaborate training and precautions are taken. For instance, Herbies are the reason for flagged routes and the guide ropes connecting key structures around McMurdo. Herbies are responsible for "survival school" where we learn to make emergency snow structures and erect tents in a gale. Herbies dictate when the weather is in Code 1, 2, or 3, depending on the degree of danger. In short, Herbies are an ever-present but unpredictable menace: the Al-Qaeda of Antarctica.

Back on the *Green Wave*, we had left the polar storms in our wake and the seas were flattening out by degrees. During the previous night, I had experienced not only my first darkness in nearly half a year, but also a fair rollicking as the ship threaded its way through the storm systems. At some point, a tracked vehicle in the ship's hold broke loose of its tie-downs and crashed about for several hours like a deranged elephant, intimidating the ship's crew before it was at last subdued.

But now, I was back on the fantail, watching the graceful wheeling of albatross and shearwaters sliding down the deep troughs and cresting the foamy wave tops. I was again transported to Antarctica, gliding down rivers of glacial ice and cresting the ramparts of its nunataks. I was looping through the Martian landscape of the Dry Valleys with Beez at the controls of a UH-1 helicopter.

My attraction to Antarctica is something I still can't explain. Initially I went there out of curiosity but soon realized that I had traveled to a different planet. Then, I was hooked. Before long, I discovered that most people who go to Antarctica return and return and return, even, like Ernest Shackleton did, to be buried there. But why? Perhaps early Antarctic expeditions were motivated by the because-it's-there factor, which has produced so many firsts in exploration. But what about those that followed? What about all the unknown explorers who spent decades mapping Antarctica's ice-crusted coastlines? And what about all my cohorts, who have seemingly moved on, had kids, pursued careers but *still* hanker for the Ice. Why?

I think it has something to do with the purity of the place: the pureness of a simplified life, the purely ruthless conditions, the pure untrammeled beauty. Maybe that is what draws me back and holds me captive. The only thing I knew for certain as we steamed out of Antarctic waters that day was that I would return.

• • •

Kristin Larson has been an Antarctican since 1988, serving in a variety of roles including winter and summer manager of the research laboratory in McMurdo Station, and later in the development and implementation of environmental policy for the U.S. Antarctic Program. Larson has two degrees in science, is past president of the Antarctican Society, and serves on the board of directors of The Explorers Club. She resides in Washington, DC, where she is an environmental attorney.

Chapter 7

Dictator or Democrat

RANULPH FIENNES

My diary, ten days into our Antarctic crossing in 1981, recorded: "Nobody knows what lies ahead because nobody has been here before." Back in Britain I had asked the Antarctic experts in Cambridge what was known of the region. "Previous forays into your area," they wrote, "have been turned back by crevassing so it seems possible that a lot of the way ahead of you, between 79 and 89 degrees south, may be badly crevassed." This dearth of surface data made any careful route planning impossible.

For six hundred miles in this unexplored zone my team and I recorded the height of the ice surface above sea level using aneroid barometers, thereby mapping this part of Earth for the first time. Vast regions of sastrugi, ridges of ice cut out by the prevailing wind and running transverse to the line of our advance, blocked our path. We struggled over this immense plowed field against the grain of ice furrows up to four feet high.

The eighteen-inch skis at the front of our machines jammed in the furrow troughs, as did the heavily laden sledges. We used axes, shovels, manpower, and foul language to forge each mile of painfully slow progress to the south. There were four of us on this expedition: myself; my wife, Ginnie, who helped organize all of our expeditions and kept radio watch for this one; Oliver Shepard, a beer salesman whose previous experience on our polar expeditions proved invaluable; and Charlie Burton, a retired corporal from the Sussex Regiment, also a trusted veteran.

The cold was all-pervasive and numbed the brain as well as the extremities. The machines broke down frequently. Oliver somehow managed to cope with each successive mechanical trouble. As we climbed to eleven thousand feet above sea level the engines were increasingly affected by the thin air. We slowed to the pace of anemic snails and ran out of fuel within ten miles of our expected minimum range.

While our ski plane flew fuel drums from the coastal dump, we camped and waited for seventeen days. The mathematics were critical. To stock up a fuel cache in the middle of nowhere and often flying blind in blizzard conditions, our pilot, Giles, made ten flights amounting to twelve thousand miles in ninety-two hours, using up six thousand gallons. Only twenty-five drums now remained of the eleven hundred we had shipped from Cape Town the previous year, and Giles had to use up twelve to fly just once to the pole, the halfway point of our crossing journey.

Navigation was a problem every minute of the day in this featureless land. For twelve hundred miles I used the sun, my watch, and a compass with nothing solid to aim at or check against. The problem was compounded by many days of whiteout including the day we finally reached the American research station, McMurdo, at the South Pole.

My means of determining our daily position was a theodolite, an instrument used for measuring both horizontal and vertical angles, and complex navigation tables. This kit weighed thirty-two pounds. (In the 1980s I switched to a two-pound plastic sextant, thanks to research work into plastics at low temperatures, and after 1991 I began to use a global positioning system [GPS], which weighed less than nine ounces.)

We stayed for four days at the South Pole station waiting for Ginnie to be flown there by Giles. A merry Christmas, planned for the twelve resident scientists at the station, was only a day away, but we needed every hour if we were to complete the crossing during Antarctica's brief summer season. Each day of delay increased the hazards ahead. Summer was already well advanced. Crevasse bridges, weakened by the sun, would be increasingly liable to cave in beneath us. British explorer Robert Falcon Scott, sixty years before, had left this place at the bottom of the world two or three days too late, and stranded by early blizzards, had died as a result.

On March 2, the last ships and aircraft would have to leave Antarctica or risk being marooned there for eight months. After that date our own situation would revert to that of Scott's group, with zero possibility of rescue or supply.

I noticed an unusual tension in the tent among the team members as we approached the edge of the high plateau. Ahead of us lay a one-hundred-eighty-mile cliff-girt chute, the Scott Glacier, which dropped through nine thousand feet of chaotic ice to the coastal edge of the Antarctic.

One of the most treacherous zones of this glacier, never previously descended, was its upper rim. A whiteout caught us in the area of great instability, so we camped fully aware that a hidden network of trapdoors to oblivion, slits and caverns with inch-thin booby traps, and snow covers hiding dizzy drops of 150 feet and more lay all about us.

Knowing that a weather change could pin us down for two precious weeks, I decided that delay posed a greater danger than attempting to travel blind. Ollie was silent when I announced this, but Charlie, to use Ollie's words in his diary, "was very shifty and he thought we should have stayed in the tent and not traveled in the white-out through the crevasse field." Whenever my decisions appeared to be wrong, Charlie was an excellent weathervane. On this occasion I could see his point. To move through a highly volatile zone, unable to spot the hazards ahead or underfoot, could be described as stupid, but in my opinion, we ran a much greater long-term danger if we lost the race against the onrush of polar winter because of short-term caution.

If I was misunderstood through not fully communicating the logic of my decision, the fault was doubly mind, since my reason for failing to "discuss opinions" was merely the desire to avoid an argument that might not win me the most votes.

But Oliver and Charlie were not accustomed to blindly following orders they could not understand. They were strong individualists and leaders of men who disliked being told what to do at the best of times. They expected involvement in planning our moves. Normally, I respected this, and many a democratic decision took place over the years between the three of us, but when instant action and reaction was required, I reverted to the one-man-band-ism to which my past life in the army had accustomed me. For one thing, it saved precious time.

There was another, subtler fact, which sometimes stirred the chemicals between the three of us. Urgency. Charlie and Ollie were brought up by their parents in the old-fashioned way. Faced with danger they consciously avoided at all costs any outward show of haste as though it were a symbol of cowardice, as though to hurry in the face of adversity would be unseemly and ungentlemanly.

I believe my father would have had just such an effect on my own behavior had he survived the war and guided my formative years. As it was, I developed my own perhaps maverick policies and these did not include having a democratic powwow with my companions, however brief, when some imminent hazard demanded a speedy reaction. If I was confident that my way was best, what would be the point of a discussion to listen to other possible ways?

So we broke camp, crept forward, and, luckily, the whiteout lifted. Charlie, careful never to sound excited about anything, described the subsequent journey: "The descent was hair-rising, too steep for the sledges which ran down ahead of our skidoos, sometimes wrenching them sideways, even backwards, over wide, droopy snow bridges. Some of these bridges had fracture lines on both sides and were obviously ready to implode at the first excuse. How we made the bottom God only knows."

We continued day after day with few solid areas of respite. One disturbed region averaged a crevasse every six years, two-thirds of which had lost their bridges. Oliver wrote:

> *The descent was a nightmare. Ran[ulph] zigzagged in all directions to avoid the worst but with little success. At one point today we ended in a major pressure zone with great ice bubbles and blue domes rearing above us as we slithered along a maze of cracked corridors, totally lost. Nobody who wasn't there, who hasn't felt a snow bridge*

> *begin to fall away directly beneath his skidoo seat, who hasn't been forced to carry on hour after hour, day after day, through the world's worst crevasse fields can even imagine the extreme fear of it all.*

Against the expectations of the polar pundits in many countries, by this time we made the descent without loss of life and, in nine days, crossed the Ross Ice Shelf to Scott Base on the continent's Pacific rim. We had traversed the Antarctic Continent in sixty-seven days; the first one-way-only crossing of Antarctica ever made.

Giles, our resupply pilot, had saved the lives of a number of lost South African scientists during our journey. He was awarded the British Guild of Air Pilots and Air Navigators Sword of Honour. Sadly, flying a gyrocopter, he died in Antarctica some years later. He was known for his polar expertise and his critical nature, vital to a good polar pilot. Of our expedition, he said,

> *Before we even left London, I really doubted they would succeed. Their land team is after all not professionals at anything. I mean, they have learned to cook in Charlie's case, how to be a mechanic in Ollie's, and Ginnie, how to be a radio operator. Ran[ulph] is a good leader, probably a great leader, but he has had to learn about navigation. The great thing about these four people is their persistence as a group in the face of terrible difficulties in getting across; not their individual abilities.*

Unfortunately, any collective ability we may have developed as a group was soon to be reduced. Ollie's American wife had become worried about his continued absence in risky places, and after much deliberation, he responded to her urgings by agreeing to leave us.

The committee in London that funded our expedition decided to find an army replacement for Oliver. I was adamant that Oliver should be replaced only if I found that Charlie and I could not go on as a two-man group. Charlie and I had worked together for six years. We knew each other's limitations and plus points. The committee members opposed our continuing ahead without a third man. In desperation, I did what I always do in such straits: appealed directly to the boss. In this case, the relevant god was our patron, HRH The Prince of Wales. I called Prince Charles at his Gloucestershire home well after midnight and he sounded groggy. I put the third-man problem to him and his response was unequivocal. With the prince's involvement, the issue was finally resolved. We continued as a two-man group.

Meanwhile, the *Benjy B*, the ship that served as our sea base during the expedition, chugged its way north past Fiji. The vessel was designed for polar expeditions, and its crew boiled in the leaden heat of the tropics. At one point we stopped in mid-Pacific and everybody jumped overboard, including Ginnie's dog, a Jack Russell terrier, but even the sea felt warm and sticky.

We came at length to the Bering Straits, and the ship ventured into the silted shallows off the mouth of the Yukon River. To the north its way was blocked by Arctic sea ice so the plan, made eight years before, was to drop the travel group overboard in rubber boats. We would then go up the Yukon, down the Mackenzie River, through the Northwest Passage and north through the Canadian archipelago to the most northerly habitation in Canada, our old training base at Alert on Ellesmere Island.

Our two twelve-foot rubber boats were winched overboard in choppy waters sixteen miles off the Yukon. A rogue wave overturned Charlie's heavily laden inflatable and near disaster ensued. Back on the ship we watched as the skipper edged around wicked shoals until, two hundred miles farther north, we anchored off the Indian sea village of St. Michael. This time our boats made it to the coast and on to a tributary of the Yukon. But Charlie's dunking had forced me to rethink my plans for boating the infamous Northwest Passage in the rubber inflatables. The loads we each had to carry in two boats were just too heavy because of the absence of Oliver and a third boat. The only solution was to switch to a different type of boat that would cope with our load and the Arctic storms.

From an Indian village, I radioed Ginnie, who was working as a maid and waitress at the Klondike Lodge near Dawson City. This was timely employment as she had no funds, and in two weeks' time she also had the job of transporting us and our boats from a bridge six hundred miles up the Yukon to Inuvik on the Mackenzie River. I told her what we needed: a nineteen-foot Boston whaler with outboards. In between making beds and serving meals, Ginnie telephoned desperately around the world to find a boat sponsor. After five days she located a banker in Hong Kong who agreed to buy us a boat. The nearest source of a Boston whaler was in Vancouver. Ginnie made sure it was modified for ice, and then found a cargo plane boss willing to underwrite its transport to Inuvik. Its arrival there coincided with ours so no time was lost.

Anton Bowring, our boating expert, had advised against the use of an open whaler. The whaler weighed fifteen hundred pounds, plus the weight of fuel, and would be difficult to manhandle across ice floes. Unlike an inflatable, the whaler could not be flown anywhere in a floatplane. The whaler would have to be ditched along the way. But I was convinced that the whaler was our only chance. There have been many occasions, on many expeditions, when the experts have counseled against the plan I thought best for the problem ahead. When this happens I try to keep an open mind, plan for the worst-case scenario, and then go for the best compromise solution.

Advice and dire warnings from the local experts came thick and fast when Charlie and I finally reached the Arctic mouth of the Mackenzie River at Tuktoyaktuk. We said good-bye to Ginnie there on July 26. In the thirty-five summer days left when, with luck, the passage should remain at least partially ice-free, we had to complete not only the three thousand miles of the passage, in which so many ships and men have disappeared, but also cover an additional five hundred miles still farther to the north. We had to reach somewhere within skiing distance of our Arctic winter headquarters before the new ice began to crust over the sea, forcing us to abandon the whaler.

The first month of travel was a hectic and uncomfortable race with little sleep. I spent much of the time being frightened. If the rolling waves capsized us, we would undoubtedly die in the water. Long stretches of coastline offered no landing spot, and the tundra everywhere was uninhabited but for isolated radar sites.

On July 30 we plowed east for thirty-six hours without a break, for the cliffs that we skirted faced north with no stitch of cover. We were very tired, wet, cold, and cramped together. Charlie was later asked how we got on. "We do lose our tempers occasionally," he replied. "But very, very seldom and mainly when under pressure."

At the next settlement we learned that ice blocked our way east so we detoured south one hundred miles in thirty-knot winds and fog. We sheltered from one gale on a tiny island, but on August 3 my patience gave out and we ran through the storm. In a mist we grounded on shoals in the lee of dark cliffs. We escaped by luck, but that evening there were no more islands to dodge between, and we plunged all night between creaming breakers.

Finally, we limped exhausted into the isolated radar station at Gladman Point. The station boss said we must now wait for the storm to abate as, to the east, the big seas in Wellington and Victoria Straits would be lethal. We heard on his radio that the local Eskimo fisherman had been stranded for five days. "You must wait," he advised us. "The Eskimos know best."

I had no wish to ignore local knowledge, but winter was closing in fast. On August 14 we reached the passage's halfway point at the Eskimo village of Gjoa Haven.

We came to a forty-mile crossing packed with highly mobile ice floes. Fog descended and a north wind blew the ice toward us. Rather than risk being crushed in the ice pack, I told Charlie that we must turn back and search for the protection of a narrow fjord. He looked disgruntled and silence reigned. I was tempted to argue the issue, but I knew this would be a pointless exercise since I was sure mine was the correct course. The whole affair of judging risks can be intuitive and, when time is critical, I respond to my natural inclination. One key principle I hold dear, a policy much loved by the late Field Marshal Bernard Montgomery, is never move against opposition until the cards appear stacked in your favor. Nature can be a tough opponent, not given to handing out second chances.

For four anxious days, we were pinioned in a fjord. Then, we pushed north through a labyrinth of floes to Resolute Bay. Again the ice blocked our way north, which was worrying since only six days remained before the sea was likely to freeze over. In a few days we would face a nine-month delay until the following summer, so we set out on an unprecedented nine-hundred-mile journey with small chance of success.

Much of the next five days saw us bouncing through rough seas, dwarfed by huge jostling icebergs and sheer black cliffs. For one period of nine hours we saw no landing place, no inlet, however small. Our propeller blades broke, one by one, against unseen chunks of growler ice, and our speed lessened hour by hour.

Charlie spotted a tiny defile, the size of a suburban garden, between two cliffs. In desperation we nosed toward it to change propellers only to find a polar bear already in residence hunting for beluga whales. We moved in beside the bear and warily changed propellers.

Back at Resolute, Ginnie maintained an unsleeping vigil on her radio, well aware of our vulnerability along these remote coastlines. When I contacted her two days behind schedule, I could hear the tiredness and stress in her voice.

I found our intended route through Hells Gate passage ice-blocked, so we detoured around Devon Island to the only alternative sea canyon. Two anxious days and nights later we reached Great Bear Cape as the sea's surface began to congeal. We had no choice but to keep going for the last 230 northerly miles of interlocking fjords.

By the dawn of the new month, we saw to our north the dead-end beach of Tanquary Fjord. Snowcapped peaks now blocked our way north. Wolves stared from lava beaches, but nothing moved except us. Within four days the boat was frozen into the bay. It remained there undisturbed for the next seven years. With one-hundred-pound loads we skied north over the mountains of Ellesmere Island, switching to snowshoes on steep, icy sections. For 150 miles we passed no man-made object, no paths, nothing but rock and ice.

Charlie fell and cut his head open on a rock, and deep blisters festered on the soles of both his feet. Our boots broke through the snow's crust into hidden holes and Charlie jarred his spine. His left eye was swollen shut and his right heel was raw. He no longer wanted to carry his rifle.

"What about bears?" I asked him.

"Good thing," he said, "they'd put me out of my misery."

Late on September 15, we reached the foot of Omingmak Mountain, disturbing a herd of musk oxen that galloped off, snorting. Every day grew colder and the daylight hours rapidly diminished. Freezing fog banks closed over the glaciers, and we camped beneath the Boulder Hills at twenty-two hundred feet in a narrow, frozen gully.

At noon on September 26, the riverbed plunged down into a frozen waterfall, and a jagged vista of contorted pack ice stretched away to the polar horizon—the Arctic Ocean. We came by dusk to the twin huts of Alert, the most northerly buildings in the world. We had traveled around the polar axis of the world for 314 degree of latitude in 750 days. Only 46 degrees more now to Greenwich, but by far the most perilous sector lay ahead.

For the next five months Ginnie, Charlie, and I lived, with Ginnie's dog, in the huts at Alert and planned the final phase, the crossing of the Arctic Ocean via the North Pole. No man had ever crossed the Arctic Ocean in a single season, as we had to, to meet our goal. The only crossing in history, four men with forty dogs under British explorer Wally Herbert, had taken two summer seasons. Instead of waiting for the comparative comfort of March, with warmer temperatures, we had to set out in mid-February in twenty-four-hour darkness and temperatures in the minus fifties.

We left Ginnie on February 13, 1982, and four days later found our way west along the coast blocked by pressure ice. We turned north on to the sea ice. For days we axed and shoveled our way between ice walls and boulders to make way for our skidoos and heavy sledges. By February 19 we slowed to a crawl. I made a snap decision to abandon the skidoos for later collection by ski plane. We continued immediately, dragging our key stores on man-haul sledges.

Sheer exhaustion overcame any fear of bears, and a competitive sense helped us work for long hours. We knew a Norwegian team would soon be setting out to beat us across the Arctic.

One night back at base, Ginnie woke to find our main store hut on fire. She tried to put out the flames, probably ignited by an electrical spark, but with rifle bullets and flares exploding about her, she had to desist, and by morning everything was destroyed. Up until this point the entire expedition had attracted little media attention, despite its success, but our base-camp fire sparked interested all over the world. Within an hour of assessing the damage Ginnie began a forty-eight-hour sleepless vigil on her radio to London. Inside of ten days, our sponsors there reacted with replacement equipment, everything from rations to parachutes.

In the evening of March 7, my thirty-eighth birthday, in our tiny tent on the ice, we celebrated with two extra cigarettes. That day Charlie's diary recorded: "We suck ice and snow. There are times when Ran and I have to camp exhausted because we can't pick the axes up. We are shattered. But there is always light at the tunnel's end and that is what you must think about."

Back in London a committee report stated: "At this stage it is fair to say that nobody involved in the expedition would give much for its chances of reaching the Pole this year."

On March 21 our Norwegian rivals ran into trouble, and one who was suffering from frostbite was eventually rescued. The other two men continued, but they failed in their crossing attempt.

By now Charlie and I both suffered from lack of sleep; piles; many areas of raw skin; bloodshot eyes; swollen and bloody fingers, toes, noses, and lips; crotch rot; cracked fillings; and a variety of other discomforts. But there was no serious damage, and so we began to make good progress as the ice rubble lessened.

We reached the top of the world half an hour before midnight on April 10, 1982, Easter Sunday. We were the first men in history to have traveled over the Earth's surface to both poles, but many hundreds of miles and cold, wet months still lay between us and the *Benjy B*.

Two weeks after leaving the pole we completed some 230 miles of southerly progress, but all around the sea was opening up. I knew we must find a safe floe before the breakup began, but Charlie felt we should concentrate on getting much farther south before even looking for safe floes that we could use to float south. Otherwise, he believed, we would be cut off from any hope of reaching the ship before the ice refroze. We discussed our options and I took the safer course of searching for a floe sooner rather than later.

Charlie made his position clear. The decision was mine not his. The outcome of starting to float too soon from too far north might make us end up well short of the ice edge and the *Benjy B*. If so, all fingers would point at me. The popular course would be to, as we Brits say, "bash on." But the southerly sea currents were now with us. I used a 1936 Soviet guide, which showed a good mathematical chance that we could float south fast enough to just make it. My natural instinct to hurry conflicted with an inner instinct to be cautious. The outcome of ten years of work by many people depended on this single decision.

The ensuing search for a suitable floe was nearly our undoing. Charlie and I both ended up on the same narrow stretch of mobile sludge towing all our gear. We came within a few yards of breaking through into the sea. Nothing could have saved us, and I cannot to this day forget the nightmare of that moment.

At last we located a solid floe and made camp. Although there were many scares over the next three months of floating and many new cracks that slowly diminished the floe's size, it took us safely south despite the frequent storms that raged about our fragile home. Nineteen bears visited the tent during our ninety-five days on the floe. Only one was aggressive, and it was warned off by a bullet through the shin as it attacked.

On June 1, 1982, Charlie, checking his diary in the tent, muttered, "By tonight we will have been traveling from Greenwich for 1,000 days." During the entire duration of our Arctic Ocean journey, Charlie and I had no serious personal flare-ups. The secret was probably the long period of working together prior to the crossing. We knew each other's stress points so well that we subconsciously knew when to steer clear of a delicate topic.

Because of strong, southerly winds, our float rate slowed to a crawl, and the committee in London came to the conclusion that we could not reach any point to rendezvous with the ship before that winter. On July 2 the ship tried to force its way toward us but was driven back. Later that month, eighty-two miles from our floe, the *Benjy B* struck ice too hard and a key welding joint in the stern cracked open. Cleverly, the captain managed to ram another floe in such a way to run the damaged section high out of the water, and, kneeling on the floe, the engineers botched up a temporary repair.

In mid-July the committee, very worried that we would soon be out of reach in the pack ice, sent orders to Ginnie that the ski plane must try to evacuate us. But Ginnie conveniently developed rather sudden radio troubles and failed to receive this evacuation order. At the end of the month, when a wind change briefly loosed the pack, the ship tried again.

On August 3, 1982, the ship became jammed only seventeen miles from our floe. At 2 p.m. that afternoon we abandoned the floe, and using two small canoes on detachable skis, made a dash for the ship on a compass bearing. The canoe skies broke, but we hauled like madmen, and mounting a pressure ridge at 7 p.m., I spotted two tiny matchsticks to the south, the masts of the *Benjy B*.

I think that was the single most satisfactory moment of my life. For three hours we heaved, tugged, paddled, and often lost sight of the ship, but soon after midnight we climbed on board. The circle was complete. Ginnie was standing by a cargo hatch. Between us we had spent twenty years to reach this point. None of us will ever forget that moment—we shared then something that no one could ever take away from us.

On August 24 Prince Charles brought the ship back to its starting point at Greenwich, almost three years to the day since we had set out. Ten thousand cheering people lined the banks. The journey was over. Earth had been circumnavigated on its polar axis.

• • •

Sir Ranulph Fiennes has been named by *Guinness World Records* as the "World's Greatest Living Explorer." He was born in 1944 in the United Kingdom and was brought up in South Africa. In 1965, he became the youngest captain in the British Army. In 1970, he launched a series of record-breaking expeditions, some of which include first to reach both poles (with Charles Burton), first to cross the Antarctic and Arctic oceans (with Charles Burton), first to circumnavigate the world along the polar axis (with Charles Burton), the discovery in 1992 of the lost city of Ubar on the Yemeni border, and in 1992 and 1993 he and Michael Stroud completed the first unsupported crossing of the Antarctic Continent. He is the author of sixteen books. This chapter was excerpted from *Beyond the Limits* (Little, Brown, 2000).

Chapter 8

Big Heart on Baffin Island

J. ROBERT HARRIS

It was a bleak, cold Arctic day on Baffin Island. Dusk was approaching, there was less than an hour's worth of sunlight left, I was alone and scared. Since early morning, I followed an obscure trail along the eastern shoreline of Summit Lake. The trail was on a glacial moraine made up of millions of rocks, some as big as elephants. Progress was slow. The route markers were also made of stone and difficult to distinguish from the moraine itself. Even the light was gray.

I walked under the weight of my backpack. An intermittent snowfall made the boulders slippery and treacherous. The view across the lake was of a long, high wall of rock rising abruptly from the shoreline. I saw where the eastern and western shores converged. It was there, between the top of the moraine on one side and the high ground, that Summit Lake squeezes through a deep gorge as a cascading rapid. That convergence marked the beginning of the Weasel River.

When I finally arrived at the gorge, I saw my dangerous predicament. I needed to get to the other side. The only way to do that was in a weather-beaten chair that was suspended from a rusty cable anchored to the rocks on either side. The chair was too small to accommodate both me and my pack and even if it could, the cable did not look strong enough to carry the combined weight. As darkness approached, I was afraid to make the crossing but realized that turning around and going back was not an option.

In 1989, I was browsing through a magazine and came across an article about Baffin Island, the sixth-largest island in the world, the majority of it above the Arctic Circle. The article described the island as being inhabited by dozens of small Eskimo settlements and that the natives depended on hunting and fishing for their subsistence. I thought it would be exciting to undertake a trek across a remote wilderness, where there are no towns, no roads, none of the trappings of civilization. I wanted to see and experience for myself what life was like for the Inuit, whose ancestors had lived there for centuries.

When I read the article, I was forty-five years old, a marketing consultant, and a native New Yorker. I had some experience as a backpacker, having trekked in remote areas for years—much of it solo—but my roots were definitely in the city. I grew up in a working-class family and lived in city housing projects. During the gang warfare days of the 1960s, I attended neighborhood schools and walked the mean streets with a swagger. Back then, if you were street smart and not easily intimidated, then you had "heart." If someone said you had "big heart," then that was the highest compliment.

As I grew older, a hunger for the wilderness replaced the streets, and I set out to learn a new set of skills. Over time I evolved an image of myself as an adventurer who is cautious but not timid, bold but not reckless. I had heart in the wilderness too, maybe even big heart. My city friends were convinced that I was fearless. Most would not go to the South Bronx alone, and few could comprehend how I could enjoy sleeping on the ground in exotic, sometimes dangerous places, and truthfully say I liked it.

So that's why one Wednesday afternoon in late August, I took my big heart to Baffin Island, beginning with a long journey northward to a tiny settlement called Qikiqtarjuaq. While there I arranged for transportation through the pack ice to the desolate, inhospitable shore of Baffin Island. It was a half day's journey across the Davis Strait in a small wooden boat called a "freighter canoe." Once there, I would begin an eight-day overland hike to my final destination, the town of Pangnirtung. In Qikiqtarjuaq, I went to the community center, where the men of the village congregated, and introduced myself. They were cordial and curious about what life was like in faraway New York. At the same time, I could sense them subtly checking me out, wondering why a middle-aged black guy would travel so far to make this hike. They seemed impressed but wondered aloud if I realized how remote and isolated I would be when the boat got to Baffin and left me there alone to sort out what would be a treacherous hike. They puffed on their pipes, shook their heads, and finally wished me luck.

My next stop was the Auyuittuq National Park ranger's office, where I registered and got a hiking permit. The ranger was a younger man in his thirties, lean and fit, with calloused hands and deep lines of experience around his eyes. Like the village men, he took a few long moments to size me up. If the guys at the community center were politely dubious about my chances, the warden was openly skeptical and tried to discourage me. When I insisted that I was good to go, he made me write and sign a disclaimer absolving Parks Canada—and himself—of responsibility for any harm that might come to me. I signed, anxious to be on my way.

A young Inuit couple, with their baby daughter in tow, took me in their boat to the Baffin coast. When we reached the shore, I unloaded my gear, paid them, and waved good-bye, watching as they chugged away. The sound of the outboard motor fading into silence made me realize that I could not turn back. It was now impossible to return to Qikiqtarjuaq. I had to get to Pang. I also knew that the summer season was over and I was likely the last and only person hiking this route in either direction.

Four days later, at about 8 p.m., I arrived at the chair crossing over the Summit Lake gorge. I'd been hiking over the boulders for more than ten hours. My feet, the muscles in my calves, thighs, lower back, and shoulders were locked in pain. The sky was overcast and a chilly breeze was blowing through the canyon. It looked like it might snow again. I knew from the map that there was a chair crossing here.

However, I wasn't prepared for how primitive it was. Across the front of the chair, clamped to a wooden armrest on either side, was a length of cable that served as a makeshift seat belt, the only protection against falling out and being swept away. The theory was that I was to strap myself into the chair, then reach up and haul myself, hand over hand, across to the other side. If I had not been alone, the system might not have been much of a challenge. With two people, one person would cross, so that someone was on either side. Then you could lash each backpack into the chair and pull the gear across, followed by the remaining person. But I had to get myself and my pack across at the same time. There was no obvious way to do it. Even if I figured something out, I wasn't sure I would be strong enough to pull the combined load across by myself. Besides, I could not shake the feeling that the thin, fragile-looking cable would suddenly snap with me on it. The sight of this contraption creaking and swaying in the stiff breeze made me question how much heart I really had.

Fear shows itself in different ways. In a crisis that requires an instinctive and immediate reaction, you don't have time to be afraid. The fear comes later, after your breathing returns to normal. It's worse somehow when there is ample time to experience the fear, when it simmers and threatens to overwhelm. In those occasions, there are two problems: the fear itself and the unavoidable crisis. During those first few moments at the gorge, I was stunned and immobile. I suppressed a wave of panic, but the longer I stood there, the more frightening it became.

Survival experts advise that if you find yourself in a life-threatening situation, the first thing to do is to sit down and gather your thoughts. Thus, despite the fact that it was getting steadily darker and colder, I dropped my pack, sat down on it, and took a few deep breaths. I forced myself to think logically. I was intensely aware that there was nobody with me to share my anxiety, to discuss risks and options, or to give encouragement.

Meanwhile, the awesome power of the tumultuous rapids and the thunderous roar it made as it blasted through the channel were so overwhelming that I could not bring myself to look down. I felt I might be drawn into the rapids. Despite my efforts to fight it, I felt paralyzed by the thought that I might not have long to live. My thoughts drifted to my family and friends. I remembered the guys back in Qikiqtarjuaq, how I stood among them in my expensive clothing and fancy gear, pontificating on courage. I also recalled the interview with the warden, and how I insisted that I was competent. It all seemed so vain now.

The concept of big heart, which used to seem so noble and romantic, now seemed macho and stupid. The fact was that if the chair should fall, there would be no rescue. Nobody would ever hear from me again. I would disappear in an instant, without a trace. I started to hyperventilate and made a desperate bid to breathe and regain control.

I knew what I had to do, but doubted that I could do it. Nevertheless, I knew I had to make my move now. It was almost completely dark and there was no place to camp on this side of the gorge. I was shaking uncontrollably, but took a deep breath and forced myself to sit in the decrepit little seat. Instead of strapping myself in, I looped the seat belt down and through the shoulder straps on my backpack. My gear now hung beneath me under the chair. The pack was heavy and I had no idea if the seat belt could hold the weight. If the belt broke, all of my food, clothing, tent, and gear would be gone.

Mustering a little bit of courage, I shoved off, moving away from the safety of the ridge top. The chair moved fairly easily on a slightly downward trajectory as the cable sagged under the weight of its burden. Out over the gorge it was really windy and cold. When I could not see the ridge I had just left, I felt another surge of panic. I hung from a wire suspended in space, expecting it to snap at any moment. The sound of the invisible torrent, with me now directly above it, was even more menacing.

When I passed the middle of the gorge, progress suddenly became much slower and more difficult as the cable slanted up toward the far side. I yanked frantically on the pulley rope, trying to haul the load upward. Movement was made in inches. My arms ached and my fingers were numb and freezing. If I let go with one hand, or even loosened my grip, the chair would start to slide back toward the middle. With each agonizing pull, I glanced in the direction of the cliff, hoping for some sign that the crossing was almost over. Finally I could see the other side. A final blast of adrenaline propelled me to the end of the cable.

Yet, I was not out of trouble. The cable was attached to a wall of rock that sloped steeply downward toward the rapids. There was no easy way of getting both me and the backpack off the chair. If I was careless, I could slide down the cliff and into the swirling, frigid water. Taking my time, I managed to crawl up the inclined rock face to the top of the cliff and safety.

The next morning, before continuing my journey, I walked back to the gorge for a final look. From the safety of the other side, the crossing looked much less intimidating. I tried to convince myself that I had not been all that frightened. It didn't work. That episode, which took maybe half an hour, remains vivid in my mind even now. I learned on that cross not to be afraid of fear. From then on, I was confident that I could somehow rise above panic and maintain control of rampaging emotions. I found what big heart really is: not the absence of fear, but the acceptance of it.

• • •

James Robert "J. R." Harris is an explorer by avocation, having completed twenty-three expeditions worldwide, many of them solo. He works as a marketing consultant in New York.

Chapter 9

Life When Hell Freezes Over

BRANDON WILSON

It's a glorious summer day by Arctic standards. At a sunny 36 degrees, with just enough wind to carry the aroma of fermenting walrus carcasses far away from our Inupiaq Eskimo village, this day has been a long time coming. In fact, it's been nearly a year since my wife, Cheryl, and I landed on this remote outpost of civilization.

We've traveled to some extreme places on Earth, but this place epitomizes the phrase "when hell freezes over." Barrow is the end of terra firma, some 330 miles above the Arctic Circle. You can go no farther, even if you dared. Pitted dirt tracks peter out at the edge of a thick sheet of ice, a floe that only vanishes for a few short months of the year. Even today, in June, it's still lurking, taunting us just offshore.

The "road," if you generously call it that, extends only as far as the former Distant Early Warning (DEW) Line station, some five miles away. It was 1981, and this former bastion that protected America from menacing Communist hordes is mostly a watering hole and pool hall. It offers *tunniks* (that disparaging term given to us white folks by the locals) the promise of a drink ("hold the ice") in this otherwise supposedly alcohol-free icebox of isolation.

That dirt track continues another mile or so to "Hollywood," the ramshackle remains of a movie set used for filming *Nanook of the North* back in 1922. It's also home to the windswept Wiley Post Memorial, commemorating the tragic downing of the American flying ace who ended his days here in this godforsaken gulag.

Yes, today promises a day of unbridled freedom after a winter that could try the patience of Gandhi. Since arriving last August at this remote settlement of twenty-five hundred natives, pioneers, dreamers, and social outcasts, we've been welcomed with all the warmth of a summer cold. First, my wife and I found jobs. I became the mayor's assistant. A simple apartment was its primary perk. Within months, I kissed them both good-bye for pledging loyalty in His Honor's power struggle and refusing to "submit" to the new city manager's authority. So we were summarily plunked out onto the streets.

Truth is, our lonely village of mostly thrown-together houses, many looking like they'd been constructed of driftwood, is not a hotbed of housing options. So we've been forced to camp out on couches and floors over these past six months and rely on the kindness of strangers.

"Why don't you just leave?" you might ask.

Well, there's a point to be made and we stubbornly refuse to be run out of town. Besides, this being quirky Barrow, I was immediately offered a better job by a lady with ties to the other "tribe," just to get back at my nemesis. So, this year has been a daily, ongoing opera on ice.

Next, as if this wasn't enough to discourage all but the true masochist, there's the weather, always the weather. Mark Twain's lament that "everyone talks about the weather, but nobody does anything about it" should be the village motto, inscribed on its official seal.

Soon after our arrival, temperatures dropped dramatically in this barren, beachside desert. Days grew increasingly shorter as the town braced itself for its annual fiesta of darkness—complete and utter blackness from November 18 to January 24. Even the famous northern lights chose to vacation elsewhere. By then, the winds howled across this eerie lunar landscape while the wind chill sometimes brought this garden spot of the north down to a bone-numbing minus sixty degrees Fahrenheit.

Then, to make matters worse, the locals' welcome has often been just as bitterly cold. Our charming hamlet is base camp for the oil industry's Roto-Rootering Prudhoe Bay to our east, as well as home to well-moneyed native corporations and the seat of a county the size of California. Unfortunately, it's going through a major transition. The Inupiaq have leapfrogged centuries of development in just a few short years, morphing from a seminomadic, fishing and whale-hunting society to a corn-chip munching, cable-watching bureaucracy awash in money.

It's been a tough year for our hosts. They haven't caught a bowhead whale from their skin boats, called "umiacs," so there will be no Nalukataq whaling celebration. Bad juju, I guess. Meanwhile, more of their kids are leaving for the lower forty-eight to get their piece of Uncle Sam's pie, but many return. One lady we know who went to Seattle couldn't cope with the heat until she filled her bathtub with ice cubes and stretched out in cool, arctic comfort.

Ah, just like home.

Many of us *tunniks* have been innocently lured to this remote outpost to help its inhabitants build a modern infrastructure. There has been no raping, pillaging, nude sunbathing, or otherwise frowned-upon behavior that I know of. We've set up schools, utilities, banks, stores, churches, cultural programs, health care, social programs, and even "honey bucket" trucks to retrieve plastic bags of human refuse. (Indoor plumbing will still take its time to arrive in every home.)

Out of necessity, we've banded together in a kind of MASH-type unit for friendship and psychological survival. Together we've suffered through winter anxiously awaiting nature's annual renewal. But nature has had other plans in this icy colony of sensory deprivation. Sure, days have grudgingly grown longer and warmer one minute at a time, but there's been no welcome burst of color. No trees have budded, since there *are* no trees. No bluebirds of happiness chirp from our windowsills. No merry "Hi ya, neighbors" resonate across the vast stillness of our barren yards.

It's life, same as it ever was. Only now, depression weighs on everyone's back as we realize that things really aren't any better than they were last winter. Only now, we can see the barren bleakness where fate has dropped us. Plus, all those missing bags of human waste tossed into the snow in winter darkness are thawing and a less than springtime-fresh aroma wafts across our quaint village.

So today, now that our one-year anniversary and vowed departure looms on the horizon, we do the nearly unthinkable. We decide to wander away from the security of town. Besides, it's sunny, already warmed up to freezing—and it's finally warm enough to snow. All winter long the snow has just whipped in horizontally from the nearby North Pole with no new accumulation, no snow drifts, no chance for my wife to make snow angels in fresh powder.

However, we're still cautious. We've listened to daily radio warnings about polar bears wandering through our village, digging through the dumpsite, stalking the school. We know that polar bears are the only mammal to actively stalk humans, and a hungry bear is a persistent bear. So we're a little reluctant to venture too far out of town during the dark of winter. That unmistakable "crunch, crunch, crunch" of snow in the distance always sets our hair on edge, since those cuddly critters can outrun even the fastest human.

Today is different. With a buddy of mine, Speedo (who, incidentally, carries a .457 Magnum whenever leaving town), we've arranged to borrow two three-wheelers from a friend and take off down the barren beach and across the boggy tundra to Hollywood and beyond. Eager to get started, Cheryl and I sit atop one shiny red bike with Speedo on the other. Being a much more experienced rider, he quickly takes the lead.

It's exhilarating to be moving again, the wind whipping against our faces and finally free of our heavy winter fur-trimmed parkas, free of our frustrations, free to explore. We've waited all winter for this, and although I've never driven a three-wheeler before, I'm caught up in the moment: Easy Rider of the Tundra.

"This isn't hard at all," I think, charging up another dune.

As our minds race ahead, we try our best to forget all the pain of the past ten months. We and the bike sail as one across the hard-packed beach, then up over one small sand dune after another. Farther and farther the three of us head west until the village quickly dips from sight. Even Speedo, riding solo and faster, soon becomes a speck on the flat, western horizon.

Laughing together, ecstatic, our spirits soar each time we hurdle over another dune and become momentarily airborne. Then unexpectedly, these rises come in quick succession and we no longer feel any sand beneath our tires. We're airborne. I frantically jerk the wheel, but it's too late. We plunge like pelicans into the Arctic Ocean.

As you might expect, our bike quickly sinks, but we hold on tight and then struggle with all our fortitude to push, pull, and jiggle our reluctant, waterlogged three-wheeler back to the water's edge.

Now if this had happened at any other place on a sunny day, I think, we'd have a good laugh and take a leisurely stroll back home. But this is different. We're drenched, it's freezing, and we're miles from town—in polar bear country.

Without wasting a moment, we decide that our best option is to take off our clothes, wring them out, and begin the long slog back into town. Again, in another place and time, we'd start a fire. But here, there's no wood, not even dung to burn like in Tibet.

"This would be hilarious, if only . . ." I mumble between chattering teeth. "Imagine seeing two ghostly white, naked *tunniks* on an Arctic beach, shivering madly as they prance and hop to keep warm while wringing out their clothes."

Mission quickly accomplished, we attempt to restart our bike, but it's uncooperative and useless. It'll never start now that the engine is flooded (*literally*). And I hate to risk leaving our friend's three-wheeler out here on the tundra.

"Best to keep moving before hypothermia sets in," I remind Cheryl, but my brave companion is already steps ahead of me, head tucked down against the wind. Reluctantly, we begin our slow trudge back to the village with me pushing the bike. However, it only takes one hundred yards to convince me of that folly.

"It's hopeless. I'll never make it back pushing this, especially while shivering uncontrollably and growing colder every second," I said.

At just that moment, we catch the drone of Speedo's engine. He's finally realized that we are missing and returns to check on us—or perhaps to see if there's anything left after the polar bear's picnic.

With obvious relief, Cheryl hops on the back of his three-wheeler for the ride back into town. Meanwhile, I jog as far as my lungs will carry me along the beach for miles, trying desperately to keep my body temperature up. Until finally, in what seems like an hour, my friend returns and I'm more than relieved to catch a ride with him and forgo the earlier adrenaline rush of any more dune racing—or swimming.

This was my first and last dip in ice-packed waters. But that July, just before we left Barrow for good, Cheryl and a few other crazies decide to join the local Polar Bear Club for their annual dip. They huddle in heated cars until the appointed hour, then rush like penguins to dive into the glacial sea. A few exuberant Mexican workers even swim out far enough to hop onto chunks of ice bobbing offshore and pose for a quick photo.

"Ah, the shrinkage! The shrinkage!"

As for me, well, I always like to say that I'll try anything once. And in this case, for both icebox living and Arctic swimming, once is certainly enough.

• • •

Brandon Wilson is an award-winning author/photographer who has explored nearly one hundred countries. He is now an expert long-distance lite trekker, having walked the Camino de Santiago across Spain (twice), the Via Francigena from Canterbury to Rome, the St. Olav's Way across Norway, and a 650-mile pilgrimage trail from Lhasa, Tibet, to Kathmandu. He is the author of the critically acclaimed books *Yak Butter Blues: A Tibetan Trek of Faith* (Heliographica, 2004) and *Dead Men Don't Leave Tips: Adventures X Africa* (Pilgrim's Tales, Inc., 2005). His new book, *Along the Templar Trail,* is about a 2,600-mile peace trek to Jerusalem and will be published in 2008 (Pilgrim's Tales, Inc.).

PART THREE

Chapter 10

Thieves of Baghdad

MATTHEW BOGDANOS

On May 2, 2003, I was working my way through Iraq's National Museum in the heart of Baghdad, investigating the rampage and the looting that had taken place during the 2003 war. With me were other members of the multiservice, multiagency unit that I led, military trigger-pullers and analysts teamed up with law enforcement officers from a dozen other agencies.

As we passed through the museum's long, central corridor—the musty, poorly lit room that had just been on the cover of *Newsweek*—our guide was Nawala al-Mutwali, the museum's director. We stepped over rubble and shattered glass, cracked sarcophagi, and the broken heads of ancient statues. The large objects that had fared better were surrounded by sandbags or wrapped in foam-rubber padding. While most people found Nawala to be dour and difficult, we had become friends. In fact, our affection for each other was so obvious that the team joked relentlessly about my carrying on some mad affair with this imposing and somewhat older woman.

After two weeks of laborious, room-by-room inspections, we were ready to examine the underground storage area, the first portion of the museum that was virgin territory, completely undisturbed since the looting. That meant it was our first clean crime scene and offered the possibility of a significant investigative breakthrough. We might even get something we had seen little of so far: evidence. On that day, we had a BBC film crew tagging along. They wanted the story, and I wanted to be able to use their footage to document our findings. Like everything else in a war zone, their presence was a quid pro quo, a horse trade.

The list of missing objects already read like a compilation of Mesopotamia's greatest hits. There was the sacred Vase of Warka, the world's oldest carved stone ritual vessel. There was the Mask of Warka, the first naturalistic sculpture of the human face. There was the gold bull's head that had adorned Queen Shub-Ad's Golden Harp of Ur, discovered in 1929 by a team that included Sir Leonard Woolley, Sir Max Mallowan, and Mallowan's future wife, Agatha Christie. There was the Bassetki Statue, one of the earliest known examples of the lost wax technique of casting copper, as well as the Lioness Attacking a Nubian ivory, and the twin copper Ninhursag Bulls. These pieces alone were a year's course in art history. They were all in one museum. And they were all gone.

We had repeatedly tried to open the heavy, steel doors that would lead us down into the basement. So had the looters—some of the doors bore sledgehammer marks. Others were covered over by heavy grates wrapped with the kind of cable locks we use in Manhattan so that motorcycles stay put. Much later, watching the BBC footage while back home, I noted how one of Nawala's AK-47-toting assistants showed up behind me with a set of keys. The museum had this curious arrangement of overlapping circles of security, born out of their even more curious system of centralized authority and interdepartmental animosities. Not only did staff from one department have no idea about the inventories or practices of other departments, no one person had the keys to every sector. None of the keys were ever marked, and this set was no exception. Nawala had to try every single one, and even then she could not find the key that would get us into the sanctum sanctorum of the underground storage room.

We took the difficulty as cause for optimism. Actually, given that this area held some of the museum's most highly valuable and most easily transportable objects, it was closer to elation. If we couldn't get in, chances are the bad guys didn't either.

As we would later determine, there were four underground rooms in an L-shaped configuration, plus a fifth that had to be accessed through a different route. In the deepest, darkest corner were two rows of ordinary, unmarked lockers that would have fit right in at the gym where I'd learned to box as a kid growing up in New York City. Only instead of sweaty workout clothes, these held the world's greatest collection of ancient gold and silver coins. In these same brown and beat-up lockers, in the same dark corner, was also the world's greatest collection of ancient cylinder seals, highly prized by collectors and, accordingly, highly prized by thieves. About the size of a piece of chalk, these intricately carved pieces of lapis lazuli, carnelian, or other stones had once been worn on a string around the neck by upscale citizens of ancient Mesopotamia. These were the people who'd invented writing, scratching wedge-shaped (*cuneus forma* in Latin, hence, cuneiform) symbols into soft clay with a stylus beginning about 5,500 years ago. As the final touch to any correspondence, they would use the seal the way my Greek grandmother used a rolling pin to smooth out phyllo. The impression left in the soft clay by the inscribed seal was the distinctive signature of that individual.

Nawala, a descendant of these ancient and inventive people, was one tough lady—I had watched her break her toe just a few days earlier and not utter a sound. On that day, we had also been trying to open a locked door, one that was ten inches thick. When it finally gave, she could have jumped back out of the way, but in doing so she would have touched me—a violation of sharia, the religious law. So she stayed put, the heavy steel door raked across her toe, and she silently crumbled into herself, biting one of her thumbs.

In the hot glare of the BBC cameras, Nawala was frustrated by the endless number of unmarked keys. I heard her mutter to herself in Arabic, and then she said, "There is the other way." I glanced at my guys from the Bureau of Immigration and Customs Enforcement (ICE). "It has been sealed off with bricks," she said. "So there is no way anyone could enter." I didn't know if it was the custom in Iraq, but my thought was, "Knock on wood when you say that."

This back door Nawala told us about was at the bottom of a narrow stairwell, accessed from a landing just off a room displaying Roman antiquities from Hatra. Those are the ruins of an ancient commercial crossroads that you see in the opening scene from *The Exorcist* when a Mesopotamian demon escapes from an archaeological dig. We went through the Assyrian and Babylonian galleries and entered the Hatran Gallery. All we noticed at first were some three-foot-high partitions in front of a doorway in the corner. Walking closer, we moved the partitions. The lower portion of the locked glass door was smashed, and behind that, down about knee level, the steel grate across the door had been bent with a crowbar.

Nawala threw up her hands, gasping out the Arabic equivalent of "Oh my God!" The small area beyond the glass door was like a broom closet beneath a stairway. In fact, the underside of the museum's main stairs passed overhead, ascending from right to left. But immediately inside the small alcove, to the right, was another extremely narrow stairway going down to the basement. At the bottom of this narrow stairs, the metal door was wide open, but—as we had come to expect by now—there were no signs that it had been forced open. We could see the cinder blocks that had been mortared into place behind this door to seal the actual opening itself. We could also see that two cinder blocks from the top row and two from the second row had been pried loose and removed. At this point, we asked the BBC crew to stay behind and politely appropriated their equipment.

Steve Mocsary, the senior ICE agent on my team, picked up the big Ampex camera and started filming. His most immediate purpose, though, was to direct the TV lights into the cavernous area beyond the doorway as Bud Rogers and I prepared to go over the wall. Bud was also ICE, as well as a former member of the U.S. Army Special Forces. He had been on a classified operation in Romania when we'd first entered Iraq, but as soon as we decided to undertake the museum investigation, Steve told me Bud was the best in the business and requested permission to bring him into the country. One phone call later, Bud was getting off a Black Hawk, and I learned quickly that Steve had not been exaggerating.

For his own part, Steve may have been a bit long in the tooth—this was certainly his last shot in the field before a desk job and then retirement—but he was no slouch. A former U.S. Navy SEAL, the nation's premier special forces unit, he was also a veteran of the navy's elite Underwater Demolition Team; he was tough and seasoned, utterly unflappable, and he knew explosives.

The hole in the cinder blocks was big enough for only one of us to go through at a time. On the other side of the wall, the stairway continued on down. I went first, like a diver—head foremost, arms extended. I'd like to say that I landed in a perfect combat roll with catlike reflexes, peering into the unknown darkness, my 9 mm poised and ready to fell any evildoer with a double tap to center mass. In fact, I landed in a clump and scratched both elbows—but at least my pistol was ready.

Then Bud Rogers dropped down beside me.

In Iraq, every place at every moment is hotter than hell, but underground it was hotter than the hinges of hell, specifically, the hinges of Dante's eighth circle, the one he reserved for thieves and hypocrites to suffer together for eternity. The room was airless and, aside from the BBC camera's light shining over my head, pitch dark. Steve maneuvered the beam so we could assess the situation before we moved. We could not be 100 percent certain that we were alone down here, and holding a flashlight in front of your body is like wearing a nice big target pinned to your chest.

I looked ahead and tried not to blink as the salty sweat trickled down, burning my eyes. Then I saw footprints in the dust making a beeline across the floor. These thieves had a clear idea of where they were going and, presumably, what they were after: the coins and the cylinder seals, some of which were worth $250,000 a pop. Given their size, anyone could carry off a million dollars' worth in a single fanny pack.

What I didn't know was whether they had reached their objective. But of more immediate concern, had they left any surprises for us? We had found rocket-propelled grenades, hand grenades, Iraqi uniforms, and assorted small arms scattered throughout the museum. This last corner of the basement would have been an excellent place to leave a parting gift wired with explosives. As an investigator, I was thinking about that straight line in the dust. As a marine, I was thinking about rods, cones, and night vision—in the dark you're supposed to look slightly off center—and trigger pull. As a classical-history buff, passing sarcophagi and amphorae I was thinking, "Wow, this is like the catacombs."

Slowly, and with great care, we crept down the few remaining steps and followed the path of the footprints. The smell of damp clay was overpowering. We stayed just astride the beam of Steve's camera light, which showed the way ahead, but only directly ahead. We went as far as we could in that one direction, dust motes swirling above us like snowflakes. Then we turned around and retraced our steps.

I had dispatched a couple of other ICE guys—Claude Davenport, our computer whiz; and Bud Adada, one of three fluent Arabic speakers on the team—to wire up the basement to our generator outside. We needed to get the lights back on before we started exploring more broadly. Unfortunately, air-conditioning was not an option.

Once we were back to the sealed doorway on the stairs, Steve extended a meter-long pry bar through the small opening. It would have been much easier to break down the wall from the outside, but the steel bar was too long to maneuver in the narrow space. The guys who last passed this way had been better prepared. Somehow, they knew to bring a hammer and chisel. Doing the best we could from the inside out, Bud and I took turns chipping away at the mortar holding those big gray cinder blocks. It took us over an hour to loosen another seven or eight rows, removing enough blocks for the rest of the team, including Nawala, to make it through. We generated buckets of sweat,, as well as buckets of dust and rubble, sucking down water and struggling to breathe.

When the wall was about knee-high, Nawala climbed over. Her two assistants with the AK-47s seemed eager to tag along. One of them raced forward, but I put my hand on his chest and he stopped. He looked at me, I looked at him, and he backed down. But not out of fear. He was acknowledging the obvious: that I was in charge—for now. He was also letting me know that my authority did not extend beyond this moment. In that one look, we understood each other perfectly. In other circumstances, we would each go for the trigger, and I made a mental note never to turn my back on him.

"I had no idea," Nawala muttered to herself in Arabic as she followed on my heels. "No idea," she repeated in English, ostensibly for me. We were doing it my way, in single file, stepping in the footprints already made. Even before we had passed through the first room, she had begun to hyperventilate. Her face was flushed, but not just from the heat. It was as if she had a child trapped down here, and she had to know if that child was dead or alive. It did not help that she was covered from head to toe, including the *khimar* that swathed her head.

The overhead lights were on now, and we could easily make out the footprints leading into the next room. We could also see that while everything in this storage area was filthy, dusty, dank, and jam-packed with pots and statuettes, it was also totally, and incongruously, undisturbed. Clearly, the people who had entered before us were not impulse shoppers.

We continued following the footprints, turned a corner, and then it was as if we had crossed paths with a tornado. The entire floor was strewn with what were, essentially, plastic fishing-tackle boxes. Some were upside down, some had been flung aside, and others had been smashed into the walls. It looked as if the intruders had simply thrown a fit. Remnants of burned foam-rubber padding lay on the floor everywhere, still giving off an acrid smell. And behind all this, standing silently, were the thirty brown storage cabinets containing the coins and the seals.

The first of these cabinets stood open and empty.

Nawala went down on one knee. She had hoped against hope that the looters had failed, but now that hope seemed dashed. Bud Rogers pulled over a chair for her and she sat down. Then her head listed to one side and she hit the floor.

I motioned to Steve to turn off the camera. I also noticed that a couple of the BBC guys were following us now at a distance. "Clear the room!" I yelled. Then I sent for Claude, our computer whiz, who was also an emergency medical technician. I knelt down and touched Nawala's face. She was out cold. Her skin felt clammy, and she had only the faintest suggestion of a pulse. She was in shock—acute circulatory failure, with barely enough blood pressure to transport oxygen to the brain. And it doesn't take much of this before brain cells start dying from hypoxia.

We elevated her feet and fanned her face, but she gave no response. Claude came running and knelt down beside her. He was around Steve's age and I could see the sweat soaking his graying goatee. He looked her over. Then he turned to me and said, "Colonel, she might go out of the picture." Now I was the one feeling light-headed. Nawala and I had become close. But it was also true that if she died, we were in deep trouble. I could see the headlines now: FAMED IRAQI EXPERT DIES IN U.S. CUSTODY.

"We've got to get her headgear off," Claude said.

That much was obvious. But I also knew that Nawala was no "Ash Wednesday, Palm Sunday" sort of Muslim. I thought back to the way she had broken her toe to avoid touching me. For all the hours we'd worked together and the friendship we'd struck—and my team's nonstop girlfriend jokes notwithstanding—she and I had never so much as shaken hands. My team's mission in Baghdad was delicate enough without scandalizing Muslim sensibilities.

"We've got to get some women down here," I said. Bud Rogers took off, running back up to the main floor, looking for some of the young women who were conducting the inventory of what was left of the museum's collection. Trying to carry Nawala up to the first floor would be a sure way to kill her. In fact, given the absurdly narrow stairs, we were not at all sure that we *could* carry her back up to the first floor. We had no choice but to revive her where she was. But for that, we had to get her out from under all that fabric so she could breathe. If the female assistants had already left, we were screwed. Given the chaos that still reigned on the streets, their male relatives usually came to pick them up in the early afternoon so that they could make it home well before dusk.

Bud came back with two young women who spoke no English but still understood what we were asking them to do. They too were covered head to toe. One of them, in addition to the *khimar* covering her head, wore a scarf as a veil over her face. Looking down at Nawala, they shook their heads, and I could see that their hands were trembling. Even as women they could not do this—uncover another Muslim woman's head in the presence of men, especially non-Muslim men.

I told all the guys except for Claude to turn their backs. While one of the women unbuttoned Nawala's jacket, it fell to me to remove her *khimar*. For whatever damage it would do to U.S.-Iraq relations, I also held her hand. I remember wishing in that moment that I had learned enough Arabic to coax Nawala back to consciousness. Meanwhile, the other side of my brain was stressing over what was happening to my evidence. Rumors of Nawala's demise had brought museum staffers and even journalists creeping downstairs until there must have been forty people in the basement.

"Steve, crime scene," I yelled. It was all he needed to hear. Pro that he was, he got everyone to back out slowly, and in the same footprints that they had made when they'd entered.

I turned my focus back to Nawala, and waited.

Half an hour later, her eyes began to flutter. We let her take her time. She was still woozy, but she was going to recover. She wasn't ready to stand, but we helped her into a chair, positioning it so that she was not facing the cabinets. She kept turning around to look at them. So I came back to her several times to redirect her gaze, and each time I'd shift the chair. Then each time she would simply crane her neck still farther to look back at the lockers. By the time we were done, I had rotated her chair beyond the one-hundred-eighty-degree mark, so that now she was looking back over her *other* shoulder. It was another hour before Nawala was able to stand up and go home. This day's discoveries had come to an end. We would have to wait until she was in better shape to see what was or was not inside those cabinets.

I was desperate to know what was behind the rest of those cabinet doors, but we had to maintain discipline in assessing the only undisturbed crime scene in the entire museum. A rookie would have gone straight to the lockers the very next day, but then I would have put that rookie on a C-130 plane heading home before nightfall. We needed to bring in a proper forensic unit and have them with us the next time we went down there. A crime-scene analysis is like losing your virginity—you only get to do it once—because as you examine the evidence, you disturb the evidence. So we sealed up the entrance to the basement with crime-scene tape and went back upstairs.

This was a war zone halfway around the world, not the New York City District Attorney's Office where I was a homicide prosecutor before being recalled to active duty on September 11, and I had no idea what resources were available to me. At the very least, I needed a fingerprint unit and a forensic videographer. But I also wanted the ability to collect and analyze whatever else I might find: blood, fibers, skin, footprints—all the stuff you see on *CSI*—and I needed them all at the same place, namely, the Iraqi National Museum, at the same time, namely, as soon as possible. But I had no idea when that would be.

Given that some of the experts I needed might be in Frankfurt, some might be in London, and, for all I knew, some might be in Fort Hood, Texas, I knew that this could take a while to line up. And I didn't even know which agency had which of the necessary specialists available. And if they were coming to Iraq, they'd need anthrax shots. Were they up to date on their other vaccinations? And what if I needed a locksmith? Or luminol testing as a preliminary to blood analysis? Once you've picked up a piece of paper off the floor, you can't ask the rest of the team to stand like statues while you go find someone to check out the dried brown droplets underneath.

Practicalities aside, even the idea of requesting a crime-scene investigation team in a combat zone was highly unusual. So over the next several days, I received several calls on my satellite phone from perplexed officers. "Sorry, Colonel, but can you explain to me exactly what the hell you need, and why?"

And so the days passed, and we did our job examining other rooms in the museum, all the while wanting to examine *that* room. For Nawala, life was governed by Insha' Allah (God's will). Where we tolerated the suspense through immersion in our work, she did so by resignation to Allah's plan.

Ten days later, on the morning of the twelfth, the assembled crime-scene technicians arrived, and we went back into the underground storage rooms to begin a methodical forensic investigation. Almost immediately, we recovered several readable sets of fingerprints from the doors of the lockers themselves. Two ICE agents later hand-delivered those prints to the FBI's lab in Quantico, Virginia, for comparison against all U.S. databases of known criminals, federal employees, and U.S. military personnel.

Meanwhile, we continued to play it by the book, assessing every square meter, one millimeter at a time, on our hands and knees with feather dusters. On top of the lockers were small cardboard cartons stacked six feet high. A few had been knocked to the floor, but seemingly by accident. The rest were untouched, in sharp contrast to the 103 tackle boxes that had been thrown around and left on the floor.

More of these cardboard cartons rested atop a row of combination safes standing directly across from the lockers. Steel gray, manufactured in Germany, and evidently procured at great expense, they had never been used. In fact, they were still partially covered with clear plastic, like a new washer and dryer delivered from Sears. It would appear that they had been acquired to provide a more secure storage place for the goods that were in the lockers. So why had the coins and the cylinder seals never been transferred? And while we were at it, why had the thieves ransacked the tackle boxes but left the more numerous cardboard cartons undisturbed? Not until we took down the cartons and examined them did we discover that they were all empty. How could the looters have known that in advance? Judging from the evidence in front of us, they had not even bothered to check.

I was just beginning the mental calculation, trying to add up these random thoughts, when another ICE agent, Kevin Power, said, "Look what I found." He pointed to a set of keys on a string, jumbled inside one of the plastic boxes. We brought Nawala over to identify them. Slowly, hesitantly, she said, "They were hidden."

I said, "Show me where."

She took me to a dusty shelf in a remote corner of the room and pulled out a long drawer. She then showed me the place where the keys had been stuffed behind a fat collection of index cards. The cards were where they had always been. Neither they nor anything else in the drawer had been disturbed.

At this point, within the pinball machine inside my DA's head, the quarter finally dropped. The subterranean rampage that had left all this debris had already come into focus for me, and from the moment we discovered the breached wall I had no doubt we were dealing with an inside job. Probably many dozens of people in the world knew what was in those cabinets but did not have enough knowledge to lay their hands on the keys. "Eliminate the impossible and whatever remains, however improbable, must be the truth," Sherlock Holmes had told Dr. Watson. We had just eliminated an entire universe of archivists, archaeologists, and stock clerks as impossible, leaving—however improbable it might be—a small and select group of managers as possible suspects.

The scenario I had worked out so far went like this. There was no electricity while the thieves had been down here. After years of embargo, batteries were scarce in Iraq. So forget about flashlights. The bad guys had improvised. They had gone back up to the galleries where the staff had prepared for the invasion by sandbagging all the friezes and wrapping large pieces of foam rubber around the statues. The bad guys then brought some of these hunks of foam back downstairs, set fire to them, and tried to use them as torches. The fumes in that sealed basement must have been awful, not to mention the singed fingers. Maybe they got dizzy or even sick. But one thing we know for sure—one of them dropped the keys. Not only that—he dropped the keys into one of the 103 plastic tackle boxes that had been on the floor in front of the lockers. We found over four hundred cylinder seals left behind in those boxes, so very likely more had been taken. (Later, we would determine just how many.) But only inches away from one of the world's great treasures, some genius had screwed the pooch, and the rest of the gang had gone nuts in frustration, looking for that string of keys.

For the first time I allowed myself to feel a glimmer of hope. I nodded to the lockers, then asked Nawala, "Are you strong enough?"

She took a deep breath and said, "Yes, but we do it together."

"As you wish," I said. I had made a little joke. *As you wish* was an expression she used again and again during our time together at the museum. You would have needed a shutter speed of about 1/800th of a second to capture it, but I believe Nawala smiled. As we stood side by side, I inserted the key into the first lock, turned it, and opened the metal door. Nawala let out a shriek. Her knees buckled, but she held her ground.

All the gold and all the silver—more than one hundred thousand pieces—were exactly where they were supposed to be. As were the rows upon rows of exquisite cylinder seals, each revealing its delicately carved scene of ancient myths, ritual dances, and moments from ordinary life five thousand years ago. My mouth dry and pulse thumping, I went down the line, opening each locker in turn. All thirty were untouched. Every last piece of treasure under lock and key was in its proper place. Nawala began to sob, her chest heaving with relief. Setting aside, at least for a moment, more than thirteen hundred years of Islamic tradition, she also gave me a hug that I thought would break my neck.

• • •

Matthew Bogdanos has been an assistant district attorney in Manhattan since 1988. A colonel in the Marine Reserves, middleweight boxer, and native New Yorker, he holds advanced degrees in law, the classics, and military strategy. Recalled to active duty after September 11, 2001, he received a Bronze Star for counterterrorist operations in Afghanistan, served two tours in Iraq, and received a 2005 National Humanities Medal for his work recovering Iraq's treasures. This story is excerpted from *Thieves of Baghdad: One Marine's Passion to Recover the World's Greatest Stolen Treasures* (Bloomsbury, 2005), copyright 2005 by Matthew Bogdanos, and published by arrangement with Bloomsbury USA. Royalties from his book are donated to the Iraqi National Museum.

Chapter 11

The Making of Iraq's First Lady

MARY ANN SMOTHERS BRUNI

When I spoke to The Explorers Club about the Kurds in 1992 I wore the khaki, baggy pants suit of a *peshmerga*, a Kurdish guerilla fighter. The suit was a gift from my friend Hero Talabani, now the First Lady of Iraq. She sewed it for me the previous August as we sat chatting on the floor of the Talabani peshmerga camp at Qala Chwalan, the ancient capital of the Kurdish emirate of Soran. I wore the suit by choice for the talk in 1992, but Hero insisted I wear it at the camp, accessorized with her own blue gun belt. After all, we could see—and be seen—by Saddam Hussein's troops, who surrounded and still occupied the city of Suleymaniyah right down the mountains from us. "You could be in great danger were Saddam to learn there was an American at the camp," Hero warned.

The first time I saw Hero, in June 1991, was at the Sulaf Hotel near Amadiya. She and her husband, Kurdish leader Jalal Talabani, now Iraq's president, were traveling to Turkey and had come to the hotel to leave their guards. Hero is petite, but that day she strode into the hotel at the side of her husband, her steps as sure and as strong as his. She was dressed like Jalal, in the khaki, baggy trousers of the peshmerga. She wore a sleeveless, short khaki jacket, and the handle of a small pistol peaked from under a dark gun belt that hugged her waist. Her thick, black, curly hair fell loose. Her large, almost black eyes caught mine, and she smiled.

Hero moved liked a squirrel—gracefully but quickly, a woman sure of herself but accustomed to caution. A large entourage of peshmerga, maybe two hundred and fifty strong, armed with Kalashnikovs, shoulder rocket launchers, and other fighting paraphernalia marched behind Hero and Jalal into the hotel. These were the Talabanis' private guards, the most skilled and bravest of the peshmerga.

I met Hero again in late July that year when I was photographing and she was videotaping a peshmerga rally at a hotel in Shaqlawa. After the shoot, over tea, she explained that she was a peshmerga but carried a video camera into battle zones rather than a Kalashnikov and recorded Iraqi air attacks on Kurdish villages. "Peshmerga also are cooks and administrators, not just warriors," she explained. "Why don't you travel with my father and me to our camp at Qala Chwalan tomorrow? You can see firsthand how the peshmerga live." Little did I realize what a profound effect the visit to Qala Chwalan would have on my perception of the odd challenges we encounter in these grave times and how women can adapt under adversity, and change the world as we know it.

Early the next morning a peshmerga loaded me into the front seat of a Land Cruiser at the Talabani home. Ibrahim Ahmet, Hero's father, a legendary writer who is celebrated for introducing liberal political thought into Kurdistan, climbed into the back. His step was lively. Years had not dimmed the twinkle in his eye. He wore a gray peshmerga suit, but did not cover his balding head with a turban. He greeted me with a firm handshake, a mischievous smile, and said: "When you embark upon a strange journey in a strange land with strange men, you must try *everything* once!" Then, the Kurdistan's premier political philosopher handed me a bright pink Kurdish Popsicle he had concealed behind his back. Two young boys on the curb who were selling iced sweets giggled.

Hero, flustered by preparations for the journey, appeared a little later. Soon, we were off, I in front with my cameras, father and daughter in back with water, lemonade, and cookies. A Land Cruiser of armed peshmerga led the way and two more followed.

Fifteen minutes out of Shaqlawa, the road wound through a lush green meadow filled with brooks and shaded by aspens and cottonwood trees. Children played amid rubble on the grass. Young men cooled soft drinks in the stream to sell to travelers. The pastoral scene had a brutal past. "Kurdish songs celebrate the pomegranates of Heran. Saddam couldn't destroy the town with bulldozers, so he blew up over five hundred houses with TNT. That was 1987," Hero said.

We started our tour through the Balisan Valley. Each pile of rubble we passed had a name and a history. Heran, Nazanin, Nezihan. "Saddam destroyed twenty-eight villages in this valley alone," explained Hero. "Kurds are a village people. By destroying our villages Saddam hoped to obliterate our way of life." We passed the remains of Sheikh Wasan, the first village that Saddam attacked with chemical weapons.

Our road dead-ended into a highway. "This is the last peshmerga checkpoint. Those are Saddam's men over there," said Hero, pointing to tents about half a mile away.

After witnessing such destruction, the dust and bustle of the town of Ranya was a welcome change of scenery. As we left the town, a lake appeared framed by yellow mountains. "The lake is man made," Hero explained. "It backs up against Dukan Dam and provides water for southern Iraq. Beneath it lies our most fertile land."

While we waited in the shade for our ferry, Hero traded at a market for kitchen tools, three chopped tomatoes and cucumbers, plates, and a colorful oilcloth. Her father listened to BBC reports on his shortwave radio. Hero unwrapped cooked kebabs that she bought earlier in Ranya. Soon, lunch was ready. "It's simple fare, Mariana, but you will learn how we poor peshmerga live," she said.

The road on this side of the lake had been bombed into misshapen bits. Rock pile after rock pile marked the sites of once vibrant villages. Pieces of a few buildings had survived at Maluma. "Villagers live in the hospital over there, and about fifteen families are in the remains of the schoolhouse," Ahmet told me.

"You see that cave?" He pointed midway up the mountain. "It was my home for two years in the 1960s." Months after being reported dead, the revered philosopher was discovered by a surprised British journalist who announced that Ahmet was safe in a cave in Kurdistan. The journalist found Ahmet writing his memoirs and reading the works of Dostoyevsky.

Villagers gathered around Hero's father, chatting with him as if he were a long lost brother. A woman invited us to tea. Her home consisted of part of a wall, blankets spread on the grass, and kitchen utensils that hung from the tree, which also served as a roof. "The tree protects us from the sun," said our hostess, "but before winter, we must build something more."

Twenty minutes down the road we came to Balik. "An old town on a trade route established when the area was part of the Ottoman Empire," Ahmet told us. Families lived in tents and huts they had fashioned from tree boughs. The villagers welcomed Ahmet even more warmly than those in Maluma. Years ago, he'd been their lawyer when the villagers won back titles of their land from tribal chiefs.

Saddam destroyed Balik and sent villagers to concentration villages or to southern Iraq. Those who were able fled to the mountains and Iran. "But uprising families returned to rebuild. Kurdistan and its villages will not be destroyed. The Kurds cannot be stopped easily," Ahmet said.

I asked if the rebuilt villages would be able to band into an independent nation. He was quiet for a moment. "The distinction between Arabs and Kurds came with Western nationalism after World War I. Ethnic minorities—Kurds, Christians, and Jews—had more freedom in the days of the Ottoman Empire than they do now. We need more unity in this part of the world, not more division," he replied. Unity however is as elusive as independence.

We bumped past more destroyed villages, two peshmerga camps, and arrived at Qala Chwalan, now reduced to a few battered buildings. We turned down a dirt road between the building, and a peshmerga opened a barrier for us. To our right stood a long cinder-block dormitory. Directly ahead was headquarters, a one-story building faced with cut stone.

"The camp was miserable when we first arrived," Hero said. "What the shelling didn't destroy, the people here did. Iraqi soldiers had forced them out of their houses without allowing them to take anything with them. They were angry and irrational when they attacked the fort." Inside, headquarters was stark but clean. The floors were worn terrazzo, the walls plaster. Furniture was sparse and battered.

"Take your rest," Hero invited, showing me to a room void of furniture except for a torn carpet, blankets, and pillows in a corner. "I'm afraid this is all that we peshmerga can offer."

After breakfast the next morning, Hero and I sat on the floor and together watched the peshmerga-camerawoman's videotapes. The first was of the bombing of a village. "My hand was shaking. My body was shaking. Even my mind was shaking. I had lived in that village. I knew the people," Hero said. "Each time I film an attack, something happens to my mind," she said. "I hurt for my people."

On the video, Hero pointed at a single haunting image—a fern growing out of a bombshell in front of a school. The teachers at the school planted the fern and left a message in writing. The message said: A present to the children of Kurdistan from Saddam Hussein and his Ba'ath Party. Next, children appeared on the screen covered with terrible blisters, the victims of Saddam's chemical warfare. The video was taken two years before the tragedy of the poison gas attack at Halabja. Hero showed it to friends, to the press, to politicians. No one believed her.

I slept on the floor that summer, spent mornings learning elementary Kurdish from the peshmerga and afternoons chatting on the back porch with Hero's father. "I don't know how Saddam can watch men being tortured to death," he told me, "when I can hardly bear to assassinate these pesky flies."

Mornings, a barefooted Hero climbed up to clean windows, sat on the floor to sew curtains, and fretted over what to do about the destroyed ceiling with its protruding steel rods. In the afternoons, she consoled widows, advised young peshmerga, and encouraged independence in the young women who visited from Suleymaniyah. "Don't be like your grandmother. Educate your daughters. Don't make them servants of your sons," she said. In addition, she told them of Kurdish women who had become engineers, doctors, and attorneys. "Men will honor your choices, but you as women must recognize your own worth first."

Hero had first come to the Kurdish area with Jalal in 1980, leaving behind an infant son and his seven-year-old brother in London. When she saw the situation, she decided to stay, and left her boys with her parents. In many places, she became the first woman to sit in meetings with men. In this way, Hero paved the way for other women to be included in conferences with men.

Kafiya Suleiman, Hero's peshmerga colleague, lived close by with her husband, Kurdish commander Omar Fatah, and his mother, Aisha Khan. Earlier, Hero and Kafiya started a woman's group, Zhinan, which means simply "women," an organization to help women support themselves and "keep them from becoming beggars," as Kafiya put it.

"A sewing machine can support a village," said Nazanin Mohammed, their schoolteacher friend who ran Zhinan in Suleymaniyah. The schoolteacher invited me to visit Suleymaniyah, but Hero was against the idea. Kurdish civilians had taken the city from Saddam's men only two weeks before, and their hold was tenuous. The peshmerga now ruled, but some Iraqi soldiers were still in the city, and Saddam's troops, armed with heavy artillery, had it surrounded. At any moment the city might be engulfed in more fighting.

I knew that I might never have another chance to see a Kurdish city and wanted to go. "If you insist on going, you must be very careful," Hero warned me. "Don't tell a single peshmerga of your plans. If Saddam's men were to learn of your trip—and they easily could—you would be picked up in a minute."

To get past the Iraqi soldiers at the checkpoint who would ask for identification, Kafiya suggested I disguise myself as a Kurdish woman, which would not be easy. Nazanin advised that I wear my peshmerga suit, but Hero said that was out of the question. I had a Kurdish dress, but it came from the wrong province. Kafiya's mother-in-law offered a dress but Hero thought it "too traditional." A woman of my age in a Sorani city like Suleymaniyah would wear traditional Kurdish clothing only on special occasions.

Finally, Kafiya produced a pleated navy skirt. Nazanin contributed a print blouse from her bag. The mother-in-law fetched me a white scarf.

Hero added her sunglasses. I had on a pair of tennis shoes. Hero looked at them with a frown. No self-respecting Kurdish woman, it seemed, would wear tennis shoes. She handed me a pair of her own shoes, which were a size too small.

When I was finally dressed in disguise, Nazanin said I looked like a proper Kurdish schoolteacher. Soon, the three of us—Kafiya and Aisha Khan, the mother-in-law—were ready to go. Hero was still dubious. Kafiya had a price on her head. If Saddam caught us, he would have an American and two Kurdish women—all friends of Hero's—in a single sweep.

Nevertheless, Hero wished us well and saw us off in a taxi to Suleymaniyah. The taxi driver and traditionally dressed Aisha sat in front. We three Kurdish "schoolteachers" sat in the back. I was between the others, with my cameras stowed in an innocent-looking shopping bag.

At the top of the hill, we reached the checkpoint. An Iraqi soldier and a peshmerga approached the car. I held my breath. But they waved us through with no questions. We'd passed the first hurdle.

On the other side of the hill, Iraqi soldiers, tents, and artillery stretched as far as the eye could see. Hundreds of sons of Iraqi mothers napped, wrote letters, and hung freshly washed clothes to dry. They looked very young and reminded me of American Boy Scouts, too inexperienced to understand the personal tragedies that an all-out attack would bring to the Kurds below. As we drove through the troops, it was impossible not to have compassion for all those involved in this tragic civil war.

Just as we entered Suleymaniyah, the taxi driver let off Kafiya and Aisha in a pleasant neighborhood. Tall stucco walls and wooden gates lined the streets. At Nazanin's, the gate opened into an attractive patio filled with flowers. A one-story, white stucco house sat at the back. Oriental rugs were thrown on the terrazzo floor in the spacious living room, and overstuffed velvet and mahogany sofas and chairs faced a mahogany chest full of mementos from Nazanin's visits to Venice and Rome. We sat to have tea.

"I wanted to join the peshmerga, like Hero and Kafiya. Go to the mountains and fight for Kurdistan. But it's not possible for a single woman," said

Nazanin, with a sigh. "I work for the Kurdish resistance in the city. I teach women and young people about Kurdistan, about the West." By necessity, she's found indirect ways to teach. Ali Hasan al-Magid, Saddam's cousin who is known as "Chemical Ali," lives close by in Kirkuk. "When you Americans leave, we all are dead," she said, with certainty.

Inside a chest, she keeps Frank Sinatra records. She uses them to teach Kurdish friends American idioms, music, language, and values. "I know all of the words to all his songs, but 'Strangers in the Night' is my favorite," she said, as she put that song on her antiquated record player. Soon the sound of the ballad filled the room.

I tried not to wince. What were Kurds learning from Frank Sinatra? Perhaps that when Americans are inflamed, we commit to the quick fix like no others. American soldiers had been prominent in the international effort to bring the Kurds safely out of the mountains and resettle them in the safe haven we created. An American colonel coordinated the ongoing relief effort. American planes stationed across the border at Incirlik, Turkey, continued to fly over the area to protect the Kurds.

Kurds wanted to believe that Americans loved them and could offer permanent answers to complex questions. I feared that they risked mistaking impassioned glances for longtime commitment.

"The women you know—Hero, Kafiya—they are not *normal* Kurds," Nazanin confided to me. "I can show you how normal Kurds live." Soon, we were off.

Suleymaniyah proved an attractive city. Modern buildings and statues celebrating Saddam punctuated broad avenues. An occasional destroyed building, another riddled with bullets, and armed peshmerga in the streets testified to the recent uprising. As we turned onto the main street, about twenty Iraqi soldiers appeared. Farther down, six more stood on a street corner. We turned, pulled into a driveway and stopped in front of a two-story building.

"This is my school." Nazanin opened the door.

"The soldiers are too close," I said. "I don't think we should go in."

"They'll think we're just teachers checking the building," she said, marching toward the school with confidence. I reluctantly followed. The hallway smelled of dust and chalk. Classrooms lined the hall on the left, and dirty windows provided some light on the right. Nazanin charged into each room like a general inspecting her field after a battle.

"What animal would smash the children's chalkboards?" she asked, pointing to remains of a slate board clinging precariously to a wall. She turned to broken furniture and battered books in a corner. "Why would soldiers destroy clarinets and easels?"

"At least the city children have school houses," I blurted out, remembering the families living in a destroyed school in Maluma.

"This is about culture," she said. "When you destroy education, you destroy a culture."

"What if those soldiers come in and check our identification?"

"I don't care," she said. "This is my schoolhouse, and I shall come and go as I please. Just like the peshmerga come and go in the mountains." But there were many well-armed peshmerga and we were two women. The resigned, silent anxiety that I suffered as we examined the rest of the battered schoolhouse taught me that fears of sudden disappearance that Kurdish city folk endured are as difficult as the villagers' preoccupation with chemical weapons and bomb attacks.

After we left the school, we visited a few homes. Ahmad pulled the car into a patio at the first house, got out of the car, and closed the gate behind us. Only then did Nazanin and I emerge from the car. "Don't worry," Nazanin assured me. "This precaution is not for you. It is to protect those we were visiting. Should Saddam retake the city, they could be severely punished for receiving you."

Women at the homes we visited nervously changed television stations, rearranged lace doilies, uneasily poured tea. They whispered: "Please don't take pictures of our children." "Don't use my name." "Don't quote me." The signs of normal life were everywhere in these homes—*Sesame Street* and televised mosque prayers, doilies and dollies and whatnots, overstuffed furniture and orange-flavored soft drinks were the accoutrements of the bourgeois hell of which Nazanin spoke. The gardens were abundant with flowers, and the big-screen televisions did not allay the terrible fears of being swept away in the night.

When I returned to Qala Chwalan, the peshmerga were watching a Western cowboy movie that was set in Texas. They had their Kalashnikovs stashed in a corner. The cowboys did not charm them as Frank Sinatra had Nazanin. "We're not coming to visit you in Texas," one said. "You have too many guns there." The peshmerga laughed, and I laughed too. But as I thought through my day, I realized that it wasn't the guys with the guns, the cowboys and peshmerga, who frightened me. It was the guys armed with words, the city politicians, the strangers in the night who had me worried.

Meanwhile, Hero refused invitations to Suleymaniyah. Saddam's men remained there, and she was a prize they would like to capture. Then one morning a favorite peshmerga came to call. He and Hero argued, but he left with a big smile on his face.

"That peshmerga," said Hero, as she shook her head. "Long ago I promised to be a witness at his wedding. His fiancée's brothers finally agreed to the marriage, so tomorrow we are going to a peshmerga wedding in Suleymaniyah."

The next day, Hero, dressed in her peshmerga suit, was calm but quiet as our four Land Cruiser peshmerga escort drove through Saddam's troops. We could hear a loudspeaker and music blocks before we reached the house.

Peshmerga whisked Hero away to sit with the bride. A band played electronic music. Men wore peshmerga outfits and women the colorful sequined party dresses for which Suleymaniyah is famous. Men and women joined arms in a circle and danced in the front garden. The bride received guests in a red traditional Kurdish bridal outfit. Peshmerga guards stood on the garden wall, Kalashnikovs on the ready.

The bride disappeared for a moment and returned in a white Western wedding dress. Her sisters and friends gathered to drape her with gold jewelry—a necklace, pins, and bracelets. Hero put gold earrings on her ears. A smiling groom slipped a golden bracelet on his bride's arm, placed a gold ring on her finger, and then took her by the hand to join the dancers.

"We want to thank Hero Talabani," a man announced over the loudspeaker. Hero flinched. "We are so proud to have Hero Khan with us." I turned my head and saw Hero disappear. A peshmerga grabbed my arm and pushed me toward the gate. Hero was already in the Land Cruiser. "What was that man thinking?" said Hero. "Anyone could have heard that I was at the wedding."

"Everything is fine," her assistant said, trying to soothe her. But Hero lit one cigarette after another during the thirty-minute drive to Qala Chwalan. She was still tense as we sat down at the kitchen table. I thanked her for taking me to the wedding. She talked quietly about the strength of the Kurds. "Everyone at the party has lost a family member, yet we continue to dance, sing, and celebrate life," she said. "We give each emotion its due and no more; we laugh in the face of death if we must."

I thought about all the men killed, the children orphaned, the villages destroyed. What was worth such a price? Was human rights worth it? An independent Kurdistan?

"Kurds don't need independence," Hero answered. "If Iraq achieves a democracy, if we can live in peace, go to school in peace, send our husbands to work in peace—that is all we want. But for now we must fight now or be destroyed like the villages. Human rights? Maybe in a few years you won't find a human here. Our fight now is to survive."

When next I visited Qala Chwalan in April 2006 I slept in a featherbed in a suite complete with a WiFi-outfitted office. A man in a Western suit with a British accent served me Johnny Walker Blue Label Scotch and left silver trays laden with fruit in my private reception area.

Hero's rebel husband was now the first elected president of Iraq—the first Kurdish president of Iraq.

As for Hero, she traded her peshmerga garb for tight jeans and high-heeled sandals. Still, she was clear that her life is more multidimensional than the traditional American idea of a First Lady. "I don't do First Lady," she told me emphatically. "And I am not some sort of Greek 'hero.' I am Hirau, a wild hollyhock. Kurdish women don't use our husband's name. I am Hirau Ibrahim Ahmet."

"So still a daddy's girl?" I asked.

"*Always* Ibrahim Ahmet's daughter."

"Peshmerga or First Lady?"

"*Always* a peshmerga," she vowed.

Ibrahim Ahmet is buried in his beloved Suleymaniyah. Kafiya heads Zhinan, now forty-thousand women strong. Nazanin works with women in Afghanistan. Hero is producing *Qali*, a feature film based on her father's novel of the same name. These women carry within them the history of the Kurdish way of life and the hope of a new Iraq.

• • •

Mary Ann Smothers Bruni is a writer and photographer who lives in San Antonio, Texas. She first met Iraqi Kurds in 1991 when their uprising failed. Her book, *Journey Through Kurdistan* (Texas Memorial Museum, 1995), documents the destruction of a Kurdish village and the Kurds' way of life. She is currently working on a documentary, *Zhinan: Architects of the New Iraq*, about the role of Kurdish women in the rebuilding of their lives and country.

Chapter 12

Ghost Call

CATHERINE NIXON COOKE

April 2001
I hear birds screeching, followed by the rumble of distant thunder. A thick mist surrounds me and it is difficult to see. Ice is falling from the sky like sharp shards of glass. I am very cold. I can barely discern a track of some sort, ghostly footsteps in the snow. I follow.

The dream has come again, both scary and seductive. In darkness so complete that the roof of my tent is invisible, I zip my sleeping bag so that just my face is exposed. Then, I listen. Yes, the thunder is real.

A ghost has lured me to Nepal. For the past two years, his pale blue eyes have stared at me from a small silver-framed photo. His many letters, now yellowed with time, gave me entry to a private world of dreams and visions. Images have haunted me—snowy mountains, hidden valleys, sacred caves, and mysterious creatures. Now, I can't resist the call to his imaginary Shangri-la. Like dreamers everywhere, I believe that I might find answers just over that mythic farthest horizon.

I have convinced five friends to join me, and boldly calling ourselves "twenty-first-century explorers," we have organized our quest—an expedition to Nepal's remotest region, where mountain gods still control the rain and snow, and hidden *beyuls* (valleys) hold the promise of grail-like discovery. East of Mount Everest, in the shadow of Mount Makalu, the world's fifth highest peak, our task is to trace the route once taken by the blue-eyed "ghost" nearly half a century ago. He searched for the mysterious Yeti, or Abominable Snowman, whose legend has inspired expeditions to the diminutive Himalayan kingdom for more than one hundred years. We are not only looking for the Yeti, but also for the ghost of my uncle, Thomas Baker Slick Jr., an explorer who made three trips to the Himalayas in the 1950s in search of the elusive creature. The same powerful magnet to explore the unknown that pulled Slick now pulls us.

We have brought expensive night-vision equipment—infrared binoculars and cameras—and state-of-the-art satellite maps to help us chart our course over a terrain where there are few existing trails and inhabitants. We have *not* brought along any communication equipment—no satellite cell phone, no laptop powered by a portable generator, not even a radio. For the next three weeks, we will be in a faraway world, unable to hear the news and noises of our Western lives, experiencing a frontier of mystery the way that Slick did so many years ago.

Our expedition members all are fit by Western standards, but no one has climbed much above twelve thousand feet before. The thought of no bath for three weeks is a daunting idea. We all have our private questions. Can we endure the physical challenges? Will two months of training in a gym in Texas be enough for the constant ups and downs of peaks and beyuls in the little-explored Upper Arun Valley? Can we put aside our Western mind-sets to look for the serenity and magic that might await us in the Himalayas?

With a special expedition flag awarded to our group by The Explorers Club, a sirdar (lead guide), more than twenty-five porters, the latest in hiking boots and expedition clothing, cameras, and our shared excitement, we are ready for adventure.

The roar of the big Russian helicopter reverberates through every part of our bodies. We reach for our earplugs and grip the narrow metal benches as the chopper lifts off, leaving dusty Kathmandu behind. Our backs to the windows, we face a large pile of duffel bags and equipment in the middle of the helicopter's floor. In the small space, I turn uncomfortably to look out the small Plexiglas windows. Soon we've climbed to nine thousand feet and are skirting the foothills of the Himalayas. Nepal has the most dramatic elevation changes in the world—from nearly sea level in the south to the towering peaks of Mount Everest, Kanchenjunga, Lhotse, Makalu, and Cham Lang, all more than eight thousand meters high. As we bounce over air pockets, heading northeast, voices muffled by the noise, each team member thinks about the days ahead. With a tinge of dread, I remember my dreams of the ice storm. However, the bright blue sky and sunshine soon chase those thoughts away.

After an hour of flight, the taciturn Russian pilot peers anxiously at the ground below. It turns out he has never flown to NagiTar and is not quite sure where to land. It is a tiny village, just above Tamku at sixty-five hundred feet, far enough from the populated Everest region that the villagers have never seen a helicopter. We touch down in a different world.

Our sirdar is waiting on the ground with about twenty-five porters and a nurse practitioner named Paru. They walked four days from Tumlingtar, where there is a small slip of an airstrip, carrying all of the tents, food, and kitchen equipment. Our camp is set up in the flat meadow just below NagiTar.

Descending through the green terraced fields, I'm struck by the spectacular beauty that surrounds us. Past journeys to the turquoise waters of the Mediterranean, the lush jungles of Africa, the white and craggy cliffs of England, the burnt orange desert of the American Southwest, and the dense green rice paddies of Indonesia, inspired me with their visual and spiritual power. But these mountains in the distance, with their snowy peaks hidden by mist, and these unspoiled valleys where gentle-eyed Nepalese look at us with curiosity, create an electrifying sensation of awe.

Later, after dinner, we sit in the dark around a kerosene lamp and wait for our first visitor from the past. He is Dawa Tshering Sherpa, a sixty-three-year old porter who accompanied Slick on his expeditions here in 1957 and 1958. Today, Dawa walked for about forty-five minutes barefoot, wearing a light jacket, without light of any kind. Ghostlike, he appears at the entrance of the dining tent, just slightly over five feet tall, weighing less than one hundred pounds but still very strong. He accepts a cup of tea and lets his memories speak:

> *It was a long time ago. I am an old man now and most of my friends have died. But I am living longer because I am small in stature. I am very strong—it was my job on the Slick expedition to carry the tents. They were much heavier than the tents you have now because they were made of canvas.*
>
> *We were looking for the Yeti near a waterfall close to the village of Wallung, where you will go in a few days. Some of the expedition members also wanted to find a Ban Kati [wild woman or forest girl] that everyone knew lived there, but they couldn't find her. Instead they captured a baby bear.*
>
> *There are no Ban Katis close to NagiTar, but there still are some on the other side of Sedua, a few ridges over that way, where you will also go. Bankatis are very wild; they have very long breasts, which they flip over their shoulders when they run. They turn over rocks and eat frogs. I have never seen a Ban Kati, but I have seen the frog remains that they leave on the rocks in the forest. And I have heard the sounds they make.*
>
> *Heeeeeeee . . . heeeeeee!*

An eerie high-pitched wail echoes in the quiet darkness, and the young porters from our expedition gather around the tent, eyes as big as teacups, to listen to the old man. He told us about the strange trained bloodhounds that the Slick expedition brought to Nepal to track the elusive Yeti. Throwing back his scrawny head to the dark night sky, Dawa imitated the howls of Slick's hunting dogs with eerie precision. He told us about the only order on the expedition that he could not bring himself to obey. When he was told to kill a goat, Dawa, a Buddhist, realized he could not comply and ran away from the camp. All these years later, he remembers details of an expedition that took place more than forty-five years ago. Though Dawa does not read or tell time, he wears a watch that his son has sent him from India. Around 9:00 p.m., without even stars to guide him, he starts his walk home in total darkness.

The next morning, the trek begins. For days, we walk up steep ridges and then descend rocky slopes without trails. Soon, all semblance of civilization (for that is now how we remember tiny NagiTar) disappear. We chop our way through bamboo forests, eventually get used to the leeches that somehow slip through layers of clothing to find fresh blood, and head toward the distant Mount Makalu, hidden by the mist and rain that are our constant companions.

For two weeks, our team walks for six to eleven hours each day. Wet, cold, and tired, we struggle into camp at nightfall. The physical challenges are offset by incredible visual gifts of beauty—sacred chortens draped with prayer flags on the top of remote ridges, and giant rhododendron trees, more than thirty feet tall, bursting with scarlet blooms. Every day is filled with experiences of both suffering and redemption.

At last we arrive in Dobatok, the halfway point of our journey. It is a virtual metropolis, with six miniature homes and a beautiful prayer wheel. Again, we squeeze our tents onto a small bit of empty, flat land. As our porters drink *chang* and drum and sing to relax after a hard day, we nestle in our sleeping bags, listening to a mountain lullaby, drifting into dreams about tomorrow's journey to the sacred Khembalung Cave.

The Khembalung Cave is one of the legendary holy places in the Himalayas. According to local lore, centuries ago the cave was hidden by Guru Rinpoche, whose followers regard as a second Buddha. Today, it is revered by Sherpas, Rais, Khumbos, Shingsapas, and Tibetans of Kharte and Dingri. In her chapter in *Mandala and Landscape*, a 1997 book edited by A. W. McDonald (D. K. Printworld, 1997), famed anthropologist Hildegard Diemberger describes the slopes of the beyul where the cave is located through the phantasmagorical lens that locals view the region. Diemberger writes that the valley is "covered with thick forest, inhabited by wild animals, and surmounted by the white Himalayan peaks. . . . in the *beyul* lives the snow lion, the plants know no seasons, there are fruits and flowers and many streams, there is a poisonous burning lake, there are medicinal springs, clouds and mists darken the whole atmosphere, there is a lot of rain; and from the sky you hear the roar of the dragon (thunder)."

During the past days, we heard the dragon and felt the rain. We saw the clouds and mist and were amazed by the plants and flowers that bloomed from trees as big as skyscrapers. During moments of clear weather, we glimpsed the white peaks of the mountains. By the time we arrived, I was tired and giddy and certain that the poisonous, burning lake would be just around the next bend.

However, our climb to the mouth of the cave proved uneventful. More than one hundred once colorful prayer flags waving in a blur of faded red, green, blue, yellow, and white greeted us when we reached the high ridge. The flags surrounded a simple stone structure with aluminum siding and wooden benches, where we removed our boots and anything else made of leather. A lone monk invited us to say a prayer and light a butter lamp, then led us outside to wash our feet in a sacred waterfall. With bare feet, we walked down a rocky slope to the entrance of the cave that is considered a sacred oracle, visible and accessible only to those who are meant to enter.

Just inside, we saw paintings of the ancient Tara, the feminine goddess who watches over the cave, and a rusted trident and bell. The trident represents the masculine gender; the bell is symbolic of the feminine.

I'd read warnings in academic journals that the cave is not for anyone claustrophobic or plump. Yet, when I saw the smallness of the opening of the cave, I was astonished and more than a little worried. I wondered if our Western bodies would be able to pass through the cave's winding and narrow chambers. With nervous smiles, we turned on our headlamps and entered the dark, tight space.

Once inside the cave, we either crawled like bears on all fours or slithered like snakes with bellies to the ground, using our arms to inch our bodies forward. Occasionally, we reached a chamber big enough to achieve a sitting position. In each tiny room, there was always a stone Buddha figure or other carved deity to greet us, and we were careful to follow custom, leaving a coin or butter lamp or some other offering with a prayer for health, wealth, fertility, abundant crops, or whatever blessing we sought. Alone, deep inside the earth, with my headlamp flickering uncertainly, I realized that the cave was indeed a transpersonal space that made this journey to Nepal as much an inner exploration as an adventure on the raw, physical level.

At the deepest point, we reached a particularly tight passage that is called the "Purification Chamber." Pilgrims must slide through a narrow, tubelike passageway, circling a rock column clockwise. At one point, I realized my body was contorted in the shape of the letter C, and panic seized me. To calm myself, I remembered that I'd come halfway around the world for this experience and said my mantra softly to myself. Soon, I felt slightly calmer and slithered further along the rocky path.

But panic struck again as I began to imagine getting stuck in the cave; I was aware that I couldn't sit or stand or even raise my head in the tight passageway. I felt myself sink into internal darkness far more frightening than the cave's blackness. Then, out of the darkness, I felt the small hand of the Nepalese girl who had gone through the chamber just ahead of me. She reached back and grabbed my hand just when I thought I could not go on. I inched my way forward.

When I pulled out of the C-shaped tunnel, I heard the voices of other team members who decided to avoid that passage. Later, after we left the cave, several told me why they had bypassed the route, explaining that a huge spider had hovered over me, just inches from my head, during my entire purification effort. At that moment, I felt purified—at least from the fear of small spaces and hairy spiders.

The entire traversal through the cave took only about forty-five minutes, but it seemed like forever. The final crawl into daylight left me with a clarifying absence of fear and renewed sense of life's gifts. According to Buddhist texts, three trips through the Khembalung Cave brings a pilgrim to sainthood. One-third saint was good enough for me.

The next morning, the mountain gods sent a message of approval. For the first time on the expedition, the day was absolutely clear. There was not a cloud or snowflake or raindrop in the sky. The view of the mountains was unobstructed and spectacular. Were they really there yesterday, just hidden by the mist and snow?

The oracle at Khembalung Cave, the waterfall where the Ban Kati shrieked at night, the footprints we photographed, perhaps of an elusive snow leopard, are our rewards for answering that compelling call to explore. When the mist and mystery surrounding my uncle's long-ago quest lifted, I realized that nothing much has changed in the beyuls of Nepal since Slick was last there. But I had changed. For me, this possibility of transformation is the real motivation of exploration. I followed Slick's snowy footsteps to Nepal in search of his mysteries, but I left with a renewed sense of my own life journey.

• • •

Catherine Nixon Cooke is a fellow of The Explorers Club, elected shortly after the organization began admitting women in 1981. She has been awarded three Explorers Club flags for expeditions to Nepal, Bhutan, and Belize, and has served as a director and officer of the club. She is the former president and chief executive officer of the Mountain Institute, an international conservation and development organization operating in the Andes, Himalayas, and Appalachian mountain ranges. Previously, she was executive director of the Mind Science Foundation and editor in chief of *Coronet* magazine. She is the author of *Tom Slick Mystery Hunter* (Paraview, 2005), and has been published extensively in national magazines and newspapers.

Chapter 13

The Weather Prayer

SCOTT HAMILTON

The climbing season on Everest was drawing to a close as we packed up our gear, having spent six weeks undertaking high-altitude biomedical research. Everest had provided an ideal location for torture testing both equipment and people in a harsh, oxygen-deprived environment. Understanding human adaptation to such low barometric pressure is critical for future space exploration, including a manned mission to Mars.

We'd spent the last two weeks on the Khumbu Glacier, sleeping on ice 17,500 feet above sea level. Avalanches awakened us nightly with a thunderous roar and billowing winds and snow enveloping our desolate camp. We yearned for the Hotel Yak & Yeti in Kathmandu, with its hot showers, clean sheets, cold beers, and bowls of tasty borscht—amenities we had forgone for seemingly a lifetime. The problem was simply one of getting there.

Kathmandu was a mere hour-long flight away by Twin Otter from the Lukla airstrip, a short, narrow slope of dirt carved into a hillside. Our trek from Lukla to Everest had taken twelve days. Our plan was to make the return trip in only five. The early monsoon rains were fast approaching from the Bay of Bengal, their arrival heralded by massive black clouds that filled the sky. For us to get a flight out would take a miracle.

As we began to descend the knee-destroying trail from Namche Bazaar to Lukla, we encountered the blustering winds and rain of the arriving monsoon. It was not long before the trail grapevine was filled with news that the Lukla airstrip had been shut down by bad weather. Local tea shops were reported to be packed with stranded climbers, perhaps two hundred of them, running out of money and hope. Some climbers had already opted for a grueling, five-day trek along slippery trails to Jiri, where they could catch a public bus to Kathmandu. We were still a day's hike from Lukla in what could only be termed "deteriorating weather conditions." Things did not look good.

Air travel in Nepal is unique. Suppose, for example, one has a reservation for a 10:00 a.m. flight on Tuesday. If the plane actually shows up, you get priority for boarding, assuming you have engaged in the judicious use of baksheesh, a term used to describe both charitable giving and bribery, and are near the head of the queue. If, for whatever reason, the scheduled flight does not arrive, all bets are off. Your "reservation" vanishes like a prayer flag in the mist. Once a confident ticket holder, you are now little more than part of a multicultural human chain of hundreds that encircles the airstrip. A Twin Otter carries but fourteen passengers. Planes are few and far between. Do the math. Those near the front of the line tend to be optimistic, but as the days of fruitless, hypothermic waiting pass, they begin to exhibit fear, resignation, and finally despair. We did not want to join this unhappy lot.

Along the trail we were met by a blind man from the village of Munjo. He was a young schoolteacher we had examined previously while conducting one of many free medical clinics for villagers along the road to Everest. We had been touched by his plight, and thought he might be treated surgically in Kathmandu. Our team had agreed collectively to sponsor the cost of his transportation and treatment, and told him to meet up with us on our return. Our entourage increased by one as the blind man from Munjo joined us on the trail. We were greeted with an ankle-deep, muddy rivulet cascading down the path as we entered the village of Phakding, our last stop en route to Lukla. It was time for a plan.

We could make out the silhouettes of a few prayer flags waving in the mist high on the mountainside above Phakding. We had been told that there was a small Buddhist monastery perched atop the cloud-cloaked ridge just an hour's hike from the trail. Our only hope, I thought, would to be to ask the monks for a weather prayer. Explaining my plan to skeptical comrades, I managed to collect five hundred rupees for an offering.

Climbing through the cloud layers, I ascended a narrow path that zigzagged up the hillside. An hour later, with much anticipation, I finally crested the hill where the prayer flags flew. Alas, there was no monastery, just a few rough dwellings. I walked around for a while exploring the thickly wooded trails above the tiny hamlet, but found nothing. Soaked with sweat and rain I finally approached a tiny hut. The door swung open while I was still some distance away, as its inhabitants had been watching me. A large mastiff barked ferociously. Clasping my hands together, prayerlike, I uttered "Namaste" the traditional greeting in Nepal, followed by "Guru, Lama, monastery?" hoping that one of the words might convey my quest.

A young woman, who appeared afraid at first, smiled at my feeble effort to speak Nepali and replied, "Monastery," pointing farther up the hillside into the clouds. She then sent her son, perhaps six years of age, to take my hand and show me the trail. We meandered through the tiny village to a place with a watering trough carved out of a log. I had passed by it in my earlier search. He pointed to an obscure opening in the trees, then turned his eyes up to mine and implored, "Baksheesh." With ten rupees clutched in his hand, the kid ran happily back down the muddy trail. I stood alone, in the mist and rain at the edge of the mountain plateau.

I ascended through an enchanted forest of tangled roots and trees. I soon came upon the Choling Monastery. Seemingly devoid of life, it was dark, damp, and very quiet, the forest eerily melting into the mountain mist. I slowly walked around, spinning a prayer wheel as I passed in the hope that its bells would announce my arrival. It was now twilight as I stood in the rain, rapping my knuckles on a large wooden door. There was no response—no lights and no sounds beyond the rain dripping from the roof onto the rough wooden steps.

I waited awhile, and knocked again, harder this time. I heard distant footsteps, then a bolt slid back, and the hinges creaked as the ancient door slowly swung open. A young monk, clearly surprised, cautiously greeted me, then invited me into the monastery. Lama Pasang Sherpa's English was better than my Nepali, but not much. The lama was quite accommodating and gave me a brief tour of the sanctuary. It was almost completely dark inside, illuminated only by a few flickering candles. The air had a deep, musty scent of ancient wood smoke, damp prayer books, candles, incense, and yak butter tea. The walls were decorated with thangkas, scrolls, and paintings, magnificent even though dulled by centuries of dust and soot. Steeped in centuries of powerful juju, the monastery was permeated with an overwhelming spiritual energy. Built in the twelfth century, the Choling Monastery once was bustling with several dozen monks. Now, it is tended by only four.

Respectfully bowing my head, I quietly placed our expedition's offering upon the altar and attempted to convey my request to the lama. Asking a weather prayer from a monk living an ascetic existence devoid of worldly attachments suddenly seemed inappropriate. I chose instead to ask for "safe and timely passage" for our expedition team. That way, I figured, a prayer for fair weather would be implicitly included. The young lama listened intently and seemed to understand my request. "Would it be all right if the monks offered the prayers in Nepali instead of Tibetan?" Sure, I replied, even though I was aware the sounds of the spoken Tibetan language are said to have magical powers. He promised the monks would pray for us during a special *puja* prayer service the following day, which was a particularly auspicious time in the Tibetan calendar. I thanked Lama Pasang Sherpa profusely, promising to send prayer flags to the Choling Monastery. I bid farewell and began my descent into the damp, dark night.

As our team entered Lukla Village the following afternoon, things seemed pretty grim. Some two hundred trekkers were stranded because of monsoon rains and the resulting lack of flights. Having sent a runner ahead two days earlier, we managed to grab a few rooms in a local tea shop for an uncomfortable night of howling dogs, crowing roosters, and drunks beating drums in the muddy streets. In the dark of the night we could hear rats crawling in the walls next to our bunks.

In a series of late-night meetings we hatched a plan to escape from Lukla, weather permitting. We bartered generator motor oil, specialty food items along with a few other things, paid baksheesh, and played heavily off friendships forged on our past expeditions. The plan was good as far as our obtaining an optimal place in line, but the weather would be the ultimate authority.

Not wanting to divulge our arrangements to the unhappy campers surrounding us, we stealthily crept from our lodge at 4:30 a.m., quietly making our way in the darkness to the airstrip. As sunrise approached, a miracle of sorts occurred. The clouds parted and the sun began to shine. Within half an hour a plane arrived. A short time later several of our group were given seats on the oversold Yeti Airlines' Twin Otter. Airborne, they soon disappeared on the Western horizon.

A while later a huge Russian MI-17 helicopter thunderously arrived at Lukla. It had been carrying a load of cargo to the higher village of Syangboche but couldn't land there because of rain and low visibility. The pilots, veterans from the war in Afghanistan, sat with protruding bellies on the chopper's fuel tanks nonchalantly smoking cigarettes. Opportunity was staring us in the face. A bit of conversation ensued, and eventually the pilots agreed to let us unload their cargo and replace it with our three thousand kilograms of expedition gear—no small task. After literally squeezing five members of our group in on top of the load, the chopper took off for a ride to remember on Cosmic Air. With clouds and rain fast closing in, one additional plane arrived. The remaining members of our team, along with the blind man from Munjo, got seats, lifting off just moments before the monsoon rains again engulfed the Lukla airstrip.

Late that afternoon we arrived at the Hotel Yak & Yeti—the place of our dreams. Amazingly, we had made it safe and sound with all our team members and gear. As promised, I arranged to have prayer flags sent to the lamas at the Choling Monastery. It had been a miraculous day; our weather prayer had been answered.

• • •

Scott Hamilton is a director of The Explorers Club. He has led and participated in numerous expeditions around the world. He works as investment professional in New York, but his true passion is exploration. His field experience includes exploratory mountaineering, biomedical research, arctic aviation, small-boat expeditions to remote areas of Patagonia, and oceanographic exploration with manned submersibles. He has also helped establish several medical clinics in remote Himalayan villages.

Chapter 14

Disaster on Everest

KENNETH KAMLER

Huge, steep, cold, and windy, Mount Everest is the highest mountain in the world—and entirely indifferent to the fate of those who try to climb it. I've made six trips to Everest, each time as expedition doctor and climber, treating people in the surrounding villages as well as my fellow mountaineers. Four of those trips were with *National Geographic* to calculate Everest's true height and to make maps and tectonic plate measurements. On my two most recent trips, I served as the chief high-altitude physician for NASA expeditions to field-test space-age medical devices and telecommunications for possible use on a space station or on Mars.

It was in 1996, on my fourth trip with *National Geographic*, that Everest inflicted the worst disaster in its history. A two-day storm took the lives of eight climbers. On the Southeast Face, relentless wind and bitter cold slowly killed five and maimed two others. Throughout that brutal storm, I was the only doctor on the mountain.

Everest is an extreme environment. The summit, at 29,035 feet, is as high as the cruising altitude for some transatlantic jets. There is only one-third as much oxygen as there is at sea level. Without enough oxygen, our body's metabolism becomes a smoldering fire that can't burn fuel efficiently enough to provide adequate heat or power. We lose the desire to eat, judgment becomes clouded, and energy is so depleted that bodies deteriorate rapidly, consuming themselves to provide a source of fuel.

On summit day, climbers arrive at the highest camp exhausted after days of relentless climbing. Breathing at sea level requires only one-twentieth of the oxygen used by the body, but here, at twenty-six thousand feet, breathing consumes two-thirds of the available oxygen. The climbers' hearts are pounding even at rest. A few hours after arriving at the last camp, they set out for the summit in the dark. Though their day is only starting, their bodies are already approaching their limit.

If things go well, they'll be out for sixteen to twenty hours in temperatures possibly as low as forty degrees Fahrenheit below zero with winds twenty to forty miles per hour or higher. Sometimes all they've had to eat before starting out is half a bowl of warm water. Yet before their day is over, they'll need to exhale one to two gallons of water and burn twelve thousand to fifteen thousand calories—ten times what they might need on an average day—and maybe more than they have in reserve.

On one of my own summit attempts I remember reaching inside my down jacket for a drink from my water bottle only to discover that the water that I had been carrying against my chest had frozen solid. That's how thin the margin of survival is near the summit and that's where the disaster occurred.

The southeast route starts from base camp at 17,500 feet. The camp is at the top of the Khumbu Glacier—the highest point we can bring our yaks. We offload our gear and supplies here, erect tents, and settle in for the next two months—the time it will take to acclimatize, build and supply our higher camps, place our fixed ropes, and find our way to the summit.

In 1996 several major expeditions were on the route, including Scott Fischer's American team, Rob Hall's New Zealand expedition, and our *National Geographic* team, for which I was carrying an Explorers Club flag. It took a month and a half for us to put everything in place. We took a few days' rest, and then each expedition began its summit attempt, Scott and Rob starting up one day ahead of us.

From base camp, the route mounts two thousand feet through the Ice Fall—a chaotic jumble of highly unstable blocks of ice. We climb through at night when the ice is coldest, and therefore more solid and less likely to collapse on us. The Ice Fall is a slowly flowing waterfall, riddled with crevasses—huge cracks in the ice created by enormous pressure differentials as the ice moves downward. We cross the crevasses on aluminum ladders laid from one edge to the other and anchored in place. Sometimes five or more ladders have to be tied end to end to bridge the gap. At the midway point of that construction, your body weight might be enough to bend the ladder down nearly to the floor of the crevasse before it gradually springs up as you approach the far side.

Some crevasses may be ten stories deep or more, which may be the real reason we climb at night: if we ever had enough light to see between our feet to the bottom, we'd never have the nerve to walk across. But the world illuminated by our headlights is nothing less than phantasmagoric: bizarre and beautiful ice sculptures—from delicate fluted spires to sheer walls towering hundreds of feet over us. The shapes are alluring, like a siren's song, but lingering in the Ice Fall could prove deadly.

We reached the top just after sunrise. The maze we were climbing through opened up to the broad expanse of the Western Cwm. *Cwm* is the Welsh word for "cirque," and the Western Cwm runs two miles long and about a half mile wide. From here, Everest is clearly in view. At the first flat spot in the Cwm, we had built Camp 1 weeks before and the tents were a welcome sight for exhausted climbers.

The next day we went up the Cwm—an endlessly long but more gently sloping snow valley, moving up and down dunes of ice to reach Camp 2, two thousand feet higher, but in a more spacious, sheltered area than Camp 1. It's set up on a lateral moraine, so it's free of ice and warmer to sleep on.

Onward from here, the altitude gain is more rapid and the climbing more difficult and exposed. The higher camps are uncomfortable and there is no place to endure bad weather. This is where climbers have to make critical decisions about the weather. From Camp 2 it will take three days to get to the summit. If we wait for good weather to continue our climb, it's likely to change before we get there. Predicting how the weather will be three days later and eight thousand feet higher up is chancy at best, but after a rest day at Camp 2, Rob and Scott both felt the signs looked good.

The route up to Camp 3 is an ascent of the face of Lhotse, the fourth highest mountain in the world, but dwarfed by Everest. Since it takes two days to climb Lhotse, and its slope is a sheer forty-five-degree angle for five thousand feet, Camp 3 is made by chipping a platform into the ice halfway up.

From Camp 3 you can see the exposed black rock of the Southeast Ridge that leads to the summit. The ridge is high enough to be scoured by the jet stream so no snow accumulates on it. What appears to be a cloud behind the summit ridge is actually a plume of snow being blown off the mountain. The longer the plume, the higher the wind velocity. Watching the ridge and seeing a lull in the wind, Rob and Scott moved their teams up the following day. Near the top of Lhotse there is a traverse to the South Col, a saddle between the shoulders of Lhotse and Everest. This is where we place Camp 4, the highest camp.

Scott's and Rob's teams got into camp in the afternoon. They had to make a decision in the next few hours on whether to go for the summit that night, since at the South Col everyone is on oxygen, and oxygen supplies are limited. If they didn't go up, they'd have to go down.

Summit bids start about midnight to allow for the maximum amount of time to get to the top and back down while there is still daylight. Just before midnight the winds, which had been constant all day, suddenly slackened, the snow plume over the ridge disappeared, and the Col became still and calm. This seemed to be the break in the weather Scott and Rob had been waiting for. It seemed to be a perfect summit night.

Using headlights the two teams set off for the summit, moving up the Triangular Face—a less-steep section of the climb that can be safely negotiated in the dark. They reached the Southeast Ridge, paused for a short rest, then continued the climb, but a few hours later the winds picked up again and one by one several climbers turned back. The rest pushed on toward the summit.

The Southeast Ridge is a fifteen-hundred-degree, knife edge—precipitous, sinuous, varying in width from three to six feet, and angling about thirty degrees upward and fifteen degrees right to left. Climbing through the night and early morning and moving at different speeds, the climbers got strung out all over the mountain. We climb unroped here because the slopes are so sheer a slip would be a free fall. Your climbing partner would be unable to belay you and you'd just jerk the climber off the slope with you. If you fall to your left, you drop eight thousand feet into Nepal. To the right, you fall twelve thousand feet into Tibet.

That same day my team moved up to Camp 3, two thousand feet below the other teams, and listened to our radios awaiting news from above. In the afternoon we got word that Rob's team had summited. There was jubilation and champagne all around at the New Zealand base camp far below us as the announcement was made, but the news made us uneasy. Only three out of eighteen team members, in addition to the three guides, had reached the top, and it was already 2:30 in the afternoon—very late to be leaving the summit. Conditions were tough up there, we thought, and there wasn't much daylight left. And so far there was no word at all from the Scott Fischer group. The time passed slowly in our tents. For hours we looked at the radio hoping that the next piece of news would be that everyone was back safely.

Instead, we got the chilling report that Rob was still up near the summit with Doug Hanson, a climber who was out of oxygen and too weak to descend the Hillary Step, a technically difficult cliff just below the summit. And there was no word on the rest of the New Zealand team or on Scott's team. The fate of a third, Taiwanese, team that had attempted the summit was also unknown. It was long since dark, and it was a cold, windy night for us. It could only be colder and windier for them.

Camp 3 is a difficult place to sleep under any conditions, and that night we slept fitfully, hoping for the best, but knowing full well the gravity of the situation. We were awakened by a radio call at 5:00 a.m. Our worst fears were being realized. Rob had been out all night with Doug. They were both out of oxygen now, had no food or water, and Doug was too weak to move. Other climbers had seen a headlight just above the Hillary Step, so that was the point where they were still stuck—just below the summit.

In addition to Rob's situation, which we knew about because he had a radio, there were about eighteen people missing and apparently still not back to Camp 4. The entire Scott Fischer team had not been heard from.

From the New Zealand team, Jon Krakauer had summited and gotten back to his tent. He had a radio but didn't much know what was going on. He reported intense cold, high winds, and whiteout conditions. He was exhausted and couldn't see outside his tent. Worse, that meant that people who were trying to make it back after being out all night wouldn't find the camp.

Besides Rob, there were two other New Zealand guides: Andy Harris was carrying a radio but hadn't been heard from, and Mike Groome had made it back to Camp 4 but was hypothermic and frostbitten. The team was left leaderless. The only other New Zealand summiter, Yasuko Namba, was a Japanese woman who hadn't been seen since she summited. Another team member, Beck Weathers, hadn't summited but hadn't returned either, and the Taiwanese team reported that its leader, Makalu Gau, had summited but was missing.

There were many other reports—all were confusing and most were conflicting—but what was clear was that a horrible disaster was unfolding that morning. The temperature had plummeted overnight, and the winds were now howling so loud that it was impossible for us to talk between tents even by shouting. We had to use our radios to communicate and formulate a rescue plan.

Our two strongest climbers, Todd Burleson and Pete Athans, quickly prepared to go up to the South Col despite the fierce wind. They never discussed whether they should go. They began the conversation with how quickly they could get ready. They tried to pass a message to Rob Hall. I expected it to be something like, "Hold on, we're coming," but, facing reality, with heavy hearts they told Rob to abandon Doug and try to save himself. The situation was hopeless if they stayed together. Better to save one than to lose two.

Our Sherpas were at Camp 2, and we asked them to try to move up to help. They refused, saying it was too dangerous to climb in that wind, but nobody is braver than a Sherpa, and we felt the real reason was that they were spooked by the idea of seeing dead bodies lying all over the Col.

Again, hours went by and we waited in our tents inside our sleeping bags, trying to stay warm. Todd and Pete reached the Col and radioed back.

The Fischer team had all gotten back to Camp 4 except for Scott himself who was still missing. They all had frostbite, but were otherwise OK. The wind had abated somewhat and Todd and Pete were sending them down under their own power.

We set up a kind of way station at Camp 3, and as they passed us we dispensed hot tea and oxygen and made sure they were steady enough to continue down to Camp 2. The New Zealand team was still in complete disarray. We decided they shouldn't attempt a descent today, but rather stay in their tents to eat and drink and try to regain some energy for a safer, more controlled descent tomorrow.

Later in the day the winds came back more fiercely than before, but we got a radio report with some better news. We had been told earlier that Beck Weathers had been found dead, but now Todd called down to me saying, "You won't believe this. Beck is alive—but I don't know for how long." He had just staggered into Camp 4, like a ghost risen from the dead. An apparition, with a frozen, gloveless right hand dangling from his arm. Todd said he looked like a mummy from a grade-B horror flick and had frostbite up to his elbows.

From Camp 3 I could radio medical advice to Todd and Pete, but it was no place to treat anybody. The camp is merely a notch cut into the forty-five-degree slope of the Lhotse Face on a platform so narrow there's no room to even stand outside the tent. We agreed that if Beck survived the night he'd have to be brought down to Camp 2, a flatter, more open place where I could treat him. In addition to Beck, the Taiwanese climber, Makalu, was found alive but also severely frostbitten, and he would need intensive treatment as well.

A little good news and then more bad news. Rob's terrible ordeal continued. He was still in radio contact, but his voice was getting weaker and weaker. He said he was below the Hillary Step now and had crawled into a snow cave for shelter. It was unclear what had happened to Doug, but Rob seemed to be by himself. Doug had probably died higher up, without Rob abandoning him. Earlier Rob had gotten the radio message to leave Doug and try to save himself, but his response had been, "We're both listening."

So now he was alone, but too weak to descend any farther. A team of Sherpas with some oxygen had been trying to reach him, but they were beaten back by the ferocious winds. When Rob was told that the Sherpas weren't coming he didn't scream or curse, he just quietly said, "OK."

He asked to be patched in to his wife, who was home in New Zealand, seven months pregnant with their first child. With modern technology it was done. Rob and his wife, Jan, had their last conversation and picked a name for their unborn child. Finally Rob said he was shutting off his radio so he could rest. We hoped, by some miracle, he would turn it on again in the morning, but he never did.

That night came the strongest, most violent winds I've ever experienced. Our tents at Camp 3 were perched on a sheer slope, held in place by ice screws that we thought would pull out any second. Or else the tent would shred, sending us tumbling three thousand feet down the Lhotse face.

We spent the night fully dressed and splayed out over the tent floor, trying to hold the tent down and lessen the pull on the ice screws. In the morning we got word that Beck and Makalu had survived the night and would be brought down to me at Camp 2. The New Zealand team members, what was left of them, would be able to come down under their own power.

I climbed down three thousand feet back to Camp 2 to receive my patients. Using medical supplies that I had requested by radio, which were brought up from base camp the day before, I set up a make-shift hospital in the largest tent in the camp—the New Zealand mess tent. With a lot of help, I laid foam mats and sleeping bags on the tent floor, gathered two complete sets of dry clothes, hung IV bags through carabiners hooked into the tent frame, laid out oxygen bottles and regulators, arranged my bandages and medications, and had the Sherpas boil up as much hot water as possible.

By radio we were kept advised of our patients' progress down the mountain. There was plenty of hot water around, so the Sherpas didn't lose the opportunity to make tea for everyone. While we waited I tried to keep my thoughts focused—not easy to do at an altitude where tying your shoes can be confusing.

Makalu arrived first, covered in a bulky down suit head to toe, with an oxygen mask over his face. We laid him down on a sleeping bag and took off layer after layer of wet clothes. He was wet down to his underwear. His frostbite was horrible. His fingers were deep gray down to the knuckles and as I held his hand up to my face it radiated cold. His toes and feet were frozen and black and so were his heels. Using a scalpel, I cut away a piece of sock that was stuck to his foot. He had pulses in his feet, which I marked with a pen to keep track of his circulation. Taking off his oxygen mask was a shock. His nose was just a brittle, dried, black crust. Checking his eyes, I found that he could see, but he had snow blindness in one eye.

I started an IV giving him fluids and medication to increase blood flow to the hands and feet. This can have the side effect of dropping blood pressure, and having no blood pressure cuff, I had to monitor his pressure by regularly feeling the strength of the pulsations in his neck. We put him back on oxygen but took it off long enough to feed him some soup. We placed his limbs in tubs of warm water, monitoring the temperature carefully with little submerged thermometers. His hands and feet were literally blocks of ice and they cooled the water rapidly. It took a lot of work to keep the water at the right temperature, drawing off the cold and adding hot from a thermos.

The Sherpas were eager assistants, and though most of them had never used a thermometer before, they quickly got the hang of it, reading the temperature themselves in each tub and making their own decisions when to add hot water.

Just as we were getting Makalu under control, Beck arrived. I expected an incoherent, half-conscious phantom, but in he walked, mostly under his own power, and in an easy conversational tone he said, "Hi, Ken, where should I sit?" We moved Makalu to one side and laid Beck down next to him. Makalu had had the worst frostbite I had ever seen, but that was before I saw Beck.

His entire right hand and wrist and a third of his forearm were deep purple and frozen solid. No blisters, no pulse, no sensation, no pain. It was the hand of a dead man, but, bizarrely, he could move his fingers as the live muscles in his forearm were able to pull on the dead bones in his hand. On the left hand all the fingers were rock hard, frozen, and purple. His face and nose were also badly frostbitten and black.

I went through the same routine as I had for Makalu, and as I worked Beck talked casually. If you had just heard the conversation and not seen what was going on, you would have thought he just stopped by for tea. He said that he got lost and exhausted up there and couldn't find his way back to camp in the whiteout. Beck was aware his hands were numb and took his glove off to try to put his hand in his jacket, but never managed to get it inside. He collapsed in the snow, not unconscious, but unable to move. Much later someone came by, bent over him, and said, "He's dead." Beck thought, "I'm not dead, but if I don't get up, I soon will be," and with a tremendous force of will he got up and staggered into Camp 4 where Todd found him. An incredible feat, and a real testimony to this man's indomitable spirit and will to live.

I'm often asked how Beck could have survived his impossible ordeal. We always feel more comfortable if we can find an explanation for things we don't understand. As a doctor I can cobble together some medical reasons why Beck was able to reverse his irreversible hypothermia, but I don't believe it myself. The impression I had at the time is the one that stays with me now—it was a miracle.

Beck and Makalu were stabilized, but I stayed up all night with my two patients, changing their IVs, adjusting their oxygen flow, and watching them breathe. To prevent the IV bags from freezing I had to wrap chemical hand warmers around them. It was bitterly cold in the tent and we had only one propane heater, which was aimed on Beck and Makalu. My feet were freezing, but I would have felt guilty turning the heater toward me, so I just stayed cold and had a miserable night.

At 4:00 a.m. we got a radio call that the evacuation helicopter wasn't coming. It was too windy. It had been windy for days, and with no guarantee when it was going to let up, I had to make a decision: wait another day or try to get them down now. It was a hard choice. To carry them down I'd be risking further damage to them, but even more, I'd be risking the lives of the rescuers, whom I knew were ready to carry out my decision without question. But I knew Beck and Makalu would deteriorate rapidly at twenty-one thousand feet—an altitude at which even simple cuts won't heal. The need to get them down was compelling.

I decided we'd have to bring Beck and Makalu down the hard way—a combination of walking, sledding, and carrying them down the Cwm and through the Ice Fall. While teams were being organized I packed them both up for transport, wrapping their hands with bulky boxing-glove-type dressings and then covering them with down booties.

The rescue teams started off and I followed them down the Cwm. I was so intent on what was coming next—the descent through the treacherous Ice Fall and then how I would manage them at base camp—that I didn't notice the wind had died down. I was startled back into the present by the noise and then the appearance of a helicopter overhead. The lull in the wind was just what the pilot, and we all, had needed. The pilot couldn't see the crevasses from the air, so one of the climbers used a bottle of red Kool-Aid to mark an X where he thought it would be safe to land. It worked. The pilot made a delicate landing just above the Ice Fall and carried out the highest helicopter rescue in history. Beck and Makalu were in a clinic in Kathmandu before the rest of us were down to base camp.

Back at base camp we were all in a daze. No one could comprehend the loss on the mountain. A few days later we gathered at Scott Fischer's camp to share our grief in a memorial service. The Sherpas lit a fire of sacred juniper branches in a stone altar, then sat on the rocks and chanted from prayer books they rested on a crate of oxygen bottles. Climbers took turns standing on the higher rocks to speak from their hearts, at times turning to the mountain to speak directly to Scott or Rob or one of the others still up there lying in the snow. It seemed like everyone had finished and there was a long silence. Then Lap Sang, Scott Fischer's head Sherpa, got up, and crying, said in broken English: "I tried and I tried and I tried, but I couldn't save him."

None of us could save those who were lost:

Scott Fischer: on summit day, he said he wasn't feeling so good—but Scott was Scott and we thought he'd be OK.

Rob Hall: the most respected high-altitude mountaineer in the world and my friend for ten years. He died because he refused to abandon a dying climber. I would have expected no less from him.

Andy Harris: lost his way back in the whiteout, missed the camp by a few yards, and stepped off the sheer Kangchung Face.

Doug Hanson: the year before I had treated him for frostbite. We both said then that he was lucky he'd be able to climb again. This year, his luck ran out.

Yasuko Namba: she was hanging on to another climber who was trying to drag her and two others to safety. He felt her slip off and let her go. He didn't have the strength to hold her any longer.

Base camp is ringed by brightly colored Tibetan prayer flags. The Sherpas believe that if you write prayers on them, the wind will carry the message up to the gods—but that year Everest wasn't listening.

* * *

Kenneth Kamler, MD, is vice president of The Explorers Club, where he has organized a database of information about physiology and endurance. A microsurgeon specializing in the hand, Kamler is director of the Hand Treatment Center in New Hyde Park, New York. He is the author of two books: *Doctor on Everest* (Lyons Press, 2000) and *Surviving the Extremes* (St. Martin's, 2004).

Chapter 15

Journey to the Summit

BO PARFET WITH KATIE TRENKLE

As the charter flight touched ground in the city of Timika, in Papua New Guinea, our jet lag was immediately flushed out by the adrenaline that pumped through our veins. We were among the privileged few to travel to this remote part of Irian Jaya to climb the most elusive of the Seven Summits.

Carstensz Pyramid lies in the heart of the Jayawijaya mountain range in the Indonesian territory of Irian Jaya, now called Western Papua. Carstensz is the highest mountain of the Australia/Oceania Continent, and the most exotic and technically the most difficult of the Seven Summits.

Local Dani tribesmen welcomed us into a small village outside of Timika with unflinching stares. The province of Irian Jaya has had relatively little Western influence. Its jungle and rain forest are second in size only to the Amazon, and vast tracks have not been explored. The Stone Age Dani lifestyle has continued relatively uninfluenced.

From its inception the journey was difficult. Numerous permits from the state and local governments' ministries, army, and police were required for travel and climbing. And there was the additional threat of the Indonesian Army, with a long record of human rights violations. The army frequently sealed the area for indefinite periods of time, rendering all permits void.

There are dozens of guerrilla movements on the island. Some fight for control of local resources and political life, believing they've been exploited by successive Jakarta governments only interested in taking their gold, copper, timber, and land. Others form in order to maintain their ethnic identity.

In the old days the Freeport-McMoRan Grasberg mine gave quasi permission to climbers to use its road. From the pit it's only a few hours' walking to the mountain. The powerful mine is the largest gold mine and third largest copper mine in the world. Owned in large part by a Louisiana financier, much of its profit goes to the United States, another source of resentment for many natives. The Indonesian government has a 20 percent stake in the mine. Therefore, it's regarded as a national asset. In fact, it's the Indonesian government's largest taxpayer, paying out $180 million a year in taxes and royalties. The mine employs the Indonesian Army, military police, Freeport's security force, and airport security to protect it from foreigners or non-Freeport employees coming to the area, making it impossible to enter without a permit.

The alternative route through the Singa village is now also forbidden because of violence in the area. The only current possibility for climbing Carstensz is to charter a helicopter to fly directly to base camp, the Zebra Wall, at 12,800 feet.

After five days of waiting for rain and freezing sleet to clear, and with an unfavorable forecast, Johnny, the local guide we hired, announced that we had to go through the mine. Using a solution employed in countless Third World countries, we decided to try to bribe our way across.

We were told to be ready at midnight and that we would leave under the cover of darkness. In previous climbs I'd managed to steer clear of local conflicts. It appeared my luck had run out.

A car took us to a military outpost outside the mine where a bribed military escort awaited our arrival. In order to avoid detection by Indonesian military and private security guards, we were given military fatigues—hat, shirt, and pants—then told to lie down on our bellies in the back of a military vehicle. We were covered with a heavy military blanket. Wedged between our climbing gear and one another, faces down, arms out straight, and palms up, we began the six-hour drive into Indonesia's "Wild East," a conflict region where the security forces have a bad reputation for corruption and brutality.

We began our ascent from sea level to what would eventually be 11,850 feet. Posing as army soldiers and hidden under jackets, clothing, and equipment, we passed through five checkpoints where squads of soldiers with machine guns kept the area clear of trespassers. We made it through the first and second checkpoint without incident, after a brief exchange we were on our way.

As we rolled up beneath the floodlights of the third checkpoint, the doors were thrust open. I sensed the nervous tension as men in military uniforms surrounded our vehicle and started yelling. I imagined their rifles were pointed at the windows. I could see the light from several flashlights penetrating the blanket. I wondered if they could hear my heart beat. It didn't matter who was more intelligent, they were without a doubt better armed. We weren't in much of a bargaining position.

After several minutes (that felt like days) of shouting, our hired military captain got back into the vehicle and continued beyond the range of the floodlights toward the next checkpoint. The road was cripplingly steep. In fact, drivers need a special license because of the dangerous nature of the trip. It came as little surprise when the engine overheated. We each donated a water bottle that was used to cool the overworked engine and then waited. When the truck recovered, we continued our journey.

The next to overheat was an older climber in our group. The thin air makes it hard to breathe, and the packed vehicle wasn't equipped with air-conditioning. He began gasping for air and attempted to turn over on his back. His panic attack put all of us at risk. Fortunately I hadn't donated my second water bottle. I gave the man my reserve. Once hydrated, his panic subsided.

We were given no warning about the next detail of the trip. Instead of continuing to drive through the countless switchbacks and tunnels, we were to change to a Swiss-made cable car. It would get us from twenty-seven hundred to thirty-five hundred meters quickly. The truck backed into the cable car, and we were told that, on the soldier's command, we were to dive chest down (with our gear) into the cable car to avoid detection by security cameras monitoring the activity. Terrified, we did as we were told.

Undetected, we arrived safely at the top. We got back into the truck the same way we got out, diving chest down to avoid detection. Our escorts covered us with blankets and again, we were on our way.

We hadn't reached the end of the mine when the sun started to come up, and we became at risk of being spotted by mine workers. We pulled into a barracks and hid in a small container holding five to six people. Huddled on twin mattresses in a cramped, unsanitary room covered with graffiti and black holes the size of tennis balls, I sat among the four other climbers waiting again for the darkness of midnight.

Our stomachs protested and we requested a snack. Within minutes we were presented with a plateful of fried bat, followed by the second course—a hefty serving of rat. As I pulled the flesh from my meal (still covered in patches of fur), I thought about cannibals. Human flesh is said to taste much like pig. Looking down at my meal it crossed my mind that perhaps, considering their alternative fare, the natives were on to something.

For the first time since our departure, we had an opportunity to question why we had chosen to travel to a country known mostly to the rest of the world as a hotbed of police brutality, killing, torture, hostage taking, and ethnic cleansing. I nibbled on my rat and thought about the times in my life when I was faced with adversity.

Less than two hundred people have successfully climbed Carstensz Pyramid, and the goal to climb all Seven Summits had been branded into my head. Although I hadn't been prepared to take this adventure to another level, we had crossed the Rubicon. I would not be deterred by a few men with rifles and some fried rodents. After all, this was the stuff of an Indiana Jones movie. Again, I was filled with adrenaline and optimism.

At some point I dozed off and was awakened by something crawling across my cheek. As I swiped the creature with the side of my hand, I could hear the noise of its scaly flesh ripping in two. Its tail end fell to the ground, lightening the load of its head and front legs, which continued to scurry across my face. Looking around I realized that the tennis-ball-sized holes in the wall were not holes after all. Instead, they were insects of amazing shapes, sizes, and personalities.

At 1:00 a.m. we drove an hour to the Zebra Wall, the end of the mine and the beginning of our trek. Although the route is relatively straightforward, unlike the other Seven Summits, the climb is of moderate difficulty. We rearranged our backpacks and set off on the three-hour hike to base camp.

After our arrival at the camp we waited for several hours. When the six military soldiers who had been commissioned to carry our excess gear didn't show, a couple of us volunteered to retrace our path. Exhaustion had overcome the porters and each had collapsed at a different point. Without the energy to even pitch a tent, they covered themselves with the canvas to protect themselves from the sleet and snow that had begun to fall while waiting for us to come back from the truck.

We took food and other necessities and returned to base camp. For three days there was no break from the rain, sleet, and snow. We were forced again to wait it out.

It was our intention to make it from base camp to the summit and back in one day. When the weather cleared, we hastily got geared up and began the estimated twelve-hour ascent, following a line up the north face route pioneered by Heinrich Harrer in 1962.

After numerous pitches we climbed up the obvious crack system leading to an exposed, knife-edged ridge, which would eventually lead us to the summit. We climbed and rappelled down the first notch, then up and over a huge bolder, and back down onto the other side of the notch bottom.

Next was the most dangerous part of the climb, a steep thirty-five-foot rock inverted wall with a single, old fixed rope that would get us back up to the ridge. On either side of me was a two-thousand-foot vertical drop. We didn't know how long the rope had been there and what condition the anchor was in up top. To make things worse, the weather conditions had gotten worse. The steady sleet that had been with us the entire climb had now turned into heavy snow that was practically blowing horizontally.

After everything we had been through to get to this point, we were not about to turn back. I was the second to attempt the climb up the rope. My friend had gotten five feet from the ground, but the rope was frozen. He made it safely back down and was panting like a dog and his facial expression simply showed great fear.

I'll never forget his next words: "Bo, your turn."

I made it about halfway up when I heard a noise much like a freight train. It came up fast and absolutely without warning, the wind whipped me over to one side and now I was dangling over a two-thousand-foot drop. I quickly looked up to see the rope get dragged across jagged rocks with complete malevolence. My body and mind rebelled with fear, my legs dangling two thousand feet above the surface. I thought of Wile E. Coyote when he runs off a cliff—hanging in the air for a moment before plummeting to earth. Perhaps we should have left climbing to those seeking a religious experience or simply trying to rescue goats.

In that horrific moment I thought of many things. I said to myself, I miss my mom, my dad, my friends, school . . . America. I wanted to go home. But I thought again about times in my life when I had been faced with misfortune. Suddenly, with a clear head, full of resolution, I realized I had no choice but to push forward. No way was I going back to Jakarta without reaching the summit.

At the top I fell down and lay there for some time. We strive to reach the highest peaks in our lives, I thought. I wasn't doing this just for the pure adventure of it.

After many more long stretches of scrambling, steeper moves, and intense exposure, I reached the summit. I waited at the top for about an hour before the next climber emerged. "We have to go down. It's going to get dark in a couple of hours," I told him.

"What time do you think it is, Bo?" he asked.

"Four p.m."

"It's ten in the morning," he replied.

It felt so much later.

• • •

Bo Parfet grew up in Hickory Corners, Michigan. He currently lives and works in a few places (Asia, Chicago, and Michigan). His passions are conservation, exploration, hunting, the environment, mountaineering, writing, and public speaking. He has climbed all Seven Summits and raised money for educational scholarships with each climb. Parfet has a master's degree in applied economics from the University of Michigan and an MBA from the Kellogg School of Management at Northwestern University.

Katie Trenkle completed one year of law school at DePaul University in Chicago, Ilinois, after earning her BA in English from the University of Michigan, Ann Arbor. She withdrew to focus on her creative interests, completing the Professional Screenwriting Program at the University of California, Los Angeles, and the Second City Improvisational Program in Chicago. She is currently working as an actress/model/writer in Chicago, has started her own dating company, and is enjoying life with her new husband, Rodman, and lovable pug "Sushi."

Chapter 16

The Leather Rope

ROBERT McCRACKEN PECK

Itygran Island, Siberia, August 17, 2001.

Even at a distance, the barrel-chested man with a cropped, graying beard projected familiarity and strength. I had not seen him before, but his ageless face was strangely familiar. The artist J. H. Pierneef caught such a look in his woodcuts of Paul Kruger. Rockwell Kent distilled it in his Beowulf, Yousuf Karsh in Hemingway. These and other images melded in my mind as I watched him crest the windy bluff that holds the village of Yanrakynnot from the Bering Sea. He walked down the gravelly slope with the confidence of someone who had lived a long and dangerous life. His fellow villagers wore sealskins, but he wore a tunic of more recent design: a durable, homespun whose cut must have dated from the time of the czars. Wreathing his shoulder like a bandolier was a coil of stitched leather rope.

The man saw my gaze and redirected his seaward path to greet me. We exchanged friendly nods and indecipherable greetings. He followed my admiring glance to his bandolier, then proudly gestured its origin with a fist tap to his chest. "I made this myself," he said in Chukchi, removing the rope from his shoulder. He then stepped back, and with a hard overhead throw to an imaginary reindeer, pantomimed its use, scattering children on the hill behind me. Bracing his body against the animal's lunging weight, he hand over handed the antlered ghost to his side.

"It is made from the hide of a bearded seal," volunteered an English-speaking Russian who had made his way to us from a table of raw fish and whale meat on offer by the village. Like me, he was a visitor to Yanrakynnot, part of a state security force sent here to monitor the rare appearance of an

American vessel on Russian shores. I expressed my thanks to the stranger for this timely transition, though, in truth, I quietly resented his intrusion into our conversation.

"He wants you to have his rope," explained the translator. "It is very strong. Maybe you can pull your car with it." This suggestion, no doubt the Russian's own, was intended to give purpose to the proffered gift, or perhaps to redefine the rope's strength for an American car owner, someone unlikely to know the power of a lassoed reindeer. Whichever, it seemed bizarrely incongruous and out of place on this rocky, roadless coast.

"The man who made it is seventy-five years old," offered the Russian, his eyes wandering past us to others on the hillside and along the beach. I thanked him for the information, grateful to know that the man had doubled the life expectancy of the other Chukchi men in Russia's far east. The translator nodded, sand-walked back to the foot table, satisfied that my interests—and the old man's—were benign.

Making good on his offer, the herdsman pressed his rope into my hands. It was cool and weighty, smooth and redolent with use. How I longed to possess it, both as a beautiful object and as a tangible piece of an extraordinary way of life. Fingering its oily surface, I struggled with the ethics of taking home sealskin, and with the larger question of whether it was right for me to turn such a useful tool into a talisman of culture.

"Thank you very much, but I can't take it," I mumbled, unconvincingly. "It is a beautiful rope, but you need it more than I do." I held the coiled rope toward him. "This is yours," I said. "Please take it." He smiled, sensing a compliment, and leaned back against the slope of the hill to admire his handiwork.

I looked for our interpreter, but he was ambling down the beach in search of other Americans. He carried a piece of bread and whale meat in each hand. I continued to offer the rope to its maker, half hoping he would not take it. He said something to me in Chukchi, nodded affably, and folded his hands behind his back.

Sensing no change in his resolve, and fearing that to refuse his gift would be insulting, I justified accepting the rope. I returned his gesture with a gift of my own. He may not have owned American dollars before, but the herdsman knew what they were and beamed with pleasure at their promise. He thanked me by touching my shoulders with the palms of his hands. I bowed and shook his hand in return. Nodding in farewell, he turned and strode back toward the faded wooden buildings that lined the ridge above us.

• • •

Robert McCracken Peck is a naturalist, writer, and historian with a special interest in the history of exploration and travel, science, and art. As senior fellow of the Academy of Natural Sciences of Philadelphia, he has chronicled scientific research expeditions on five continents, written six books on the history of natural history, and was a guest curator for art and science exhibitions for museums and libraries throughout the United States.

Chapter 17

Almost Swept Away

FAANYA LYDIA ROSE

On every expedition there is a tale to tell of lucky escapes. I don't think this one, which occurred in 1983 in the middle of the night in India, has ever been told. John Bashford-Snell, a British explorer who was chairman of the British Chapter of The Explorers Club, is a gifted leader, but from time to time, he can be quite gung ho.

Late one night, we were traveling in northern India in a bus. It was pouring rain, the likes of which you have never seen. It was bucketing down. Because I am a bush girl and have bush experience, I know the rule: never, *never*, drive in the rain in the bush. In a torrential rain, without someone walking in front carrying a flashlight or lantern, surveying the road in front, such driving is out of the question. When rivers break their banks it is difficult to see. In a moment, everything can be swept away.

Yet there I was, a new bride, having married Robert Rose. For about half an hour I was sitting in this coach that was rushing down the road. I was frozen with fear. We were going to see Billy Singh, the author and conservationist who writes mainly about tigers in his area.

After about half an hour, I started making a fuss. My new husband was looking at me, appalled—no doubt asking himself all sorts of private questions about why he had married this angry woman. After forty minutes, I could bear it no more.

Eventually, I stood up and shouted, "Stop this bus! You should not do this. A man should be walking ahead of you with a lantern and a flag and the bus should be going at one mile an hour. This is dangerous."

Imagine the look of surprise on the faces of the other passengers. Yet they could not ignore my screaming. While the bus was still moving, I stood up and announced, "I'm getting out."

"In the middle of nowhere in India?" asked my husband.

"I am getting out," I insisted. "You stop this bus."

I went to the door and opened it. The water immediately rushed in. We were only fifty feet from the river.

It took the workers four days to get the bus out of the mud. That was the nearest I had ever been to being killed.

Initially, my husband was furious that I made the fuss, but when they saw that the river had broken its banks and we were only a few feet from being swept away, the matter was never mentioned again. A lucky escape, indeed.

• • •

Faanya Lydia Rose was elected as a director to The Explorers Club in 1998 with Thor Heydahl as her sponsor. She became the first woman president of the club in 2000, and in 2002 received the Medallion of Honor from the New York Society of American Registered Architects for the restoration of the club's headquarters, the Lowell Thomas Building. Rose was born, raised, and educated in Africa and emigrated to Great Britain in 1980 where she established a career in London's financial center. She was treasurer of two major British companies as well as financial advisor to London Ambulance Service, university lecturer, and chairman of the British Eye Research Foundation. She was a member of the Everest Extreme Expedition in 1999, and many other flag-carrying expeditions, including ones in Nepal, Bolivia, and Easter Island.

Chapter 18

Himalayan Ibex Hunting in Pakistan

THEODORE M. SIOURIS

My hunt in Pakistan was a mixture of excitement, disappointments, and surprises. When I landed in Islamabad, halfway around the world, I soon learned that everything there is done in what is described as "Pakistani time," which is nothing like the proverbial New York minute. I was grateful that Rana Moin, my outfitter, was there to cheerfully greet me and help with the grueling formalities. It was 10:45 p.m., December 4, 2000. After sixteen hours in the air, I needed a reason to smile.

Although my arrival came before the September 11, 2001, attacks on America, published accounts of growing hostilities against Americans in Pakistan were common. The U.S. State Department had issued advisories against traveling there. For security reasons, a suburban hotel was selected by Rana. Whether it was from sheer exhaustion or the reassuring sight of the stern-faced guard clutching a double-barreled shotgun stationed at the hotel entrance, I slept soundly.

My first stop in the morning was the U.S. Embassy, where I was advised to declare my itinerary and the intended date of my return to Islamabad from hunting Himalayan ibex, a large-horned wild goat that lives in the northern areas in Kashmir. Even before business hours, hundreds of Pakistanis were in line at the embassy to apply for visas. An American diplomat who received me in his office told me that lines are common. Only applicants who can guarantee their intent to return are given visas, because many remain as illegal aliens in the United States.

Next, Rana had his driver take us to the Pakistan International Airlines office to book our flight to Skardu, the capital of Baltistan, which borders

China on the north and India to the east. Afghanistan is to the west. The flight was canceled, so we reserved space on the next morning flight and spent the day shopping in Rawalpindi. Pakistan mines yield fine rubies and emeralds, and Rana arranged for a gem dealer to assemble a selection for me to see after the hunt.

Though December weather isn't bad in Islamabad, it can be terrible in the towering mountains. Skardu is in a deep valley. Pilots of Boeing 727s have to descend in tight circles to land. If conditions are bad, the pilot aborts the landing, and the airplane returns to Islamabad. If that happened to us, our one-hour flight would become a two-and-a-half day tortuous drive down the primitive Skardu Road and Karakoram Highway.

Fortunately, our flight departed Islamabad and landed smoothly in Skardu. I was invited into the cockpit where I took spectacular panoramic photos as we skimmed across row after row of the majestic Karakoram Mountains. Massud Arshad, who is a wildlife scientist with the World Wildlife Fund (WWF), joined Rana Moin and his associate, Mehmed Zahid, and me on the flight. We were together throughout my trip.

Our expedition leader, Karim, met us at the Skardu Hotel. We quickly registered and went into town to explore the local wares. Centuries ago, Skardu was a key stopover along the Silk Road trade route. It's like any frontier town, except that, as a Muslim village, no women are visible. I was amazed by the variety of weapons of war that were being peddled. We were in the heart of Kashmir, in virtually lawless northern Pakistan, where a bitter twenty-year war was raging between India and Pakistan. A shopkeeper pressed an assault rifle into my hands and gleefully urged me to buy it. But the only mementos I bought that afternoon were a brown hand-loomed wool blanket that men wear instead of coats, and *pakols* for each of the six of us. Pakols, also called "Chitrali caps," are the typical round woven wool caps with the rolled bottoms commonly worn by men in Pakistan and Afghanistan.

Early Thursday, we pulled out of Skardu in a Russian jeep-style vehicle and a van for the long drive to Hushe (pronounced *hooshay*), a remote mountain village that was to be our base camp. As we left town, we passed a prison with the usual imposing, grim high walls, corner towers, and tall fences around the perimeter. But in this case, the gates were swung open wide and the prison was empty. Apparently, there are no criminals in Skardu.

As we drove along the Indus River, we passed the road to the base camp for K2, which, after Mount Everest, is the highest peak in the world. Later on, the terrain was dry with outcrops of rock and prominent wind-blown sand dunes. The road is tolerably maintained, but bad enough to chew up one of our tires and ruin the wheel. When we caught up to our jeep, it was stalled at the bottom of an icy hill. We used steel-tipped ski poles as ice picks to clear the ice and free the jeep.

As we entered Hushe that afternoon, we were surprised by an enthusiastic reception party of over fifty welcoming male villagers and children. I suspect the joy at my arrival was because 80 percent of my hunting trophy fee would be paid to the village. That money represented much of the village's annual cash income. Such payments are part of the government plan to save the ibex by compensating the locals for preserving rather than eating them. Only two ibex hunting permits per year are issued in that area.

The cheerful children wore lightweight clothing despite the twenty-degree temperature. No one seemed to mind the cold. Several of the men wore sandals with no socks. I'm told that the bodies of people living in high and cold climates become acclimated by generating more capillaries near the surface of their skins. Also, their blood carries a higher percentage of hemoglobin to more efficiently oxygenate the tissues than is necessary for us who live in warmer climates and lower elevations.

We set up a target range below the village to sight-in my rifle. Later, we met with the village elders, who gave us a reading of the ibex sightings over the preceding days. They then selected two guides and two teams of scouts who would be with us on the hunt.

Behind a gated entry with a hand-scrawled sign that read Hillman Hotel was a large field landscaped with rubble and weeds and a car track leading to a single-level cement building with dirt floors and two rooms. One room was the kitchen and the other was the combination dining room and bunk room.

We were crowded inside with dozens of noisy, curious men and boys. Several times the exhaust pipe of the wood-burning stove was shoved loose, filling the room with choking white smoke until the hot pipes were wrestled together again. We were served a hearty Pakistani dinner of spicy lamb stew, basmati rice, and canned vegetables. A glass of wine with dinner, of course, was out of the question, as this was a Muslim community. Later, we were invited to stay in the home of a prominent resident and found those quarters much more hospitable. Rana, Massud, Zahid, and I laid out sleeping bags over the hand-loomed rugs on the floor. We shared a latrine in the next room with several goats and sheep. Huge, dry snowflakes fell throughout the night.

The village of Hushe was home to a few hundred inhabitants. Electric power was provided from sunset to sunrise by a power station that was donated by foreign hunters. At 4:00 a.m. each morning during Ramadan, the local equivalent of a town crier walked through the village, blowing a yak horn to signal the beginning of the daily fast and to call the faithful to the mosque. During the month-long religious celebration, Muslims may not eat or drink from sunrise to sundown.

In the early dawn of December 8, we walked in a northerly direction, toward the 25,663-foot Masherbrum Peak that crowds the sky. We could still hear the melodious Islamic chanting carried on the clean frigid air from the mosque a mile behind. It was Friday, the first Sabbath of Ramadan.

I grew up in the western United States, surrounded by the glorious Rocky Mountains, and never imagined that mountains anywhere could be more spectacular—until I saw Pakistan. The main block of the Karakoram Range rises in a crowded wall, ninety-three miles thick with almost one hundred peaks rising over twenty-three thousand feet. By comparison, the single highest peak in all of North America is Alaska's Mount McKinley at just 20,320 feet.

Our scouts on the opposite side of the valley spotted ibex high up the mountain. Before we could get a spotting scope on them, a snow squall moved in, so we waited for it to blow past. Our party included the local game master, curious observers, and several village elders. Everyone looked gnarled and much older than their years, a consequence of living in such a harsh environment. Though the local language is Balti, everyone spoke English.

After thirty minutes, the snow stopped and we spotted two very good ibex rams near the peak. I quickly moved to climb the right side of the ridge with Karim, Mohammed, and Hassan. Hassan was an experienced climber from the village who had appointed himself as my guardian. Two scouts began climbing the left side, intent on driving the ibex over the top to my waiting gun. It took us nearly three hours, wearing crampons, to make the steep climb through knee-deep snow.

We got into position behind a line of boulders that offered good cover and an open view of the top. I expected the ibex to cross some two hundred yards above us. Our plan worked, but the ibex burst across the top, over four hundred yards away and trotting to the right. I placed the illuminated orange triangle reticle of my Trijicon scope very high on the shoulder of one of the ibex to compensate for the distance and squeezed off a shot at the fourth ram, which had impressive horns arched over forty inches. The rifle misfired. Quick second and third shots only left him untouched as he rounded the corner.

We retraced our steps partway down and explored a ravine that curved up to the north. The humidity was low and perspiration quickly evaporated so our clothes never got wet.

On the trek back to Hushe that afternoon, Karim pointed out a favorite hunting destination of a local ruler years before. His army would drive ibex into a narrow canyon and block the escape routes, trapping them. Then the ruler rode in and shot his pick of the ibex. So much for royal sport.

The village of Hushe is situated on a plateau about one hundred feet above the pristine Hushe River Valley. As we approached every day, a crowd of men assembled at the top of the rise to see if we'd gotten the ibex. Word quickly spread through the village that my rifle had misfired. The head man later told me my rifle misfired because we hunted on the Sabbath, which is forbidden among Muslims.

Early the next morning the sun rose on a cold but perfect morning. Because I'd missed the ibex the day before, I checked the rifle sighting before we got into ibex country. I set up a target on a large boulder and a three-shot group showed the rifle was still zeroed at two hundred yards. A couple of our scouts were very interested in my rifle, so we took a little extra time for them to try their marksmanship before moving on.

We turned right into a broad valley that leads to the famous K6 and K7 peaks. Our destination was Siacho, about four hours' walk from Hushe. Siacho is a popular summer camping area for trekkers from around the world but is abandoned in the winter. Mountaineers are attracted because of the towering peaks in the area, thirteen of which remain unnamed and have never been scaled because they lie within the two-hundred-fifty-square-mile perimeter of the Pakistan war with India for control of Kashmir. The owner of the stone encampment had given us the keys to use the kitchen, pantry, and latrine facilities. Straight up the valley is the Charakusa Glacier, hundreds of yards wide, spanning the middle of the valley.

We sent two scouting teams up the valley toward the soaring K6 peak, while we cleared the snow at Siacho, pitched our tents, and cooked lunch. I was the only one who ate. No one else ate or drank from sunup until sunset because of the Ramadan fast. Later, both scouting teams returned with reports of ibex up the valley, but there wasn't enough daylight left to begin a stalk.

We awoke before sunrise on Sunday, December 10, and ate a hearty breakfast of scrambled eggs, toast, and green tea. It was bitterly cold and Rana, Massud, and Zahid had spent a miserable night. They stayed in their sleeping bags while Mohammed, another local climber, led Karim, Hassan, and me up the valley toward K6 and K7. My altimeter watch gave me a reading of over twelve thousand feet. I'm acclimated to Manhattan's sea-level elevation. Therefore, the brisk climb at high altitude had my breathing doing a double disco beat, while theirs did a slow waltz.

We were surprised to find the tracks of two snow leopards following the trail of footprints in the snow we'd made the day before. Ibex are a primary prey of the endangered snow leopard. Considering the ibex's keen vision and sense of smell, I don't imagine that hunting them is any easier for snow leopards than for us.

We took a break and I had green tea and biscuits over a compact warm fire while Mohammed scouted toward Supanse, where the Chogolisa and Charakusa glaciers meet. Mohammed didn't spot any ibex, so we moved back down the valley. It was clear that the hunting snow leopards had driven the ibex high into the valley walls, so we focused our attention up there. Soon we spotted a group of ten ibex high on the south wall, and we quickly moved back up the valley—out of sight—before crossing the glacier.

The direction of our climb was on a vertical and lateral course to intersect the ibex beyond a ridge. A prominent boulder there would provide cover and a rest for the rifle. I put on crampons again for the steep climb. As we moved up, Hassan stayed near me and watched every step I took, offering an extended hand or supporting my footing with his foot or ski pole. I could see concern and encouragement in his eyes. I was breathing heavily and explained it was because of the shortage of oxygen up there, not terror. I took off my gloves to grasp for rocky handholds, but quickly abandoned that idea because my hands, wet from snow, froze to the rock. In conversation, I learned that Hassan, though highly intelligent and articulate, had never been taught to read or write. Literacy in Pakistan was under 40 percent and in that remote northern outpost, it was under 20 percent.

We finally reached the ridge we had chosen, and I peeked from behind the boulder but couldn't see the ibex. Then Karim, with his trained mountain eyes, scanned the ridge and quickly spotted the ibex, moving up and away. I judged them at about three hundred yards, and we collectively picked out the trophy ram. I cradled the rifle against the stone, adjusted my breathing, checked my heartbeat, and set the set trigger before touching it off.

I heard the slap that a bullet makes when it hits an animal and, for an instant, was confident the shot was true. It wasn't. The bullet's impact was about thirty inches low, hitting a much smaller animal that fell and bounced down the face of the mountain. I had underestimated the distance by a substantial margin. The big ram looked down for a moment as the young ibex plunged, and then moved off with the others, out of sight. After the event, with time to use my range finder, I learned that the true distance was nearly five hundred yards. The unlucky young ram I shot had horns only six inches long. In fact, the skull was partially smashed and one horn was lost in the fall. It was a regrettable event that could not be reversed. There is no provision for legally taking a second trophy, so my hunt was over.

We broke camp early the next morning and hiked back to Hushe. An assembly of animated villagers greeted us and we were treated to lunch by the village elders, featuring meat from my ibex. They, as I, were disappointed that I hadn't taken a better trophy, but the youngster was much better eating than an old ram would have been.

The weather that had favored us on our flight into Skardu turned against us. The incoming plane was denied clearance to land and diverted back to Islamabad because of low visibility. That meant we had to make the two-and-a-half-day drive back to Islamabad. I then realized how lucky I was to have an open return business class ticket home.

The 102-mile Skardu Road is called the most dangerous road in the world because of the mountain terrain and the seismic activity. On average, there is a tremor every few minutes. In many places, the road was blasted into the vertical granite rock. The roadbed was narrow and had a vertical drop of hundreds of feet. Any vehicle that approached from the opposite direction caused us to slow to a walking speed. Though the drive had anxious moments, they were offset by exhilaration at the beauties that nature has shaped. I could see why some believe the nearby Hunza Valley is the legendary Shangri-la.

People along the roadside hailed us and excited children ran beside the vehicle. All the villages suffer desperate poverty, but the worst conditions were where a cliff had collapsed months before and buried many of the inhabitants of a village that was built steeply up the canyon wall. No visible effort had been made toward recovery or repair.

Skardu Road terminates at the Karakoram Highway, which follows the route of the Silk Road from China to the heart of Pakistan. Construction was a fifteen-year joint effort of the Pakistan Army and Chinese experts and was completed in 1978. It was blasted through those unstable, breathtaking mountains at the cost of 810 Pakistani and 82 Chinese lives. The unofficial human cost is put at one life for each of its 1,284 kilometers.

Just beyond the junction of the Skardu Road and the Karakoram Highway, we stopped at a monument where the world's three mightiest mountain ranges —the Hindu Kush, Himalayas, and Karakoram—meet. These mountain ranges were created, and continue to rise, because the subcontinent of India is being relentlessly pushed northward by the Indian tectonic plate.

In Islamabad, Rana proved himself a masterful tour guide of the many cultural and historic landmarks of that sprawling city. One evening at dinner, his friend the gem dealer presented me with a velvet bag filled with magnificent precious gems. I bought five "pigeon blood" rubies and a spectacular emerald for my wife, Aida.

We drove to Lahore to visit a long-time South African friend of mine who was an officer of the WWF, developing conservation programs for the rural northern areas of Pakistan. We related our experiences one evening over a feast of ethnic Pakistani food. We had also invited a reporter from the BBC who wanted to interview my WWF friend and me about big-game hunting and how it is an integral part of wildlife conservation programs throughout the world.

I returned home with photos, gifts, priceless memories, and my Himalayan ibex. That broken little skull with only one horn now proudly occupies its own place of honor in my trophy room, among seven other species of record-class ibex with long, arching scimitar horns, taken from around the world in other remote mountain peaks that ibex always call home. Pakistan was one of my most memorable hunting adventures.

* * *

Theodore M. Siouris retired as a Wall Street investment banker at age forty-two to become a private investor and corporate director. He travels worldwide pursuing his interests in ethology and wildlife conservation. He resides with his wife in Manhattan and Montauk Point, Long Island.

Chapter 19

Zen Adventures in West Papua

NEVILLE SHULMAN

After climbing with a team the highest mountain in Australasia, Carstensz Pyramid, which is situated on the western side of the island of New Guinea in what is part of Indonesia, I decided I wanted to climb on my own. I needed some solitude and peace. After my previous exertions, I thought climbing a few lesser mountains would not cause any real problems or difficulties. If only I had known what was to occur.

Everyone else in the team preferred to rest and read. A few waved nonchalantly as I set off after an early breakfast. Initially I passed a series of long, jutting rocks known as the "Ten Witches" because all of the rocks have pointed stone shapes at the top that look like witches' hats. The floor of the first valley I crossed is covered with more of the ultra razor-sharp rocks, very difficult and dangerous to clamber over, as one slip can easily mean a gashed leg or arm. At the base of one of the early rock wall sections someone placed some small stones to spell the message, or symbols, MU 2991. I can't work out what it means, but I enjoy the oddity of it.

I soon crossed the Dayak Pass and climbed for more than an hour, steadily gaining height as I worked my way over a number of increasingly high ridges. There were many varieties of bushes and strangely shaped prickly plants to touch and examine. The rocks were of infinite shapes and sizes, some extremely pointed, others almost flat, often in striking deep-bronzed colors; so many different environments to admire and enjoy. The gorses and mosses were unstable and sometimes I stepped on one section only to find my foot plunging immediately inside a deep hole. This was painful and I learned to tread cautiously.

The scenery was exceptional, and I felt as if I were crossing virgin territory where no one has ever been before. This whole region was completely uninhabited and only rarely visited by climbers. I trekked over a long, mossy hill. About a hundred meters down the other side, almost at the bottom, I saw an enormous ancient cedar, completely on its own, as if some giant hand plucked it out of the forests amid its companion trees and put it there as some form of a punishment. At first glance, it appeared very lonely, but as I came nearer I saw it held its own splendor and magnificence. It had a very wide circumference and when I stretched my arms around it, it was too wide for me to touch my fingers together. It was captivating to be in an extraordinary area of total peace and beauty. There were so many different kinds of interesting things to find, touch, and reflect on.

Suddenly the weather changed. The sun disappeared, the sky darkened, and clouds quickly covered most of it. The Hindi proverb seemed likely to be proved, "When clouds are spread across the sky like partridge feathers, they will not go without shedding rain." Reluctantly I turned around and climbed back in the direction of the camp. I tried to work out which would be the fastest and possibly the least difficult. There seemed to be an easier rock section down below so I climbed steadily toward it and for a few moments rested on a ledge overlooking the valley.

The rolling, wild countryside, hemmed in by the mountains, made a wonderful sight. I was reluctant to leave but knew I had no choice but to move on. I was still not certain whether to climb farther down into the valley itself or continue climbing back over the high ridges.

To one side of me was a small buttress jutting out of the rocks; it looked as if it had been there for thousands of years. I leaned one hand on it, trying to decide which way to proceed. Without any prior indication whatsoever the whole rock buttress suddenly shot out of the mountain. It flashed downward like a huge javelin, ricocheting as it fell, tumbling until it landed with a shocking crash on some rocks far below. This all happened within just a few moments, although the whole incident seemed to have taken place in slow motion. I was dumbfounded, shocked, and quickly realized of course that I was resting only on air.

A complete void was beneath my hand, nothing to hold on to. I started to tumble down after it toward the rocks. I tried to protect my head with my hands and prevent myself from falling but I could see and feel the rocks as if they were leaping at me. Luckily I did not fall too far and fortunately didn't strike my head on anything. My legs were not so lucky. The pain was instant and my legs felt as if they had been cut to pieces. My right leg was pouring with blood. I was dazed and lay where I fell for several moments until I felt the first stinging drops of rain falling.

My practice of Zen hadn't totally saved me, although it helped, at least in increasing my perception and awareness in trying to lessen the impact. Ironically I recalled the words of Zen Master Ying-an: "Zen has nothing to grab onto. When people who study Zen don't see it, that is because they approach too eagerly." I have often been asked to explain Zen, but it takes a lifetime to learn and usually that would not be enough time. In response, I like to quote Louis Armstrong's words: "If you have to ask what jazz is, you'll never know." At this moment I was not certain what I know myself, except that I knew the feeling of intense pain in my legs.

It was necessary to pull myself together and deal with my wounds quickly. Nietzsche's words urgently sounded internal alarm bells: "If you gaze too long into the abyss, the abyss also gazes into you." There was no one around, no one will find me here, and I had no choice but to cope with the situation myself as best I could. A hermit once simply pronounced, "One who falls on the ground, must get up from the ground." I pushed myself unsteadily to my feet and bathed my legs with some of the water I was carrying, wiping away most of the blood and hoping that there will be no infection. I had some plasters in my pack. I used them to cover the cuts, although they were deep and still bled through. I realized they were not going to stem the blood totally but hopefully would hold on a temporary basis.

I now had to get back to the camp as fast as I could, particularly before the monsoon really set in. My right leg ached, blood seeped through the plasters, and I cautiously climbed down through the gorses to the valley still far below me. It is always said that the monsoon flushes snakes from hidden places, and I tried to step warily and avoid the many hidden holes. Mostly, I did. However, one time I stepped onto a small, mossy bush that instantly gave way beneath my weight. My left leg plunged deep into a hole and I was soon up to the knee in foul-smelling mud. My right knee twisted around to take the strain and weight and I screamed out as the muscles wrenched. I gently eased my leg out and then lay on the ground for several moments until the pain somewhat subsided and I felt able to continue.

After that, even more cautiously, I climbed steadily down to the valley floor. This area is really all one region, although divided into a series of separate valleys, each with their different wild vegetation, powerful rocks, but glorious and magnificent settings.

It was preferable not to risk my injured leg or take any further chances by climbing more rock sections and so I clambered gradually through the lower part of the valley. One section was particularly difficult and dangerous, as there were huge razor-edged rocks on the valley floor that are very difficult to traverse. I balanced myself precariously one rock to another, edging forward but sometimes having to backtrack in order to find an easier way of climbing across.

In one crevasse, a small, oddly shaped piece of wood caught my attention and I stopped to pull it out. It looked exactly like a snake's head and body, with an exceedingly baleful, single eye peering out of the head, and crisscross markings along the curved body shape that exactly convey a moving snake. It was a natural work of art and I put it carefully in my pack to carry back with me. I trekked slowly to the top of the next valley section and saw a ridge with a grouping of several huge boulders, each of which must have weighed several tons. One was shaped rather like a lion's head, and someone had obviously helped nature along by carving the markings of the lion's mane on one side. The whole rock had the majesty of the lion and it stared passively but regally over its domain. It probably always will.

It was becoming misty and I was finding it difficult to keep up any regular pace. It was also cold and wet and I felt very weary. However it was essential to keep going, otherwise, as it got darker, I could easily get lost and it would be impossible for anyone to find me. At last I reached the final part of the main Carstensz Valley and I knew that not too far ahead would be the expedition camp. The mist had closed down even further and the gloomy terrain looked harsh and stark. It was very wet on the ground and water was seeping through from one of the creeks. After I had been trekking for some while it seemed to me that Carstensz Pyramid was now on my left and that somehow I must have missed the way back and trekked up the other side and across to the right. I decided to continue on this way as it could be a worthwhile route to follow and then at least I should be able to come around the mountain from the top. Also I would be able to see the real shape of the pyramid as it is normally viewed and reach the camp from higher up the valley.

I continued on for a while but it became even more barren and bleak, and the terrain became tougher and more difficult. In the worsening conditions I could not see too far ahead and realized that if I did go on this way I might get totally lost. There was no choice but to return and try to find the entrance to the valley so I could hopefully locate the camp.

Wearily I turned around and made my way slowly back, losing even more time. It was much darker and I was feeling dejected and weaker. Then luckily in the half light I came across the group of stones I had seen at the outset that spell out MU 2991. I never found out who had created that sign and what the meaning was, but from the bottom of my heart I thank whoever put it there. The stones confirmed that I had been in fact trekking in the right part of the Carstensz Valley.

Somehow in the gloom, I missed the cutoff to the camp. It had just been a combination of factors—the considerable distance trekked, returning from a different direction, the weather conditions—that probably confused me. Once more I turned around and headed back up the valley, at least this time knowing then that I was definitely going in the right direction. After some further trekking I finally reached the sanctuary of the camp and made for the medical tent.

"How was it?" I was asked.

"Not bad, not bad at all."

• • •

Neville Shulman is a fellow of The Explorers Club, the Royal Geographical Society, and a life member of the Bhutan Society. Shulman is director of the British International Theatre Institute, chairman of the Theatre Forum, and a member of the U.K. UNESCO Culture Committee. He is a well-known travel writer, lecturer, and journalist, and his books include *Some Like It Cold* (Lyons Press, 2003).

Chapter 20

Siberian Expedition

MIKAEL STRANDBERG

Mike!" Johan whispered anxiously, "Look out!"

As I turned around I saw a big brown bear standing on the beach only twenty meters away, between us and our canoe, intensely sniffing and staring at us. It was one of the most beautiful bears I'd ever seen. Its fur was radiant in the sun, its front arms were gray from age, and it seemed startled by our presence. At that moment I had no idea whether it was the same bear I had shot at from the canoe ten minutes earlier or whether it was another one. The first bear had fallen over, having been hit at least three times in the area below its left shoulder, and before I had time to reload, the wounded bear slowly crawled into the thick taiga. This one, however, took a step forward, stopped again, and stood up on its hind legs, sniffing even more eagerly.

I took a quick look at my young partner, Johan, only twenty-one years old and on his first expedition, and I suddenly realized that he was unarmed. The Russian authorities had allowed us to bring only one rifle, and at that moment I remembered the words of my wife, Titti, before setting out on the expedition. "Don't ever forget that you have the same responsibility as any parent regarding Johan," she warned. "It is better you die if things come to that."

I handed Johan the rifle and took a step down from the steep bank and out of the thick forest. "Maybe you should have a go," I said calmly. My appearance startled the bear initially, but suddenly the giant charged up the steep slope, turned around, and came at us with determination.

"Whatever you do, don't miss," I told Johan quietly as he raised the rifle.

The bear suddenly stopped ten meters away from us and stood up on its hind legs again. Johan shot the bear in the stomach; the giant fell backward and rolled down the bank, straight into the fast current of the river. Stunned, we watched the bear being swept away. We had killed for nothing and I felt both miserable and painfully hungry. Our expedition down the Kolyma River, located in the far northeastern part of Siberia, was only one month old; it was the end of August and we were already on the verge of starvation.

"We better stay sharp and focused," I told Johan as he reloaded, "we still don't know if it's the same bear, or if there's another one out there. If it's the same one, it's dangerous."

It was useless advice. Johan was full of adrenaline. He trembled from excitement, concentration, and nervous tension. I grabbed an ax from the canoe, hoping to use it as some kind of a weapon if needed, and together we went cautiously into the dense taiga. We spent an hour doing a thorough examination of the area and concluded that it was the same bear and that its odd behavior had to do with it being badly injured from my shooting it from the canoe. (A Swedish authority on bears, after having heard measurements of its paws, estimated that it was a male bear weighing around four hundred to four hundred fifty kilograms.)

"No meat, no fur, and no food," Johan said downheartedly when we returned to the canoe, ready to continue down the river. "And we don't seem to catch enough fish. Maybe we're not good enough trappers?"

"Don't worry," I answered reassuringly, "if we keep working hard, sooner or later things will change."

But in reality I knew if we didn't get the local hunting and fishing gods on our side within a week, we would never make it to our final goal in Ambarchik Bay, ten months and thirty-five hundred kilometers of traveling farther north.

We had many aims for the Siberian expedition. One of the less important was to investigate whether our ability to hunt and fish would be sufficient enough to survive the wild Siberian taiga and tundra along the Kolyma

River. More important was to make a full record of this unknown part of our world. This was a vital task, since in the course of our extensive research we realized that not even the Russians or the Siberians themselves had a comprehensive picture of the area along the Kolyma River. The obstacles were the cold, the distance, the size, and the isolation. The area was untouched, remote, and unknown.

The main aim was to build a bridge between our cultures and widen the Western world's knowledge about Russian and Siberian ways. We wanted to study the Russian and Siberian temperament. We believed this could provide a perspective on the way of life of these people in the future. In particular, we wanted to ascertain how the area had been affected by the enormous changes in society that resulted from the collapse of the Soviet Union. And we knew 3.5 million people had lost their lives in Stalin's concentration camps—gulags—along the river. The documentation of the native peoples was another important issue: the Yakut, the Even, the Chukchi, and especially the Yukaghir, of whom only four hundred individuals had survived the Soviet era, despite living in one of the coldest areas on Earth.

We wanted to know if the native peoples along the Kolyma were genetically different from Western Europeans when it came to their ability to cope with this extreme cold. And, during our research, we became conscious that polar travel throughout its short history—a record full of frostbite and death—had been dominated by people who were being brought up and living in cities. We believed that people like ourselves, born, bred, and still living in the north Scandinavian outback, were more physically tolerant when it came to handling the cold and hardships of the polar areas.

To prepare, Johan and I used the old lumberjack tradition of putting on enormous amounts of extra weight in the shape of fat, before the arrival of winter. By the beginning of August when we first put the canoe down the river, we had put on twenty extra kilos each. However, it was all gone by the time we had the hunting incident with the bear, only after a month of paddling, because of the fact that we had been pushed to our limits physically and mentally since the first day we put the canoe down into the river.

Immediately a violent current of the river capsized the canoe. "Johan!" I shouted in panic, "I am stuck under the canoe!"

Johan, with all his strength, managed to pull the canoe away from me. I went under the rapids and was quickly pulled away by the strong current. It tossed me around like a piece of paper. I would have drowned if I hadn't been lucky enough to end up on the sandbank, which we had tried to avoid.

"Are you OK?" Johan asked exhaustedly.

"Yes," I answered terrified, "but I am scared stiff every second we spend in the canoe. If the canoe turns over, we're dead."

"We better not turn over then," Johan said quietly, which made us laugh and relax for a moment.

We pulled the overloaded canoe up on the bank and took a short break to give us some time to sharpen our concentration. Enormous masses of water passed us on both sides. Rain was pouring down, it was the third day on our expedition, and our lives had immediately turned into a constant struggle for survival. A nasty typhoon had hit this unpopulated, untouched, and very wild mountainous area, and this reality made the water level of the river rise seven meters in a couple of days. We had expected a fairly calm river, with relatively easy paddling, since it was the beginning of autumn. Instead the typhoon turned it into a torrent of fast-moving logs, violent rapids, and unpredictable sandbanks that were hard to spot while we steered through high waves.

"Time to concentrate fully again," I told Johan as we pushed out the canoe from the sandbank straight into another rapid.

I was terrified every single second as I was sitting in the front of the canoe. Our survival depended a lot on the knowledge of my young comrade and his ability to steer through the rapids, avoiding getting run over by fast-moving logs or getting stuck on a log that had come to a halt. We didn't talk at all. That would have meant a dangerous loss of concentration. I just sat in the front and waited for Johan's screaming instructions when we hit a stretch of high waves: "Paddle harder!"

At that moment I paddled for my life. After a couple of hours of paddling we saw a cloud of water spray and heard a thunderous noise ahead of us and we realized that something even worse awaited us. Amazingly enough we spotted a stretch of calm water to our left and I yelled in a slight, panicky voice: "We have to get out of the canoe and check that stretch out now!"

"Look out!" Johan yelled back. "I will turn the canoe around and when I scream 'Paddle,' we need all your strength to make it!"

To my amazement he managed to turn the canoe in a nasty rapid and we ended up front to front with the current. We crossed the river, paddling like mad for what seemed like ages. Eventually we made it over to the other side of the river. We hadn't come across such calm water since we began paddling. For a short moment it felt as if we had entered a sanctuary of peace.

Then clouds of mosquitoes arrived and caused havoc. We tied the canoe to a tree and entered the taiga. It was our first contact with the wild Siberian taiga and it was a nasty surprise. We were true forest people, but we were used to the easy, cultivated Scandinavian taiga, where one can travel easily. Now we couldn't even move forward one single step.

"It'll get better once we've made it inside the forest," I told Johan reassuringly, "the same way it is in all jungles all over the world."

It didn't. The forest was almost impenetrable and it took us one hour to advance only one hundred meters. And it took the same time to return to the canoe. We never got to see what waited ahead of us. "We just have to give it a try and hope for the best," I said, "And if we keep our concentration, we'll get through."

We tried to traverse the river once again, since we figured we had a better choice of routes from that side. But once we made it to the middle, the current and the rapids were too strong. Whether we liked it or not, we ended up in the worst possible route through the rapids. Before I had a chance to yell out my feelings of terror, we went into a series of high waves. The waves just tossed us around, uncontrollably, and the canoe moaned from the damage it was taking. Suddenly, just as I was sure we had had it, we were on the other side.

"I have never been as scared as that in my twenty years of extreme exploration," I told Johan in relief.

"I love it!" Johan yelled happily, "I want more of this!"

If my rifle had been next to me at that moment, I would have shot him. Luckily, he didn't say anything more for the next two hours. We went through one series of rapids after another, and after five hours of avoiding turning over, we were too knackered to continue. We stopped at the first high ground we could find. It was a muddy opening in the taiga covered with clouds of mosquitoes. It took us two hours to carry our equipment a few hundred meters inland to avoid getting flooded.

Once we started pitching the tepee, we realized we wouldn't get any sleep that night. The level of the river was quickly rising. At 7:00 p.m., it got dark and we set our alarm clock for every fifteen minutes to remind us to check the level of the river. At 11:00 p.m. we knew that we would get flooded during the night, and we were well aware that paddling in the dark would kill us instantly. We just had to hang on somehow until dawn. Working in the dark, we packed the canoe, attacked by uncountable amounts of mosquitoes, gnats, and flies, and stood by the boat until water reached above our knees at 3:00 a.m. in the morning. Then we took our seats in the canoe, tied it to a sturdy tree, and waited. It was an uncomfortable wait because we were freezing cold from being constantly wet and soaked to the bone. As soon as dawn arrived, we took a deep breath, untied the rope and set off for another day of uncertainty.

We didn't get any sleep for ten days, and the lack of rest made it difficult to stay focused. We had many near accidents every day. Most difficult of all, however, was the lack of food. Even though we carried three hundred and fifty kilograms of equipment, only a small percentage was provisions, such as rice, pasta, cooking oil, wheat flower, salt, and sugar, thirty portions of dried frozen food, coffee, teabags, stock cubes, and oats. Our original plan was to fish and hunt not only to survive, but to collect enough meat and fish to dry for the upcoming winter. The flooding, of course, made this impossible.

By the time we encountered the brown bear, after four weeks of troublesome and demanding paddling, it was pure survival instinct that made us shoot. We shot the bear in order to eat it. One of the aims of the expedition was to hunt and fish like the local people in order to understand their reality.We had pretty much run out of all supplies, except salt and pasta. The loss of the bear sharpened our instincts dramatically and made us more concentrated on the need to be better hunters in order to survive. This was indeed the reality of daily life.

A couple of days after losing the bear, nature finally sided with us. The flooding stopped and we caught fifteen kilograms of trout and indigenous fish in our net, and shot two massive hares and a pheasant. During the upcoming two months, September and October, we caught over one hundred and fifty kilograms of fish, and very few of them were caught with Western lures or flies. Every day, a couple of hours before darkness, we took turns pretending to be hunting dogs forcing giant Siberian hares out of their hiding. We established the area where they hid, and one of us took the role of a barking dog and went off into the dense taiga. The one with the rifle took position waiting eagerly for the dog to do its work. It was some of the most interesting hunting I've ever done. When the human dog barked once it meant a hare had been spotted. Two barks meant that it was coming straight for the spot, and three barks in a row meant that the hare should be in front of the shooter. We managed to hunt enough game and catch an adequate amount of fish not only to survive but also to put on additional body weight to face one of the coldest climates on Earth—the Kolyma winter.

"That's frostbite," Johan said, pointing to one of his fingers through his face mask in despair. "That means I've got it on every finger."

He was having another bout of diarrhea. It was the third time in an hour he had to squat down and pull his trousers off. And his third set of gloves. On every occasion he had experienced that burning feeling followed by numbness in one of his fingers, which marked the first stage of frostbite. I could barely make him out in the eternal darkness of midwinter, and I shivered violently. The same way I had every day since we left the settlement of Zyryanka four weeks earlier, in the middle of November.

"I think we better move on," I whispered.

Then I exhaled, coughed, and heard that familiar tinkling sound that occurs when someone's breath turns into a shower of ice crystals, locally referred to as "the whispers of the stars." It was minus seventy degrees Fahrenheit and it was impossible to form a decent thought or even to daydream. Or feel any worries. By pure survival instinct, we knew we had to keep moving and never stop. Therefore, we continued with great effort in the darkness, pulling our three hundred thirty pounds each behind us.

Even though the river was covered with only a couple of inches of snow, it still felt like pulling the sledges over sand. It didn't help that we both were walking, not skiing, since our ski bindings had broken, as with most of the metal parts of our equipment, when the temperature dropped below minus fifty-eight degrees Fahrenheit. The heavy load made us sweat profusely the whole time, but we just couldn't stop and take a break. Every time we did, we seemed to pick up more frostbite on our fingers or cheeks. Consequently we kept moving in complete darkness. Hour after hour, we steadily put one foot in front of the other. The darkness didn't matter since our eyebrows were always iced up, making it hard to see anything. But, as long as we kept moving, at least it made us aware that we were still alive—until that dreadful moment it was time to get inside the tent.

After sixteen hours of skiing it only took us a few minutes to pitch the tent, but it took at least an hour to get the stove going. Some nights it didn't work at all. Poor-quality Russian petrol was the problem. It froze solid. As a result, we carried the petrol bottle under our armpit the last hour of the day to keep it warm. We always knew when it was usable, since the bottle would then leak. It still took an hour to get the stove going, as it was completely frozen and we had to pour petrol in a cup and light it to defrost the stove. We both had to keep busy during these attempts in order to keep dangerous apathy at bay. The cold still made us tremble, sometimes almost hysterically.

When the stove finally worked, we could momentarily form a thought, but unfortunately this relief just made us more aware of how cold it was.

Once inside the sleeping bag, we knew we had to cope with at least six hours of unrelenting pain. It took at least three hours to gain control over our bodies. During this time, we lay on our backs, bodies arched, trying to keep the worst shivering away, and rest as much as possible. We hardly slept at all. Sharing the sleeping bag with the face mask, satellite phone, torch, spare batteries, boots, stove, and gloves didn't help. It was absolutely silent outside. Sometimes we heard a lone howling wolf in the distance or the odd explosion when a tree detonated from the cold. We didn't thaw up completely this night either.

"It is time to get up," I said through my breathing hole in the sleeping bag. "Four days to go before we reach Srednekolymsk."

"What time is it?" Johan groaned.

My answer was simple: "I don't know. Does it matter? It's dark all the time anyway."

As quickly as I moved, cold snow fell into my face. It was pitch-black and it always took some time to find the torch. I'd slept on it most of the night. When I switched it on, still inside the sleeping bag, I noticed as usual that our breath had formed giant stalactites of snow hanging down from the tent roof. And when I heard Johan moving, I realized I had to try to get out of the sleeping bag. It felt almost impossible. My body was still stiff. Every muscle ached; my cheeks, nose, and hands burned. I felt no energy at all.

Johan was first out of the bag and immediately put his down jacket on, followed by his face mask, and then started the struggle to get his boots on. He was very weak after days of diarrhea, but still worked heroically hard and did everything purely by instinct. He handed me the stove. To work it I had to remove a layer of gloves and I had problems getting the lighter to work, even though I'd kept it in my underpants all night. My hands were too stiff. And the stove was frozen solid. Johan gave it a try with no luck.

"I think we have to give breakfast a miss today," I told Johan. "We forgot to take the petrol bottle and stove into the sleeping bag last night."

The only positive aspect about not being able to cook was that we didn't have to suffer condensation, which iced everything up badly. It took us just a few minutes to get all the equipment out of the tent, disassemble it, and pack everything together in the dark. Then came one of the coldest moments of the day, when it was time to take our down jackets off and start moving. It took at least three hours to feel relatively warm. During this time our face, nostrils, and eyes were covered by ice again, breathing was difficult, and we coughed continuously. To save batteries we traveled all day in the darkness. Three days later we reached the Yakut settlement of Srednekolymsk.

We spent January thawing out in Srednekolymsk among some of the nicest, most generous people on Earth. Temperatures were constantly below minus sixty degrees Fahrenheit. We put on a lot of weight needed for the remaining fifteen hundred kilometers to reach Ambarchik Bay before the end of April. We sampled the local delicacies like *stroganina*, frozen raw fish eaten like ice cream; *maxa*, frozen raw liver eaten the same way; cooked moose nostrils, stewed moose heart, fried liver from wild caribou, cooked moose muzzle with pasta, raw frozen horse testicles, and much more.

The local people gave us a healthy perspective on the extreme cold. Some of them had amputated fingers, arms, and legs. Almost all had scarred cheeks and had lost the tip of their nose. And, as they told us, it could have been worse. We could have been unfortunate prisoners in one of Stalin's gulags whose remains dotted the Kolyma. Many of the prisoners froze to death within two weeks.

Even though we encountered temperatures below minus fifty-five degrees Fahrenheit most of February, traveling during the end of the worst winter period turned out to be a holiday in comparison with the dark mid-winter travel. The darkness was an extreme challenge. We froze badly throughout the month, but at noon every day the temperatures rose to minus thirty degrees Fahrenheit and that was enough to thaw. We even stopped for short breaks without getting frostbite. We pulled the sledges from early morning until a couple of hours before darkness and then we pitched our tent and spent a couple of hours trying to get the stove working. Eventually it did. Equipment continued to break in the cold, but we came across trappers almost every three or four days, and their log cabins gave us enough warmth to do decent repairs.

In March we had plenty of daylight, and temperatures rose to minus forty degrees Fahrenheit even in the night, and we experienced day temperatures up to zero degrees Fahrenheit, which seemed like heaven. We reached the tundra in April and traveled quickly over the sastrugi and made it to our goal in Ambarchik Bay at the end of April 2005.

Half a year has passed since we returned home to Sweden. It hasn't been easy returning. I miss Kolyma every day. Naturally, I don't miss the hardships, the suffering, or the extreme cold, but I continue to think about the people. In twenty-five years of exploration, the people of Kolyma were among the best I've ever encountered—generous, funny, intelligent, knowledgeable, open-minded, and as warm as their environment is cold.

• • •

Mikael Strandberg was born in 1962 in Sweden. He started his professional career as an explorer nineteen years ago. Mikael is currently working as an explorer, lecturer, and writer. He has also produced three internationally renowned documentaries for television *Patagonia—3,000 Kilometres by Horse* (Panvision, 1998), *The Masai People—1,000 Kilometres by Foot* (Panvision, 2002), and his much awarded, -58 *Degrees—Exploring Siberia on Skis* (Panvision, 2007).

Chapter 21

Exploring Myanmar's Forbidden Wilderness

STEVE WINTER WITH SHARON GUYNUP

I trained my lens on the lush, unbroken forest passing one thousand feet below us and on the jagged, icy mountains in the distance. I adjusted my shutter speed to compensate for the teeth-rattling vibration of the Polish Cold War–era military helicopter we were flying in. Our destination: Tahundan, the last village in the remote, uncharted, northernmost peaks of Myanmar (formerly known as Burma). I was traveling with a team of four Burmese wildlife biologists headed by Alan Rabinowitz, an American whom the *New York Times* once dubbed "the Indiana Jones of zoology." Our quest: to meet with village elders to try to stem the growing wildlife trade with China.

When I lowered the camera, I gasped. Instead of opening up, the canyon we were flying through ended abruptly. Directly in front of us loomed a sheer cliff. I reached for the door handle, preparing to jump, as the pilot manhandled the helicopter into a one-hundred-eighty-degree turn. The craft felt like it stopped in midair, shaking like a blender—it felt like every rivet in the thing was going to pop—but somehow we barely avoided crashing into the mountain.

For a good ten minutes, strong downdrafts buffeted the craft and we kept dropping altitude. Finally the helicopter stabilized and the pilot landed in a field beside a tiny village of just a few huts. I wondered where our sixty porters and military escorts were—they were supposed to be waiting for us.

The pilot insisted that we were in Tahundan. He brandished the global positioning system (GPS)—which read "0"—as proof. Alan looked at him like he was crazy: he'd been there before and knew this was not the place.

But the pilot refused to take us farther and ordered us out of the helicopter. For the next hour, we watched him fly north toward Tibet, then east toward China, then west into India; this triangular tip of Myanmar borders all three countries. Finally, he must have found "0" on his GPS again, because he landed back where he dropped us off, out of fuel. By the time he radioed headquarters, we were two hours overdue at Tahundan. Rumors that we'd crashed or been kidnapped flew around Yangon among government officials and on the news. The army was already looking for us—dead or alive.

Before we boarded the helicopter, we'd spent three days waiting for the pass to clear enough to fly out of the northern city of Putao. Every day we went to the airfield to check the weather, and when we couldn't fly, Alan hung around teaching the military pilot how to use a GPS. He only knew line-of-sight navigation using a map and a compass. We figured that was how he almost ran into that precipice: he and the copilot must have been fiddling with the GPS instead of looking out the window!

This was my welcome to Myanmar. I had been invited in January 2000 by Alan, director of science and exploration at the New York–based Wildlife Conservation Society (WCS), to join a five-week expedition into Myanmar's "icy mountains." Alan's prior field studies had spurred the government to create the 1,472-square-mile Hkakabo Razi National Park two years before.

It was my job to document the trip. Of particular concern was the trade in salt and tea with the Chinese for animal parts used in traditional Asian medicine, which was decimating wildlife populations. While we were there, we also planned to visit and photograph the last of the Taron people, the only known Mongolian Pygmies.

We had actually landed in Talahtu, a good twelve miles from Tahundan. The villagers had seen few foreigners—or helicopters—so we were a great curiosity, watched by all and trailed by a shy pack of children. Local custom dictated that visitors were welcomed into the home of the village headman, which is where we slept, huddled around a smoky central hearth.

We hired porters and left the next morning at first light, picking our way along a river trail through a gauzy, ethereal mist. Crossing the first hanging bamboo bridge was a bit tricky in the fog. The local people had lashed three pieces of bamboo together for the floor, constructing a swinging, tight rope bridge over the fast-running, icy waters.

It was the first of many such crossings. We hiked all day through labyrinthine valleys, crisscrossing the many rivers that intertwined as they flow out of the mountains, trudging up and down slippery rock slopes, and inching across jagged rock ledges. We covered eight miles, arriving in Karaung, the next village, just before nightfall. We hoped to find Dawi there, the head male Taron, but no luck. So we bedded down, again welcomed into the headman's home—given the place of honor, the room with the fire pit, which smoldered warmth throughout the frosty night.

At dawn, we headed out and by early afternoon we made Tahundan, a small village nestled in a sheltering valley at sixty-three thousand feet. Our team and military escorts awaited us, having just arrived after thirty days of walking from Putao to get there. Our greeting: the soldiers informed us that permission for our expedition had been revoked because we had "disobeyed orders." Foreigners are not normally allowed in Myanmar outside of a few tourist areas. Special authorization had been granted to us for a strict itinerary. We later learned that our helicopter pilot told authorities we'd left him and "walked off into the forest on our own" in an attempt to save his hide.

But a great deal of money had been spent to get here, and we weren't going to leave without a fight. Over the next few days, we argued, pleaded, and bargained with the northern regional commander on a staticky circa World War II radio. First, he told us to walk back to Putao, about two hundred fifty miles through rugged mountains. Then he insisted on coming to get us. In the end, the commander granted us just ten days to do our work there.

Tahundan's only monk, U Tilawka, was a friend of Alan's. We were invited to stay with him in the "monastery"—a one-room cabin sitting on a hilltop above the village. It had a large, triangular-shaped "window" (an open space below the roof) that offered a stunning view of the snowcapped peaks in the distance, and also gave the devout the experience of human suffering. It was freezing, with icy winds sweeping off the mountains and through the simple structure that lacked a hearth to warm us. I shivered through those nights in my zero-degree sleeping bag, but at least the room was clean and quiet. Alan noted the lack of bones, rotting animal skins, fleas, bedbugs, dogs, and chickens.

We were clearly the local entertainment. In the morning, a few women would come supposedly to bring breakfast to U Tilawka, but they inevitably stayed, clustering in the corner to observe us carefully as we ate, brushed our teeth, read. They even watched us sleep. Whenever we looked at them, the women beamed wide smiles at us and giggled. In the village, many eyes watched our every move.

During the day, Alan held workshops for both the Burmese biologists and local people on wildlife conservation. We huddled around the fire for many hours, interviewing local hunters over tea. What animals and how many of them still roamed these mountains? We also questioned them about their trade with the Chinese. After being translated through four languages, Alan joked that sometimes he forgot the question by the time the answer came.

Gout was a huge problem for these people. They were trading away red panda skins, musk deer glands, horns and hooves of local deer species, and other animal parts in exchange for precious salt—and for tea. Some of these animals were endangered, and all were becoming increasingly hard to find. Alan promised to supply them with these needed staples if they would hunt only for food, not for trade. Given the difficulty of tracking dwindling wildlife through the punishing mountain terrain, they eagerly accepted the deal.

Over dinner that night we told our host about our harrowing helicopter trip. He told us that the Taron used to worship the mountain that we almost crashed into. It was home to La, the Spirit of the Mountain. The Taron once made sacrifices to La to ensure a successful hunt.

The military unit was about to fly back for us and we still hadn't met Dawi. So we went off to search for him, trekking the four miles back to Karaung—and found him there. As far as we know, Dawi is the last living pure-blooded male Taron left on Earth, and his two sisters are the only females. He is the size of a child—only forty-six inches tall but is extremely muscular. Everywhere he went, he was surrounded by an entourage of village children who were about his size.

At first, he was shy and quiet in our presence. Only two or three Westerners had ever ventured this far north, so we must have taken some getting used to. But we were given the gift of time: a snowfall kept the helicopter from coming to get us, so we were able to spend five days with him. Slowly he relaxed, and we forged a fast friendship.

Sitting around the fire, through a series of interpreters, he told us the history of his tribe. For many years, the Taron had only married each other, but their children were born with small brains and small bodies. Long ago, they decided not to have babies together anymore. If they couldn't marry into another tribe, they died alone.

The military finally arrived. We were sad to bid Dawi and this beautiful land farewell, but little did I know that our flight back to Yangon would spark a return to Myanmar. Alan pointed to a sprawling slab of green that spread to the Indian border west of Myitkina. He told me it was Myanmar's Hukawng Valley. The so-called Valley of Death was home to animals that had disappeared or were in trouble elsewhere: clouded leopard, sambar, barking deer, elephant, bear, and the second largest tiger population in Asia. He had recently launched a large "camera trapping" project there using remote-sensor cameras to document and count the wildlife, gathering data he hoped would convince the government to protect the region. I boarded my plane back to New York wondering how the Valley of Death got its name.

Back at home, I began researching a possible story on the valley for *National Geographic*. The Valley of Death nickname came from the construction of the five-hundred-mile Ledo Road that was forged through the Hukawng Valley from 1942 to 1944 by American General Joseph "Vinegar Joe" Stillwell. The road came at great cost, with Stillwell losing "a man a mile" to malaria, typhus, and snipers. I also discovered that there was important news from the valley: as a result of Alan's work there, the Burmese government designated a 2,494-square-mile area as the Hukaung Valley Wildlife Reserve in April 2001. But, with additional help from Alan and WCS, the government agreed to triple it, creating the world's largest tiger reserve—an area nearly the size of Vermont.

The tigers needed protection. TRAFFIC, an agency that monitors international wildlife trade, estimated that during the 1980s and 1990s, between fifty and one hundred tigers were poached each year for use in traditional Asian medicine. Most of the animal is used either as a treatment for a wide range of ailments—or as a talisman. Tiger bone is highly prized as an anti-inflammatory treatment for joint pain. Tiger feet, when dipped in palm oil and hung in front of a door, are used to ward off evil spirits, while the skin is said to cure a fever caused by ghosts. Tiger penis is used as an aphrodisiac. The trade is very lucrative. A tiger skeleton fetches the equivalent of a ten-year salary in Myanmar.

It wouldn't be easy to photograph in the valley. I'd been warned by Burmese forestry staff that the area was essentially unexplored. It had been used by local hunters for centuries, but there were no formal trails or villages inside the central valley—which made it the perfect place to photograph. My story proposal was approved, and I returned to Myanmar in November 2002.

When I arrived in Yangon, I was joined by U San Hlaing, the "fixer" who would make all arrangements and accompany me and Pathi, an assistant and cook. San Hlaing, who was assigned to me by the government, had never set foot in the jungle, but Pathi had served in the military, traveling all over the country, and had worked for the forest service.

We flew from Yangon to Myitkina in northwest Myanmar. There we rented two pickup trucks, loaded our gear (twenty bags and waterproof Pelican cases) and headed west on the World War II Ledo Road. Although the trucks had been modified with extra shocks, it was a bone-crushing, eight-hour drive to Tanai, like riding a bucking bronco all day long.

Tanai was a frontier town at the edge of the reserve. Tigers had been the king of the jungle here until miners moved into the valley. Gold had recently been discovered about fifty miles away, sparking a gold rush that bumped the population from a few thousand to about fifty thousand within a few months. The town was overflowing and chaotic. It was also incredibly noisy—especially at night. The Burmese have a national obsession with karaoke. With the flow of quick money and lots of locally brewed alcohol, giant speakers in rows of open-air restaurants howled bad Karaoke into the wee hours. There were several nights that I had obsessive thoughts of cutting the electricity. This was, however, a futile fantasy, as the only power came from diesel generators that also shrieked like sick and tortured animals.

We spent a few days there, gathering supplies and hiring a team. My plan was to trek deep into the jungle to meet up with the joint WCS and Ministry of Forestry "tiger team"—about thirty-five men plus a support staff. They would spend three consecutive dry seasons there to learn which animals—and how many—still survived in the valley. Camera traps had been set up along animal trails, especially where the team spotted tiger tracks.

The biologists had enlisted the aid of the area's best hunters—Lisu tribesmen, who originally came from Hkakabo Razi, near where Alan and I had been the previous year. Some returned home after weeks of hunting, but others stayed in Hukaung. Ah Puh was legendary, both as the most renowned among them and as their headman. He had probably killed more tigers in the valley than all the other hunters combined. His family, who lived just outside Tanai, helped us find a support team. I hired a photo assistant whom I nicknamed "Happy Man" because of his constant singing and whistling while we walked.

We also needed a team to carry our equipment into the forest. In that part of the country, heavy work, including gold mining, is done by elephants. We found four brothers who worked as *mahouts* (elephant handlers) and who owned their own elephants. San Hlaing quietly pulled them aside for a private talk—which he was too polite to disclose at the time. Later, he told me that Au Puh's family warned him that mahouts were notorious opium smokers. He needed to be sure that they realized they were taking one of the first Westerners since World War II into the jungle, and warned them to watch their smoking while they were with us.

The next morning our caravan set off along the Tawang River, walking on sandy beaches, rock-hopping through shallows, fording the tepid, waist-high river a dozen times. We crossed fields of elephant grass that reached well over my head. After an hour, we spotted tiger tracks. Stories of hunting tigers on elephants, the beaters yelling and thrashing the tall grasses with bamboo poles, flashed through my head. As a photographer, I wanted a clear shot, but since I was on foot, I needed to have the elephants up ahead of me for safety's sake. By sunset, exhausted, we set up camp.

By early afternoon of the next day we made it to the rather comfy tiger camp, a warren of bamboo platforms raised about a foot off the ground that was sheltered by palm roofs. I was greeted by Tony Lynam, who headed the WCS team, and Myint Maung, the reserve's new warden, who helped me formulate a game plan on how to photograph the elusive species that lived there. So far, fifty of their seventy camera traps had been set up throughout the area.

It soon became obvious why this forest had remained pristine. Lynam and others who had recently been in the jungle were covered with blisters, scrapes, and infected leech marks, and they looked dead tired. We cooked them a hot meal and presented them with a few gallons of Kachin whiskey, the local moonshine—which made us instant members of the team.

To get the lay of the land, we took a ten-mile tour up the river and through the woods—which taught us that the river was by far the best route. Even equipped with my trusty Central American–bought machete, the bamboo and rattan made travel through the forest incredibly slow and difficult. We made it back by dusk, and set to work removing whole colonies of leeches that had moved into our pants, shoes, and the backs of our shirts during the day's river crossings. Fifteen leeches came off one leg, thirteen off the other. Blood streamed down my back after Happy Man picked off two dozen or so. Then we disinfected the wounds. This became our daily routine.

The next day we loaded a camera trap into a pack and headed off with Ah Puh and five others to find tiger tracks that were spotted the day before. On the river, we met a party of five people with two elephants. They were headed to camp in the jungle about five days north of us and to mine for gold. The collateral damage from large numbers of itinerant miners and ever-larger mining operations was growing: they leveled parts of the forest for small settlements, poisoned the river with mercury, and hunted many species for food and quick cash—as evidenced by this group's weapons, an old British flintlock and crossbows with poison arrows.

Five miles upriver, we found fresh tiger tracks, maybe four or five hours old. Ah Puh followed the tracks, with me right behind him. I watched him quickly tiptoe across an open sandy area, thinking, "Great, he's really excited, maybe this tiger's nearby." But the moment I stepped on the sand, I was instantly up to my shins. It was quicksand! Ah Puh was about five feet tall and maybe one hundred pounds soaking wet, so he made it across, but not me, a husky American weighted down by an additional forty pounds of camera gear.

I yelled for help and tried to pull myself out, an instinctual but dangerous reaction—forgetting that moving is the worst thing you can do. The more I struggled, the faster I sank. Within minutes, I was up to my waist, but then my LowePro fanny pack stopped me from sinking further. Meanwhile, Ah Puh and the rest of the group stood watching, absolutely cracking up.

After they were done getting their jollies, one of them came over to try to rescue my cameras. He, too, started sinking, but immediately fell straight back. That must be the thing to do if you fall into quicksand; he got out. Someone threw me a large branch that was nearby to steady myself. Happy Man ferried my cameras to safety. Using a large piece of bamboo, I slowly worked myself free—managing to keep my boots on. When I got out—after about twenty minutes that felt like a year—I got lots of pats on the back. It felt like a rite of passage.

We set up the camera trap and headed back toward camp. On an island in the middle of the river, we encountered a group of six men who had just bathed their elephants. I photographed them in the golden, late-afternoon light, a picture that ran in the story two years later—a great end to the day.

I spent every day for the next three weeks in the forest photographing the researchers at work and the animals we encountered, mostly birds and monkeys—but we never glimpsed a tiger, though the forest floor was crisscrossed by tracks. It was the first of two trips. I returned for another two and a half months in March 2003. On my second trip, I knew what I needed to document: the slapdash settlements thrown together by itinerant gold miners and the devastation their mining activities had wreaked. Pockets of jungle were razed, the soil blasted away by high-powered hoses, leaving a muddy moonscape. And these migrant hordes needed to eat, sparking a robust bushmeat trade that was leaving little alive in the radius surrounding their mining operations. The trade was decimating the prey species that tigers relied on to survive.

The last thing that I needed to photograph was local culture. I contacted two Burmese researchers who were studying the indigenous people of the region. They brought me to a Naga village located high in the mountains near the Indian border, a place never visited by Westerners. The fiercely independent Naga warriors are famous for having been headhunters, and still hold animistic beliefs. Upon arrival, the anthropologists introduced me to the village shaman. He quickly ducked back inside his bamboo and palm hut. He leaped out at me moments later thrusting a spear, garbed in a beaded loincloth, a tiger-skin hat, and with a long necklace made of "mountain coral" and tiger teeth hanging nearly to his navel. He proceeded to laugh himself silly. The next day was my birthday and he blessed me with the appropriate Naga song.

As I photographed the villagers, I also shot Polaroids. The impact of these images was profound: Since these people did not have mirrors, I was able to show them what they looked like for the first time in their lives. WCS surveys ultimately proved that between eighty and one hundred tigers prowled the Hukuang Valley. My photographs ran in the April 2004 issue of *National Geographic*, accompanied by Alan's text. Late that year, the government protected the Valley of Death, creating the world's largest tiger reserve.

Myanmar is an enchanted land, and my time there was among my most fascinating adventures—to date.

* * *

Steve Winter has traveled the world as a photographer for *National Geographic*. His photographs have also appeared in *Newsweek*, *Audubon*, and *GEO*, among other publications. His areas of special interest include conservation biology, natural history, marine ecology, and indigenous cultural practices.

Sharon Guynup is a science/environmental writer, editor, and photojournalist. She is the author of *State of the Wild* (Island Press, 2005).

PART FOUR

Europe and North America

Chapter 22

A Bad Day at the Office

ROBERT D. BALLARD

I was lying on my stomach looking out of my office window. It was 1977, and I was trying to see the bottom of the ocean from the tiny Plexiglas window of the U.S. Navy's bathyscaphe *Trieste II*. I knew the bottom was coming up fast, but our bright lights had turned the jet-black waters of the Cayman Trough into a ball of haze, and it was almost impossible to see more than twenty feet below the craft.

Seated above me was the officer in charge of the sub, Lieutenant Commander Kurt Newell, and next to him was his copilot, Chief George Ellis. I could hear Ellis calling out our altitude—five hundred fifty feet, five hundred feet, four hundred fifty feet—as we plunged toward the bottom. It is always fun to explore places on Earth no one has ever seen before, and I was excited to see some of the deepest volcanoes on Earth waiting for me underwater.

Normally, the deepest reaches of Earth are found in great undersea trenches. In the Mariana Trench off Guam, for example, two enormous crustal plates are poised for a head-on collision. One plate is bucked up by the impact, forming an island arc or folded mountain range, while the other plate plunges back into the Earth, forming the trench. In the case of Guam, the trench holds the deepest spot on the planet, 35,800 feet down. Our bathyscaphe's cousin, *Trieste*, had reached that depth in January 1960, some seventeen years before our arrival.

Now, here off the tiny Cayman Islands, the twenty-thousand-foot depth we are about to reach is a whole other kettle of fish. It's called a "leaky" transform fault. What's that, you might ask? The great crustal plates of the world are in constant motion, moving in relative relationship to one another. They either move apart, crash into one another, or grind past each other, as is the case of the San Andreas Fault in California where the plate boundary is called a "transform fault."

On rare occasions you can get various combinations of the three plate motions. And this is the case with the Cayman Trough. To the north of the trough where Cayman Island lies, the North American plate is moving to the west. Across the trough on the south side on which Jamaica rests, the Caribbean plate is moving to the east, with the boundary between them forming a transform fault. But this is not your normal transform fault. Instead of forming a straight line, it has a ninety-mile right-angle bend in its middle where it is leaking lava. That is because the plates are not only moving past one another, they are also separating slightly, causing the floor of the trough to "leak" molten lava. It is both a transform fault and, for ninety miles, a spreading center, making it "a leaky transform fault."

In 1976, we had lowered our remote camera sled "Angus" to explore this leak. We almost needed sunglasses to view the color film that night after the film was processed in our tiny lab. The bottom was covered with fresh ropey lava like you see on the Big Island of Hawaii. The lights of Angus reflected off the lava's black, glassy surface. When walking over similar pahoehoe flows in Hawaii, the glass crunched beneath our feet as if we were stepping on millions of lightbulbs.

When I heard Ellis say, "four hundred feet," my mind quickly shifted from science to survival. Our one-hundred-ton bathyscaphe was still on a collision course with the bottom, and we needed to begin dropping ballast very soon to slow our descent. Normally that occurs when we are one hundred to two hundred feet above bottom.

Ellis was staring at a printout of the echo sounder mounted on the stern of *Trieste II*. Every few seconds the sonar sent out a 12 kHz "ping" that traveled downward through the water until it hit something, bouncing back up to be "heard" by the sonar and printed out on our display panel inside the tiny six-foot-diameter steel sphere in which we were all huddled in the shivering cold.

"Bottom!" I suddenly shouted.

"Impossible," Ellis responded.

"I tell you, I see bottom and it is coming up fast," I insisted.

Without further argument Commander Newell immediately began dropping ballast to slow our descent. Our sub had two large tanks, or tubs, mounted within its steel frame. Each tub was full of tiny steel shot, a little larger than buckshot in a shotgun shell. The bottom of the tub was shaped like a funnel with a hole in it. Normally, the shot would fall out through the hole, but our batteries magnetized the tubs and the millions of tiny shot clung together forming a giant wad of steel.

But in a heartbeat, Commander Newell had turned on two timers with a twist of his hands to momentarily demagnetize the tubs of ballast, letting the shot fall out like sand in an hourglass, lightening the sub's load.

But we didn't have hours, and spitting out a few pounds of shot a second doesn't slow the momentum of a one-hundred-ton sub. Within moments the bow of *Trieste II* crashed into the side of the volcano.

The echo sounder Ellis had been looking at was at the rear of the sub, seventy feet away from our quickly deforming bow. The wall of the volcano was so steep the echo sounder simply didn't see it, as its signal had nothing to bounce off.

The scene outside my view port was moving in slow motion. We weren't traveling that fast, one hundred feet a minute, but we weren't exactly stopping either. As I gazed out my window, it was as if a giant had grabbed the bow of the sub and was slowly bending it into a steel pretzel.

Then the bottom fell out of my stomach as I shouted, "I see gasoline in the water! There are a bunch of tiny bubbles going by my window." The bubbles of gasoline could only mean one thing. We had ruptured one of our primary flotation tanks.

A bathyscaphe is an underwater balloon. In fact, its designer, Swiss physicist Auguste Piccard, began his explorations years before as a balloonist. Instead of filling the bathyscaphe with helium or hydrogen to make it light, he had filled it with gasoline, which would be unaffected by the crushing pressure of the depths. The gasoline was placed inside a thin tank of steel, which our collision with the bottom had apparently ruptured, letting out its precious cargo.

It was the gasoline-filled shell of *Trieste II* that made it float. When you wanted to become "light" and go up, you released the steel shot inside its ballast tubs, just like a balloonist would drop bags of sand out of the gondola. I always wondered if those heavy bags of sand ever hit anyone. But that was the least of our worries at this point.

If you rupture your gasoline floatation tanks, they will take on water and the sub will get even heavier than it was. Leak too much gasoline and there is no going home.

When I said, "I see gasoline," Commander Newell immediately dumped our entire load of ballast. The bottom of the ballast tubs fell open as tons of shot fell out. We were now in an uncontrolled free ascent to the surface, but we still had twenty thousand feet to go, and like a wounded beast, our life-sustaining blood was flowing out of our body. If we bled too much gasoline we would die instantly. It was a waiting game as all eyes were glued to the tiny meter inside our pressure hull that told us our rate of ascent. Our depth sensor told us we were rising, but, more important, this meter told us how fast.

If this was a "normal" dive, and it most definitely was not, the meter would have held steady at a terminal ascent velocity of one hundred feet per minute, just as it had been on the way down. Our cross-section through the water was the same regardless of whether we were rising or falling, so the drag was the same and so was the rate of descent or ascent.

Unfortunately, the meter was not that precise so the numbers displayed on its glowing red tubes jumped all over the place. This is where you truly discover whether you are an optimist or a pessimist.

As I stared at the meter, not a word was uttered. Each of us knew there was absolutely nothing we could do. Our fate was in someone else's hands. Sitting in the quiet dark and damp sphere, I remembered how just four years prior another bathyscaphe dive had nearly killed me.

It was during the first dives into the Mid-Atlantic Ridge during Project FAMOUS (French-American Mid-Ocean Undersea Study). That was when humans had the first opportunity to see what happens when two great plates, the North American and African plates in this case, spread apart and molten lava flows out of the resulting crack or "rift."

Our dives in the summer of 1973 were the first reconnaissance dives of the project by the French bathyscaphe *Archimède*. These would be followed the next summer when our submersible *Alvin* and the French submersible *Cyana* would join *Archimède* for a much more extensive series of dives.

I was the only American on the French dive team, and it had been an honor to have been asked by the expedition's chief scientist, Xavier Le Pichon, to make the second dive into the rift valley that morning. Le Pichon had made the first dive a few days before, and the *Archimède* was now reaching for its second descent.

The first dive explored a small, active volcano called Mount Venus on the floor of the rift at its very center where the plates were moving apart. The mission of our dive was to explore the region to the east of Mount Venus all the way to the base of the steep, inward-facing rift valley wall.

When I woke up the morning of the dive, I felt like hell. I had contracted strep throat. My bunk was wet with sweat and a fever racked my body. I was in no shape to dive, but the next dive in an expedition could be the last dive of the campaign. I had waited five long years for this moment, and I wasn't going to let a sore throat stop me.

Before I knew it, I was plowing through the waves in a tiny Zodiac as the bright yellow conning tower of *Archimède*, wallowing in the North Atlantic swell, came into view. The sun was bright, but there was a chill in the air that made me feel even worse.

Quickly my pilot, Lieutenant Gilbert Harismendy, and our engineer for the dive who went by the name "Semac," scurried on top of the bathyscaphe, disappearing down the long tube that passed through its floatation tank to the small gondola, or pressure sphere, that hung beneath it. I followed as fast as I could and banged my throbbing head on the steel hatch.

Our nine-thousand-foot descent to the bottom was fairly routine as we came to rest on the fresh lava flows that cover the inner rift valley. The dive was going extremely well as we headed east toward the valley wall—that was until I heard "*Merde*!" and turned to see Semac staring at one of his many gauges.

The bathyscaphe had experienced a power outage. Within seconds, the sub pitched violently forward as I was slammed into Harismendy's back. The power failure had instantly caused the bathyscaphe to automatically drop its load of ballast and we were being propelled toward the surface. Since the dive was almost over, I was not that alarmed, that is, until I began to smell the stench of burning insulation. An electrical fire inside the sub's instrument panel was filling our tiny sphere with black eye-burning smoke.

Quickly Harismendy and Semac donned their emergency breathing masks as I followed suit. At first, I could not breathe until Harismendy realized he had forgotten to turn on the valve that fed oxygen to my mask. With the value turned on, all was well as we safely returned to the surface.

But all was not going well in *Trieste II* as gasoline continued to bleed from our wound. Our ascent to the surface in *Archimède* had taken ninety minutes; today's was taking much longer—close to six hours. With nothing to do but pray, I spent that time staring out of our tiny view port.

Slowly, the dark, black abyss outside my window began to turn a dim blue. I could make out small creatures passing by our rising sub. Then I began to feel a gentle rocking moment as the surface swell welcomed us home.

• • •

Robert D. Ballard is an honorary director of The Explorers Club, explorer in residence for the National Geographic Society, president of the Institute for Exploration, and director of the Institute for Archaeological Oceanography. He has conducted more than one hundred twenty deep-sea expeditions around the globe, including the first manned exploration of the Mid-Ocean Ridge; the discovery of hydrothermal vents; the discovery of "Black Smokers"; the discovery of the wrecks of RMS *Titanic*, the German battleship *Bismarck*, the aircraft carrier USS *Yorktown*, and President John F. Kennedy's PT-109; and many ancient shipwrecks dating from the time of the Greek poet Homer.

Chapter 23

Explorations in the Heart of Hell

PIOTR CHMIELINSKI

Washington, DC, September 11, 2001

My hands are trembling as I fumble for CNN on my TV remote. On my way to work I had heard on the radio that one of the towers of the World Trade Center had been struck by an airplane and a fire had broken out in the building.

The picture comes on, and I see that the northern tower is indeed smoking. The airplane is on fire, wedged inside. And people . . . We are standing in the office transfixed before the television screen. "My God!" the whole world must have unanimously exclaimed at the sight of another airplane approaching the southern tower, of the conflagration, and of people hurling themselves from the windows. Speechless, we are staring at the skyscrapers burning like torches. Suddenly, the upper part of the second tower tilts strangely to the side, breaks off from the rest and . . . the twin towers collapse. They were supposed to be indestructible.

Indestructible. . . . It was with this conviction that I had left New York in 1993, following several weeks of work on the reconstruction of the damaged site of the World Trade Center after the first time it was bombed. The tragedy I now witnessed affirmed my belief that it is the extraordinary will to live that helps people survive the worst of tragedies that is indestructible. Buildings can always fall.

New York, February 26, 1993

My measuring instruments were packed, and with only a few more trifles to be stuffed into a suitcase, I was ready to be on my way to the airport and then back home to Virginia. The two weeks I had spent in New York taking samples for toxic and chemical contamination after a hotel fire on Lexington Avenue had passed quickly. I had been completely absorbed by the analyses, consultations, and meetings with the building's owners who hired our company, HP Environmental, to protect the site from indoor contamination.

Then the telephone rang.

A trembling voice introduced himself as a representative of the Port Authority of New York and New Jersey and asked me to go to the crisis center at the World Trade Center. What crisis center? The words resonated in my ears with foreboding. In the cab, I heard on the radio that a bomb had exploded in the basement of Tower 1.

Our company was assigned the task of examining the indoor contamination levels, setting the safety protocol for rescuers, and establishing procedures for decontaminating the area and reconstructing the damaged section. The explosion and the resulting fire had destroyed the main entrance hall and the first floor in the north tower. The rest of the building remained intact, as did its core structure. The support columns kept the architectural giant from collapsing. I shuddered to think what might have happened if they had been the target of the terrorist attack.

Within two months, the damage had been repaired, the dust that had disseminated throughout the building had been cleared, and the smoke-stained walls had been repainted. Offices reopened, employees resumed work, and tourists again populated the site. The monument honoring the victims' memory was the only remaining scar from the February 1993 explosion.

New York, September 18, 2001

Smoke carrying dust, ashes, and the peculiar smell of burning sweeps through the streets. I pass the first checkpoint at Canal Street, about two miles outside Ground Zero. You can move around only on foot here. An eerie silence and emptiness reign. The closer I come to the site, the dust is thicker and my anxiety deeper. Masses of scattered paper cling to the ledges and rustle disquietingly under my feet. I finally come to a stop two or three blocks from Ground Zero. Before me a void stretches where the two imposing skyscrapers used to rise. I stand as if paralyzed.

The last checkpoint. Ahead, I see only a mass of rubble a few dozen feet high. A tangle of wires and steel beams tortured into unimaginable shapes and compacted into concrete slabs. It seems a vision of war, of a city reduced to ruin by a nuclear bomb: Ground Zero, the epicenter of emptiness and the heart of hell. Yet most terrible is the thought that there may be people buried in the rubble. Shreds of clothes, shoes, or a bright scarf signal their presence amid the ruins.

I keep walking, as if in a nightmare, toward the western part of the World Financial Center, located adjacent to where the towers stood. Instead of a twenty-two-floor Marriott Hotel, I see only flat ground surrounded by buildings blackened by the soot of smoke.

It's dark when I reach a wall—about eight floors high—a fragment of the North Tower. It stands jagged and partly burned, so gentle and thin. On the right, I see another wall, this one sculpted into the shape of the Coliseum in Rome—an astonishing and gruesome similarity. In the distance, I see many moving points of light, and I realize that they are rescue workers who are looking for people who might be still alive. It is a spectacle of unspeakable pain.

That night the phone rings time and again at the hotel. Everyone wants to know what hell looks like. The only thing I manage to say is, "It's horror. Horror."

As I pack my equipment early in the morning I cannot stop wondering whether what I do has any meaning. Is it worth trying so hard? The world is fragile and transient and everything we have created can vanish in the blink of an eye.

I try to chase these thoughts away and set up my sampling containers at today's testing site. All at once the firemen working nearby become agitated. A survivor! Down on their knees, they are removing steel rods and tattered sheets of metal. As I get closer I can hear their quickened breath. A silent prayer passes through my mind: "Stay alive, please, stay alive." A face frozen into a scream emerges from the rubble. It is too late.

Yet the rescuers do not give up. Despite many failed attempts, they keep hoping to find even a single person alive. The determination in the eyes of the rescue workers revives the sense of urgency of my work: I'm here to protect them from health hazards and ensure the safety of the site. They need me.

The rescue teams are accompanied by dogs. Their barking awakens hope. And again, they are barking. I hold my breath as the firefighters dig through the rubble . . . a terrible sight: fragments of a human leg and a shoe. Most often only body parts are found. The rescuers pack them into special containers, label them, and send them for examination. As I watch this routine procedure I wonder about the identity of the person who was pulled out of the rubble. Might it have been someone I know? I imagine the victim's friends and family still hoping for a miracle, and I am crushed by the knowledge that there won't be any.

Another night is falling in New York. But here, at Ground Zero, no one pays much attention to it and work goes on uninterrupted.

I enter the Millennium Hotel. I am amazed that it hasn't collapsed with the nearby towers. An unnaturally dead silence fills the lobby. Computers, chairs, tables are mutilated and covered with a thick layer of dust that ripples like water at the touch of my hand.

An open door on the first floor beckons me into a conference room. A few jackets hang over the backs of chairs; notepads, pens, and coffee mugs sit on the table. Someone had written on the board: "I think we should leave this room." I feel a bit like an intruder disturbing the quiet of this place.

I walk up a flight of stairs. Shoes strewn all over the steps mark the escape route and speak of rush and panic. I stop somewhere between the twentieth and thirtieth floors. Abandoned articles of clothing cover the floor, mainly by the elevator. I enter a few rooms. It is as if the guests just left a moment ago; the scent of a perfume still seems to float in the air. But that's just an impression; there is only the charred odor of smoke. Scattered clothes, suitcases left open. They were trying to pack a few things. Discarded wallets and purses suggest that the only treasure worth saving is life. In the collapse of the buildings, the people died. Only the debris of their lives remained.

Back at my hotel in Chinatown the first test results from our lab in Virginia are waiting for me at the reception desk. As I glance over the figures and compare them with the admissible norms, I realize that the presence of lead and asbestos, as well as combustion by-products, constitute the main hazard. And a more precise sampling method has detected particles of asbestos that are not in typical fiber form, but are tiny, pulverized, airborne threads. The results are shocking to most experts responsible for the safety and health of people working at Ground Zero and in nearby buildings. Based on our finding they encourage the rescuers to wear masks protecting their lungs from inhaling contaminated dust.

To my own surprise, little by little, I grow accustomed to the sight of the ruins. Having spent countless hours here we are all starting to treat Ground Zero just as a workplace. During the first days of my work at the site I thought I would always be overwhelmed by the sense of disaster. Then one day I discovered I was able to live with it. That very day Marc, a *National Geographic* journalist, who was covering my river explorations and my job, accompanied me to Ground Zero. He was in a state of shock, incapable of uttering a word. His reaction reminded me of my own feelings some days earlier. Had I become numb?

"Getting used to the situation is the only way to survive," one of the firemen told me. "We have our goal and mission, just like you. We have to set aside our despair and do our job."

It is certain, however, that the experience of the World Trade Center tragedy and the impressions of Ground Zero have become a part of us. Over time it may become more and more difficult to reconstruct our experiences, or to name them, but to quote from a banner hanging from one of the World Financial Center buildings, once adjacent to the most famous skyscrapers in the world: "WE WILL NEVER FORGET."

Some time later, I am walking down the brightly colored streets of Chinatown, and have a feeling of having just returned from a long voyage. I am looking at the city as if for the first time. Music is flowing through a window upstairs: it's a salsa class. I stop to watch people laboriously practicing their steps and laughing at their own clumsiness. It has been a long time since I heard anyone laugh. I buy a bag of grapes at a fruit stand. They smell of everyday life that I wish to enjoy, if only for a moment.

I pass Chinese and Italian pubs illuminated by their moody candles. It makes me think of the many busy restaurants that used to be near Ground Zero. I glance at people inside. A couple sitting at the window is observing me with rising curiosity. No wonder: I am entirely covered with dust that disguises the blue of my shirt, the navy blue of my work pants, as well as the whiteness of my hard hat and my tool bag.

The lights of Manhattan are visible in the distance, the skyscrapers, the Empire State Building, and the Chrysler Building. The streets are animated with the usual traffic. People slowly return to normal life, because they must live, because they want to live, because the power of life is indomitable.

• • •

Piotr P. Chmielinski was born in Rzeszow, Poland, and received his master of science degree in mechanical engineering from the University of Mining and Metallurgy in Krakow, Poland. Piotr left Poland in 1979 and traveled for several years in South America. He eventually settled in Casper, Wyoming. In 1986, he moved to Washington, DC, where he founded the firm HP Environmental, Inc. In 1983, Piotr established Canoandes, Inc., a nonprofit organization that coordinates expeditions and facilitates endeavors related to geographical exploration.

Chapter 24

Finding the *Oxford*

BARRY CLIFFORD

December 19, 2004.

The call came in the middle of the night. The wind was howling out of the northwest. I whacked my bad elbow getting out of bed to answer the phone.

"Hello, Mr. Clifford. My name is Mr. Lauro," said the voice on the line. "We met at Jean-Claude's in Cap-Haïtien. The archaeologist Dr. de Bry gave me your number. He said you might consider helping us identify a shipwreck on the south coast of Haiti."

As Lauro rattled on about how dangerous times were in Haiti, my mind scrambled to remember. Slowly I did. Lauro had found a Dutch warship on the south coast. I'd let him bring that up. My guess was that he wouldn't.

"You must forgive me, Mr. Lauro," I said. "My recollections of Jean-Claude's place are rather foggy. The devil knows what he laces that rum punch with."

"Yes, yes. That was me . . . the very fat one . . . with the cane," he said.

I was right. They say Lauro sold a bronze cannon from the Dutch wreck to a German antiquities dealer for a small fortune and got thrown in jail for cutting a government minister out of the deal. With Haiti now under UN control, was Lauro looking for my help to retrieve his treasure? I'd sooner go looking for land mines in Iraq than set foot in Haiti with him.

"I'm not calling for myself, you understand," Lauro said, sensing my lack of enthusiasm. "Someone I know has the permit for Captain Morgan's flagship, the *Oxford*. In fact, he thinks he may have found it." My ears perked up.

I never heard from Lauro again, but the next day Gilbert Assad, who had done research on Morgan and the *Oxford*, called. Assad and his surrogate father and patron, Jean-Claude Figgolet, held diving permits for the coast around Île à Vache, where I knew the pirate Henry Morgan had lost half a dozen ships.

By 1668 Morgan had looted uncounted Spanish ships and towns, and Île à Vache, close to both Port Royal in Jamaica and Tortuga, was his main hideout. Morgan commanded the *Oxford*, a large thirty-two-gun warship. During a gathering of Morgan's captains at Île à Vache, some gunpowder exploded and the *Oxford* sank with the loss of over two hundred and fifty buccaneers.

Morgan quickly regrouped and took the Spanish city of Maracaibo. He assembled yet another expedition at Île à Vache the following year. The target was Panama, the richest Spanish city in the West Indies. Outfitting was again disrupted—this time by a hurricane that sank three more of Morgan's vessels.

The pirates weighed anchor in December 1670—together with a witch Morgan brought along as extra insurance. Feared by all, this tiny old woman apparently took part in all of the buccaneers' councils. Any magic she made certainly didn't hurt. Morgan crossed the Isthmus of Panama, and, against impossible odds, sacked the city.

In the meantime, England and Spain had made peace, and Morgan's victory became a serious diplomatic embarrassment. King Charles II ordered Morgan's arrest, and he was sent to England. It was not long, however, before Morgan's special talents were again in demand, and he was soon authorized to return to Jamaica as deputy governor. King Charles knighted him for good measure. "Sir Henry" sailed from London aboard the *Jamaica Merchant* in early 1676. Sure enough, she wrecked on a reef just west of Île à Vache. Morgan and other survivors swam to a tiny cay and were picked up a week later.

Morgan thereafter turned Jamaica into the keystone of English power in the Americas—despite frequent carousing with old shipmates. He died of cirrhosis of the liver in 1688. Four years later, a massive earthquake destroyed Port Royal and some say his lead coffin still rests in the murky waters of the sunken city.

Wherever Morgan's coffin might be, I was a lot more interested in finding the *Oxford*. Though many ships sank with far more treasure, a pirate wreck laden for a major invasion would make a fine addition to our pirate museum on Cape Cod. But, if I was going to do this, I had to do it now. If news of the *Oxford* leaked, treasure hunters could turn the wreck site into a bone yard.

Packing for survey expeditions is a fine art. A team can spend weeks getting ready. By the time I finished my phone call with Gilbert, I had twelve hours.

The runway at Port-au-Prince was lined with light-blue UN Hummers and trucks, most with fifty-caliber machine guns mounted over the cabs. As I stepped off the plane into the broiling sun, a pack of baggage handlers shot past me toward an American couple with cameras strung around their necks and Louis Vuitton bags. Port-au-Prince baggage handlers can spot a free lunch a mile away.

As I entered the terminal, policemen—and men in gray business suits—surrounded me. They asked me to accompany them. When we ended up in the VIP reception room where my contacts were waiting, it became clear that the Haitian government was very interested in Captain Morgan's treasure.

After quick introductions with Gilbert Assad; his mentor, Jean-Claude Figgolet; and Ernst Wilson, a flamboyant representative from the Haitian Ministry of Culture, a heavily armored caravan drove us to the upper-class neighborhood of Pétionville.

No matter how many times you've been there, Haiti overwhelms all your senses: the brightly painted "tap-taps" (buses) crammed with folks coming and going to work, the monstrous hog rooting in an open sewer, lopsided jalopies sputtering up impossible hills, women striding with the grace of runway models with bundles the size of small pianos balanced on their heads, and cook shops crawling with rats.

After a night punctured with sporadic gunfire, I was awakened by a yowling dogfight and what seemed like every rooster in Haiti crowing outside my window. After strong mountain coffee, and a delicious rice and mango porridge, we said good-bye to Gilbert's wife and kids and headed out for Île à Vache.

There is nothing like a long, dangerous road trip to get to know someone.

Gilbert told me how his great-grandfather came to Haiti from Lebanon in the late 1800s with only the clothes he wore. As he walked around the city, looking for a meal, he met a Haitian woman peddling fish. "My great-grandfather was a man of great pride," Gilbert said. "He would have rather died than beg for food." But the peddler was a fisherman's widow with three children, and Mr. Assad, Gilbert's great-grandfather, was a keen businessman.

After light conversation, Mr. Assad politely inquired if her late husband had left her with anything. "No," she replied. "But my father left me eighty acres in the mountains."

"Ahh . . . ," came the reply.

They promptly married, cleared the eighty acres, and planted coffee. Soon they began shipping coffee and fish all around Haiti.

We stopped for gas. A small boy was washing cars. His right arm was severed at the shoulder and the right side of his face was gone. When he saw that I was a *blanc* (a white man), he hid his face. I think he was concerned that his looks would frighten me. To let me know that he was OK, he placed his hand on my arm, smiled the most glorious smile I have ever seen, and then walked away.

"You smell that? They're burning tires. Lock your door and put that camera away, there's a roadblock ahead," said Gilbert as he slipped a nine-millimeter from his jacket between the seats. "You're not on Cape Cod anymore."

As we came around the corner, Gilbert skidded to a stop. A wall of stones with piles of smoldering tires blocked the road. About a dozen men with machetes and clubs surrounded our car.

"I know one of these guys," said Gilbert. "Give me fifty bucks—quick." After the money changed hands, it was like a reunion of lifelong friends.

"They say there are more roadblocks ahead. Perhaps next time they won't be so friendly," said Gilbert. "I've got to see my friend the police chief, or we'll never get through." He gunned the jeep and off we went in the opposite direction.

After two more roadblocks, we arrived at the port of Les Cayes. Gilbert stopped to get supplies for his crew. There were only canned goods, Haitian rum, bread, and a few "pharmaceuticals" like petroleum jelly and rubbing alcohol and hairspray. Gilbert bought a couple of cases of Spam, yellow mustard, bread, and rice. He was amused when I raised my eyebrows. "My crew is not sophisticated," he said. "Spam for them is like lobster for you."

Now riddled with gaps a Hummer could fall through, the wharf, built by the French in colonial days, was once a fine structure. Along its lee side, an old tramp steamer lay rusting in a great treacherous heap of jagged iron. From its fantail, a gang of naked boys begged us to throw coins in the water.

To appease the treasure gods, and help support the Les Cayes diving community, I deposited all my change and a couple of five-dollar bills into the rough, cloudy drink.

I'm often lectured about such donations. My critics, many of whom live off their inheritances, insist that I'm encouraging new generations of beggars. "It's entirely selfish," I tell them. "Watching a kid open a piece of paper with Mr. Lincoln's face looking back at him is as much fun as you can have with five bucks."

A vintage Bertram cabin cruiser rolling its way, side to side, approached the stone pier. The sea was now breaking on the wharf, and the only place the Bertram could dock was in front of the steamer. The mate of the Bertram was standing stiff-legged on the bow of the pitching cruiser with a nest of dock lines in his hand. The captain screamed at the mate to move. Still the man stood dumb. The Bertram came alongside the stone pier, gouging chunks of fiberglass from the rail of the vessel and scattering the kids like so many frantic mice into the rusty bowels of the old steamer.

As if on a Sunday cruise, Jean-Claude and Ernst were at the stern, debating shipwreck legislation, oblivious to the impending disaster, and to their *blanc* visitor. I dropped my bags, grabbed a coil of old line, and took a turn on a dock cleat. When the Bertram came up on a swell, I jumped aboard and made fast the line to the nearest cleat—slowly the Bertram eased into place inches from the wrecked steamer.

Captain Julio was a man of considerable experience. His last job had ended in tragedy, however, when his ferryboat capsized off Port-au-Prince. The *Neptune*, licensed to carry more than two hundred and fifty passengers, was carrying over two thousand people that day with no lifeboats, radios, or life jackets. Believing that a rival ferry company had engaged a voodoo witch doctor to cast a spell on the *Neptune*, relatives of the deceased promptly rioted. Julio, one of the few survivors, spent four days in the water.

After taking on supplies and fuel we departed for Île à Vache. The Coq section of Les Cayes at sundown was a place where pirate lookouts still kept watch for Spanish warships from high hills above a deep lagoon, protected by a necklace of treacherous reefs. The only lights came from the Port Morgan Hotel high above us. But for the handful of Europeans scattered about, the people of Île à Vache otherwise lived in darkness.

The next day, Pastor Raymond Bideaux, a certified cave-diving instructor, met us on the stone wharf next to his dive shop at the edge of the lagoon. Brought up in the Kentucky backwoods, Pastor Raymond began his career running moonshine. "I was roarin' straight toward hell before Daddy, a lawman, took me behind the woodshed one day. He set me straight with the Lord that day, he sure did," the pastor said. After a couple of years in the Army Rangers, "Ray" and his wife, Cathy, devoted their lives to working with orphans in Haiti.

"We spent twenty years in them mountains preachin' the gospel. I'd ride ol' Jock, my mule, where goats wouldn't go," said the pastor. "They loved seein' me comin'. . . except for a few voodoo witch doctors."

He learned the hard way that witch doctors don't have much use for gospel preachers. He told us that there are two types of witch doctors in

Haiti: the cultural kind and the devil worship kind. "I had my run-ins with the bad kind," he said. "They poisoned me once—by mistake. They meant to kill my wife. But she wasn't hungry that night." As he told the story, he'd been diving all day and ate both his food and his wife's food. "I never come so close to death. There was nothin' nobody could do," he said. "Finally, Cathy brought a colleague of mine over from the mainland to exorcize the *loa* (devil) from me. I felt the loa leave my body, and, just like that, I was like brand new."

That night at the dinner table, I looked around and thought of the old prospector in *The Treasure of the Sierra Madre* who famously said, "The brotherhood will last until the first gold is found." Who among us might sell the rest of his comrades down the river when the pile got big enough? Jean-Claude, for one, had bet his life savings on "Captain Morgan's Treasure."

Many years ago, on our first expedition to find the pirate ship *Whydah* off Cape Cod, the legendary treasure hunter Mel Fisher gave me and my crew some good advice. "Watch your back, boys," he said. Mel got that right. There are few words to describe the sight of the ocean floor glittering with gold bars and precious coins. More than once, I've caught a diver sliding a coin into the sleeve of his wet suit, or found our treasure for sale in some fly-by-night coin shop in Key West. Once we even discovered our chief archaeological conservator's sailboat packed with stolen treasure. That's like a heart surgeon dealing in body parts. I sensed the same loa lurking here on Île à Vache.

After dinner, Pastor Raymond had something to show me. I followed him to his little room. "It looks like a silver incense burner to me, the kind used in Catholic Churches," the pastor said, as he took the object from a cloth bag. He had found it concreted to the surface of what he believed was an English cannon on a reef where I knew Morgan had lost three ships.

"You might be on to something, pastor. The last place you would expect to find Catholic artifacts at the height of the Counter-Reformation is on an English shipwreck—unless it was a pirate ship," I said.

"Folks work twelve-hour days around here for less than a dollar a day," he said. "Can you imagine what will happen when they find out that their front yard's filled with treasure? Couple of years back, I was talkin' to a local spear fisherman who said he found some heavy black metal blocks and was using them for weights in his fish traps." The pastor held his hands about two feet apart. He said the fisherman told him that "the yellow shiny ones" didn't work so well as weights. He said they were all stacked up in a pile in about forty feet of water. He didn't remember exactly where he found them. "Only," as he put it, "that they was laying round with a bunch of what looked like old sewer pipes."

The pastor and I looked at each other. In our world "heavy black metal blocks" were silver ingots, "shiny yellow ones" were gold bars, and "old sewer pipes" were cannons—at least until proven otherwise.

"Yeah, there's stuff scattered all round here," the pastor said. "I've counted over sixty cannon within a few hundred yards of each other on that reef. The reason the stuff is still here, I guess, is that people are afraid. Between drug dealers and crooked dictators, this place got a lousy reputation."

At sunrise the next morning we all piled into Pastor Raymond's twenty-four-foot "Jamaica boat" and set out to find Captain Morgan's fleet. The wind had been coming out of the southeast, and big surf was crashing on the reef. The pastor's mate, Wagner, stood on the gunwales. "Come left, Pastor, yes, yes, easy now" instructed Wagner, as we cruised along the edge of the reef just outside the breakers, searching for a "flat spot" to set anchor.

"Wagner knows every reef from here to Jacmel. He's more accurate than my global positioning system. I guarantee that anchor will be right beside a cannon," said the pastor.

No sooner did the pastor say, "We're here boys," than Wagner was over the side with the anchor.

When I looked up, the top-heavy Bertram was coming down on us, rolling like a Winnebago. "Goddam, Pastor, they're going to run us down," I said. "Give me that VHF. Gilbert, this is Barry. Tell Julio to get that Bertram the hell out of here and go through that cut in the reef. We'll meet you guys inside."

Gilbert came back: "Not before we drop off Ernst Wilson. He wants to be with you guys when you dive."

After getting Wilson and his gear aboard the Jamaica boat, we peeled over the side into the swell. Wagner had put us right smack in the middle of a shipwreck graveyard. Everywhere, cannon, anchors, and ships' riggings poked into the water column like tombstones, or the bones of prehistoric beasts. The ship's timbers had held them in place until they calcified into the reef. Over time, marine organisms consumed the wood around them, leaving them freestanding.

Pastor Raymond signaled us to follow him up the incline of the reef just beneath the breakers. We came up under a huge mushroom-shaped formation of coral. As I swam around the pedestal that supported the fifty-foot-diameter mushroom, I saw that I was actually swimming along the underside of a ship, coated with a thin crust of coral.

The pastor pulled me up and took me under the lip of the mushroom. He pointed to a spot where he had scraped away a thin layer of crust. Stratified in the three-foot-thick layer, like M&Ms in chocolate ice cream, were hundreds of blue, yellow, and white trade beads, green bottles, pottery shards, and musket balls. The entire side of the ship was packed solid with artifacts.

As we continued over the top of the mushroom, large boulderlike objects appeared. I immediately recognized them as intact barrels covered with a thin patina of oxide.

Ernst listened with the intensity of a safecracker, as I thumped on the flat end of a barrel with my knuckles. Thump, thump. I tested it with my metal detector. Ziiiing . . . ziiiing. I tested the other barrels. They were likewise filled with some kind of metal.

My job was to locate, excavate, and conserve shipwrecks. Everywhere I looked, I could visualize compelling museum exhibits. But what I was seeing was something unique, something that could not be replaced or reproduced. Maybe it would be better to preserve the site intact as a national marine sanctuary.

But this was Haiti, the poorest country in the Western Hemisphere. Health care is nonexistent and the country is under martial law. Preserving historical shipwrecks is the last thing on people's minds. Outside help was needed, and a thorough archaeological survey.

Initial evidence was clear. We had discovered Morgan's lost ships. I also believed that the wreck site of Morgan's mighty flagship, *Oxford,* lay somewhere in the lee of the tall white cliffs at the west end of the Île à Vache.

My head swirled with all I had seen. I made my good-byes and promised to return soon. When I returned home, I tracked down a late-seventeenth-century map of Île à Vache. The map showed a marked anchorage that confirmed my theory of the *Oxford*'s location when it blew up.

We returned in January with my team, which included Andris Zobs and Charlie Burnham, our remote-sensing specialists; my son, Brandon, as a diver and videographer; my fiancée, Margot Hathaway, as photographer; and Bob Weihe, a rough-and-tumble former Navy salvage master and an associate of Gilbert.

After three intensive weeks of remote sensing and diving, under the constant supervision of Ernst Wilson and other government representatives, we located, recorded, filmed, and, with the government's written approval, retrieved artifacts from the wreck sites of what we believed to be Morgan's *Jamaica Merchant*, and the three Morgan wrecks off Abbaco for proof of our discovery. We also surveyed the wrecks of the famous racing schooner *Blue Nose*, and a heavily armed early-nineteenth-century former U.S. warship with huge cannon.

Gilbert and his associates had started this project as die-hard treasure hunters—just as I was when I began my career in the early seventies. By now, however, we all believed that the best way to proceed was to claim the wrecks, then persuade the government to declare the area an underwater national park for in-situ shipwreck exploration by visitors under the guidance of adventure dive tour operators. Perhaps I was dreaming, especially in a place like Haiti.

We had one final job: find the *Oxford*.

When we towed our magnetometer at the anchorage marked on the old map, it nearly jumped off the boat. "Yup, those are cannon signatures all right," said Charlie Burnham, as he and Andris Zobs evaluated the mag data streaming across the screen of the Panasonic Toughbook computer.

It soon became clear why no one had ever found the ship.

"I was afraid of that, Pastor," I said after I surfaced. "The *Oxford* is buried under a mountain of pure white sand, just like the pirate ship *Whydah* on Cape Cod."

The problem was that the *Vast Explorer*, our salvage vessel, was also on the Cape. I turned to Bob Weihe and said, "Looks like we're going to have to dig the old-fashioned way, Bob."

"Sounds good to me, sir," he said. "You point me in the right direction and I'll dig you a hole straight to China."

"In the meantime, let's get back over to Abbaco and get that goddam barrel Ernst has been hollering about."

At first, I had flatly refused to touch the barrels. Conserving them would be complicated. When I explained that to Ernst, he merely noted that failure to comply would "put our good relationship with the government at risk."

I didn't like the sound of that.

"The government needs to know immediately if the barrels contain anything of great value, . . . i.e., gold or silver," said Ernst, producing a written government order from the ministry ordering me to recover a barrel.

Against my better judgment, the next day we returned to the Abbaco site. With two policemen, Ernst, and our team we had more than a full load. "This is quite a boat you got here," I said to the pastor, as a big "gorilla wave" steamrollered past us and exploded on the reef.

We selected a barrel with about an inch of oxide conglomerate holding it to the seafloor. After measuring its location from three datum points, the barrel came loose with little more than a couple of cuts along the baseline of the coral and a good push. The problem was how to get the damn thing in the boat. We rigged two three-hundred-pound lift bags to the barrel and filled them with air. No luck. The barrel wouldn't budge.

We came back to the surface and hung off the side of the Jamaica boat. "That barrel's gotta be filled with lead," Bob said. "Or gold," said the pastor, giving me a wink. Ernst nearly capsized us when he heard that.

With the lift bags, and three of us pulling, we finally got the barrel up and alongside the little boat, and made it fast. The next day, Ernst presented another official letter. We were to open the barrel. "The government looks at this as an experiment," he explained. "We are perfectly willing to sacrifice one little barrel in the interest of science."

"OK, Ernst. Have it your way, but chances are this thing's filled with nails," I said.

As a workman began chiseling a little hole in one end of the barrel, a small crowd of onlookers watched every tap of the hammer. The concretion covering the barrel was rock solid. After about thirty minutes, I recognized the head of a boot nail. "Take a rest," I said.

When the coast was clear, I slipped shiny coppers into the hole and covered them with concretion fragments and then started to tap at the concretion. "Hey, what's that?" I said. Ernst plowed through the crowd like a linebacker. "What is it, Barry?" he demanded. "I don't know, Ernst, but it looks kinda shiny," I said.

"Like gold!" someone said. I blew away some of the concretion dust, revealing the edge of what could have been a gold coin.

"Cover it up at once!" shouted Ernst, as he flapped about like a big featherless bird.

"Let me have a look at that," I said. Out came two little boot nails and a bright new penny.

The place erupted with laughter. Even Ernst laughed—until his lower lip began to quiver. "I'm sorry, Ernst," I said. He walked across the beach, lay down in the sand under a palm tree, and stared into the sky for the rest of the day.

Then we returned to the problem of getting down to the buried *Oxford*. Finding remote-sensing targets in deep sand is never easy. After twenty years' experience, I knew what we were up against. It would have been simple with the *Vast Explorer*, but with shovels we might as well be using spoons unless we were spot-on.

By towing the magnetometer in a slow, tight pattern, Andris and Brandon "mag-truthed" the target. Based on its size and complexity, there was little doubt we were over a shipwreck—a shipwreck scattered over several hundred yards, perhaps a ship broken in two by an explosion.

"Pastor Raymond . . . Bob . . . you boys good to go?"

"Yes, sir. Let's twist her tail, Pastor," said Bob, and over the side they went, shovels in hand, like a couple of Nebraska farm boys off to the cow barn.

After about forty-five minutes, Bob surfaced holding up a cannonball.

"Congratulations Barry, you found the *Oxford*!" said Ernst, as he frantically scribbled our position in his notebook. Although the cannonball told us that the mag anomaly was archaeological, Ernst was a bit optimistic.

The sun was setting as we approached Pastor Raymond's dock where Jean-Claude waited. He had put everything he had into a search for Morgan's lost treasure, and a more desperate man you have never seen.

"Care killed a cat . . . fetch ahead for the doubloons!" I yelled, adapting the standard aphorism from curiosity to care in an effort to break the tension and motivate the troops. But Jean-Claude and Ernst just stared at each other in a hypnotic trance. Without a word, they walked off together to the side of Pastor Raymond's dive shop.

All of a sudden, Jean-Claude began screaming, completely out of his wits, "We're rich! We're rich! We got the *Oxford*! We got the *Oxford*!"

All I could do was shake my head.

The next morning, I went to check the artifact tanks and passed an armed guard talking with D. J., the owner of the Morgan Hotel (aka "l'hôtel du Dr Moreau). A few minutes later a loud shot rang out. I ducked behind a tree.

A moment after that, a group of village kids tore past me with the guard chasing them. He stopped and fired a blast over the kids, who by then had rounded the corner.

"This is not the first time ol' D. J. has done this sort of thing," said the pastor. "Couple of years back, the villagers burned the hotel to the ground after D. J. blasted somebody's stereo."

This was our last night on the island. I arrived at the palm-thatched outdoor dining room looking forward to the evening. On expedition there are few traits more endearing than being a good dinner conversationalist and listener. I had enjoyed many delightful conversations with Ernst and had come to like him. "Be careful, Barry," Gilbert kept warning me, "you do not understand the Haitian. Believe me, I am Haitian."

"Oh, Barry," Ernst casually said that night at dinner, "I need to meet with you tomorrow morning very early, say around 6:30 a.m. We can meet right here, OK?"

"No problem, Ernst, see you for coffee. Good night."

The next morning, the pastor and I watched him make his way up the steep embankment from the harbor. He seemed unusually fluttered.

"Barry, I need you to get me the artifacts at once," he told me.

We had collected five small artifacts, including the silver incense burner, a mariner's sundial from the Abacco site, and three pieces of ceramic from the *Jamaica Merchant* site. The artifacts were tagged, wrapped in bubble wrap, and submerged in water to keep them from degrading. No sooner had I packed them in a Dacor dive bag than Ernst met me outside my door. He was very nervous.

"Let me have the artifacts please," he said, grabbing them from my hands.

Off he went down the hill. "Hey, Ernst, I need a receipt for those!"

"Don't worry, Barry, you can trust me. Remember, I am very smart."

When I told Bob about this, he called Jean-Claude on his cell phone. By now, we could see that Jean-Claude's Bertram had cleared the harbor and was making a beeline for Les Cayes.

"We don't need you anymore, Bob. You and Barry can go back home now," said Jean-Claude, at the edge of losing all composure.

Bob and I just looked at each other.

"Oh my God, these characters think they've made off with the lost Ark of the Covenant," Bob said.

"That, or they've got a deal with another salver, and they will use these artifacts to perfect their salvage claim," I countered.

"You got a point there, Barry."

Within a month, the salvage vessel *Diamond* lay anchored off Île à Vache, with Ernst living aboard. The *Diamond* is home to a group of treasure hunters led by the Gregg Brooks, a partner of Sub Sea Research LLC.

Brooks has an unusual approach toward permitting requirements and archaeology. "No one told me no. Until they send out their Navy, which they don't have, or their Air Force, which they don't have, I'm just going to do it," he said in the Cyber Diver News Network newsletter on April 26, 2004.

Recently, Haitian television showed the *Diamond* under investigation at Jacmel, for allegedly attempting to smuggle artifacts. The use of dynamite on the reef has also been documented.

Whatever the exact circumstances, this episode marked the end of Gilbert's long relationship with Jean-Claude, his surrogate father, and the beginning of a mad scramble between competing salvage companies to claim what we had discovered. As Robert Louis Stevenson wrote in *Treasure Island*, you can be sure of one thing when treasure is involved—"Beware of squalls when you arrive." And so it goes.

* * *

Barry Clifford, one of the world's best-known underwater archaeological explorers, made international headlines in 1984 with his discovery of the legendary wreck of the ship *Whydah*, which went down in a storm off Cape Cod in 1717. Clifford has discovered many other shipwrecks as well, including several dozen around Cape Cod; various seventeenth- and eighteenth-century wrecks in the Indian Ocean, and more than twenty wrecks in the treacherous black waters of New York's East River. In 1989, his team located an undredged site in Boston's Inner Harbor with several shipwrecks associated with the Boston Tea Party. In 1998 and 1999, Clifford led two expeditions, under the auspices of Discovery Channel and BBC, to the Islas de Aves off the north coast of Venezuela, where he discovered late-seventeenth-century shipwrecks. In 1999 and 2000, Clifford completed three major expeditions to Île Sainte-Marie off the coast of Madagascar, as a Discovery Channel *Quest* initiative, where five shipwreck sites were discovered.

Chapter 25

The Ghost Bird

BOBBY HARRISON

"What do you think of this one?" That was the e-mail question I received from Tim Gallagher, director of and editor of *Living Bird* magazine at Cornell University's Laboratory of Ornithology. He forwarded a message he had received from Mary Scott, a fellow ivory-billed woodpecker searcher. This was one of many e-mails he had sent on the subject of the presumed extinct ivorybills.

Tim and I have been friends for almost twenty years. Both of us had a long-time interest in the ivory-billed woodpecker. We'd collected material on the "ghost bird" since our late teens. I had begun to search in earnest since 1994. As a college professor, I used school breaks to tromp through southern swamps, in muck and mire up to my knees, looking for the ivorybill. The ivorybill was my holy grail.

Tim and I had spent countless hours in libraries digging through old journals and books to find even the most minuscule tidbit about the ivorybill. We talked about why we thought it possible that the ivorybill could still exist. Forests have continued to improve since the 1940s. Habitat is getting better every year. We were convinced that the ivorybill could have made it through what Tim calls "the bottleneck," a period of maximum degradation of the southern forest. We believed that the bird's population could actually be growing, which would account for the increasing number of credible reports of sightings each year.

After we discovered that we had both been searching for the same lost bird, we decided to join forces. We exchanged ideas on why the birds are occasionally seen and then disappear when groups of searchers went into the field to investigate. We speculated on why no one who had claimed to see an ivorybill had taken a photo or captured it on a video. Little is known of the bird's natural history outside of James Tanner's monumental work on the species between 1937 and 1939. His work, *The Ivory-Billed Woodpecker* (National Audubon Society, 1942), is the only scientific study of the ivorybill, and that study only included six pairs of birds in an area that had not been hunted for almost ten years.

In time, we began to travel together in order to interview people who had actually seen ivorybills. Tim interviewed Richard Pough, John Dennis, Nancy Tanner, Don Eckellbery, and Gene Laird, son of Louisiana game warden Jessie Laird. He also spoke with elderly Cajuns of south Louisiana and aged woodsmen who survived off the southern swamps who had known the ghost bird in their youth. Together we interviewed Fielding Lewis, the dog trainer, who in 1971 took disputed photos of an ivorybill in south Louisiana. We documented sightings less than a decade old, others twenty or thirty years old, some even older. The stories were amazing. Some no doubt had seen ivorybills, while others had misidentified the smaller pileated. The key was to let each person tell his or her story, whether it was about the ivorybill or the pileated. The stories were spiced with antics and accents of the Old South and fascinating to hear.

Since Tim worked at the well-known Cornell lab of ornithology, the word soon spread that he was interested in ivorybill sightings. His telephone started ringing. Most reports were of pileated woodpeckers that the observer had misidentified. But one report sounded too good to be true. Gene Spariling, a kayaker from Hot Springs, Arkansas, said he was drifting down a bayou in eastern Arkansas when he saw what he described as a "super-big pileated with white on its back."

Once I heard Gene's report, I e-mailed Tim and said, "I've got to talk to this guy; I'm going to try and get a number for him." Within an hour and a half I received a call from Tim. "I found the guy and just got off the phone. I believe he actually saw an ivorybill," Tim said and then gave me his number.

I quickly called Gene and introduced myself. "I understand you saw something interesting in the swamp," I said, trying to contain my excitement.

"Well, I'm not sure what I saw," said Gene, in his deep, long southern voice. He said that he was floating down the bayou when a large woodpecker passed overhead and landed about ten feet up on the side of a cypress tree. The bird suddenly realized that he had landed near a human and began moving around the tree in a nervous, jerky motion.

"The back had a big white patch, but it was a dirty white—seemed to have a yellow tinge to it. The head was really strange, a big whitish beak and a pointed topknot that looked real cartoonish," Gene said. "After it saw me, it moved around the tree in jerky movements, like it was really nervous. After moving around the trunk, it hitched up the tree and flew off. When it flew, I noticed that the white on the wings were in the wrong place and too much white for a pileated."

I hung up and called Tim and said that I believed Gene's story. He described the bird perfectly, using his own words. He hadn't gotten the information from textbook descriptions. What clinched it for me was when Gene said the bird's head looked cartoonish and it moved in a nervous manner. That's exactly the way an ivorybill behaves. Even if Gene wasn't sure about what he had seen, I knew and I believed him. His sighting was only six days old when I interviewed him by phone.

"I'm going to Arkansas," I told Tim. The next day I got an e-mail from Tim; it simply said, "I'm going with you. Can you pick me up in Memphis?"

Nine days after Gene's sighting, Tim, Gene, and I were floating down the bayou, hot on the trail of the ivory-billed Woodpecker. We put our canoe in at the bridge that crossed the bayou at Arkansas Highway 38, about 1:30 p.m. on a beautiful Thursday afternoon. That first day was a little shaky. Every time I steered the canoe in one direction, Tim tried to go in the opposite. Eventually we began working together. By the end of the day we were doing better as the paddling duo.

The water level was low, and travel was arduous. At times the channel disappeared and we found ourselves in the swamp without a channel. Shallow water with submerged cypress knees can cause a canoe to capsize without notice. Often we had to get out of the canoe and slog through the mud, pulling and pushing the canoe as we went. The mud was boot-sucking muck. We clung to the edge of the canoe to keep from falling into it. Then it was back to deeper water where we could paddle for a while before again being pulled into the mud.

The cypress trees were magnificent, thrusting one hundred fifty feet or more toward the heavens with a breast-height diameter of more than three feet. The tupelo trees were smaller, but some were more than two feet in diameter and reached eighty feet skyward. "They get bigger as we go further south," said Gene. These were not giant redwoods, but they were impressive. We were in a beautiful, inhospitable spot, a place where there just might be ivorybills.

As afternoon turned into the evening we looked for a campsite. Dry land is a valuable commodity in the swamp. At the end of a long lake, the ground level rose a few inches and we found a patch of dry dirt. Hardwoods came to the edge of the swamp, and it only took a slight rise in elevation for the ecosystem to make a transition from cypress/tupelo to oak, sweet gum, and hickory. There, on the edge of the swamp we pitched our tents and made camp.

I fell asleep almost immediately, but woke up about midnight. A beaver approached the camp and decided that we were intruders. It noisily slapped its broad tail against the water. This seemed to go on forever. Later I heard a distant train and it got closer and closer. I thought it was going to come right through my tent. A train came down those tracks six times during the night. That night I did not get much sleep.

As I lay in the tent I wondered how an ivorybill could live in such a noisy environment. The habitat was right, but the noise might be a problem. Then I remembered how many times I'd seen wild turkeys on the side of a road with cars and trucks passing by at seventy miles an hour, not frightened of motion or sound. Yet when I stopped to take a photograph, the turkeys were gone in an instant. They were accustomed to the man-made noises; they adjusted over time. Perhaps the ivorybill had adjusted to the noises in the swamp as well.

If the birds had survived, they must be very wary of human movement within their range and very skilled at avoiding detection. I could well understand how Gene may have seen an ivorybill. In his kayak, Gene moves with stealth through the water. He sits low on the water and is practically invisible. On the other hand, Tim and I were too obvious in the canoe, banging our paddles against the sides. If ivorybills were present, they would see us long before we would see them. The best we could hope for was to find feeding signs, hear a double rap, or if we were really lucky, a "kent" call. At a minimum, we would be able to check out the habitat.

As the darkness gave way to morning there was a brisk chill in the air. Frost covered everything. For breakfast I filled a pot with swamp water and brought it to a boil, slipped a package of Dinty Moore beef stew into the boiling water and warmed my hands in the steam. Ten minutes later, we had hot beef stew, a real ivorybill hunter's breakfast.

Soon after breakfast, as the light of the rising sun touched the treetops we broke camp and were back on the water. As we drifted and paddled down the bayou we were amazed at how many woodpeckers we saw. Tim and I both kept thinking about Jim Tanner's statement about the ivorybill sharing the forest with an abundance of other woodpecker species. He was right. Downy, hairy, and red-bellied woodpeckers were everywhere. There were also redheaded, flickers, yellow-bellied sapsuckers, and the pileated woodpeckers—more than I have ever seen in one place. We stopped many times that morning to check out woodpecker tapping. Each time we found a pileated going about its daily routine.

About 12:45 p.m. we reached a lake. Gene went ahead to scout for dry land so we could have lunch. While paddling through the lake I told Tim that we were making too much noise to find an ivorybill.

"Maybe one will find us," said Tim laughing.

We did not know that in a few minutes our lives would change forever. The lake narrowed to an outlet channel at its south end and then made a sharp turn to the right. As we made the turn we paddled about seventy-five feet and began to drift. My eyes were drawn to the right about forty degrees off the starboard bow. Flying through the trees was a bird heading toward us. I did not say a word to Tim. I could see with peripheral vision that his sight had been drawn to the same bird.

I've been a birder for more than thirty-five years now and a bird photographer for more than twenty-six years. The bird Tim and I saw was something I had never seen before. It flew like a duck, fast with shallow, rapid wing beats. The primaries seemed to do all the flying, and in that way it reminded me of a pintail. But this bird looked black, the blackest bird I'd ever seen.

As the bird came through the trees it broke over the bayou, less than seventy feet in front of us. As it cleared the trees it tilted its body from right to left about eighty degrees, with its back toward us. It was illuminated perfectly. I saw the wing pattern immediately. The body and inner wings were a soft black, and the primaries had a slight gloss. The wings were black with white secondaries. The white secondaries were snow white, and the white extended beyond the secondaries into the three innermost primaries at an angle of about forty-five degrees. This caused the wings to appear long and narrow; a black back separated the secondaries. The image is indelibly marked in my mind. It was a pattern I knew well, a pattern that I had studied and hoped for thirty years to see one day with my own eyes.

We were so close to the bird that I could see the highlighted feather veins of the black outer primaries. I recognized the bird immediately, as did Tim, and we both shouted out "*Ivorybill*!" at exactly the same time.

The ivorybill looked like it was going to land. It swooped upward and flared its wings and tail. When Tim and I yelled out its name, the bird almost stalled in flight and then flew farther into the tree line on the east side of the bayou. It briefly landed on another tree but only for a second. Then it flew to another tree and stopped momentarily.

"Keep watching it," I told Tim. "I'm getting the camera." As Tim watched the bird, it landed on yet another tree, and then it was gone. We quickly put the canoe ashore and began chasing the ivorybill on foot in the direction it flew. But the muck and mire made a land chase impossible. By the time we had penetrated two hundred feet into the forest, the ghost bird had vanished.

Both Tim and I were emotionally overwhelmed. Tears streamed down my face and I felt weak in the knees. Tim's skin was white, as if all the blood had been drained from his body. His eyes seemed larger than normal, as big as silver dollars. He ran up beside me and said, "I don't know about you, but that's a lifer for me." It was a lifer for me as well.

As we walked back to the canoe, we realized that we had just become the first two people since 1944 to see an ivory-billed woodpecker at the same time. I sat down on a log, put my head in my hands and began to weep.

Tim's voice brought me back to the moment. "We have to make field notes right now while everything is fresh in our minds, and before we talk to each other about what just happened," he said. We took out notepads and began to write. Both of us decided to do a drawing as well.

Then we took a global positioning system reading. Tim looked across the bayou, pointed to a crooked tupelo, and said, "I believe the bird passed right across there. I remember it flying in front of that tree there." Together, we measured the distance from where we first spotted the ivorybill to the tree where it had nearly landed.

After making all our notes, we sat back down on the log. Still stunned, I felt humbled by the experience. A great gift had been given to Tim and me and perhaps the world as well. I thought of those who had come before us, including John Dennis, who, working with Davis Crompton, took the last accepted photographs of ivorybills in Cuba. Yet when Dennis discovered ivorybills in the Big Thicket in Texas in 1968, professional ornithologists ignored his sightings. Then there was George Lowery, curator of the Natural History Museum at Louisiana State University. Lowery presented photographs of a male ivorybill taken by a Louisiana duck hunter at a meeting of the American Ornithologists' Union in 1971. Most professional ornithologists thought the photographs were a hoax, but Lowery was a firm believer. His belief took a great toll on his career.

My thoughts raced to James Tanner and Arthur Allen. What would all of these ivorybill hunters say if they were sitting here with Tim and me? I was secure in the knowledge that Tim and I had just seen the bird together. Perhaps all those who had come before us would now be vindicated. The "Lord God bird," as many described the ivorybill, had been rediscovered. Would anyone believe us?

The search for proof began, but of all the highlights that followed our initial sighting, none compared to the moment, about an hour after Tim and I had seen the ivorybill woodpecker, when I telephoned my wife, Nora. Over the years, she dreamed of me seeing an ivorybill as much as I had. With shaky hands I punched in the number. "Nora," I said softly. "I found it. I saw an ivorybill."

Later, Tim returned to the ornithology lab at Cornell and told the director of our experience. I returned to Oakwood College in Huntsville, Alabama, and informed my dean. "As of 1:15 p.m., February 27, 2004, the ivory-billed woodpecker is not extinct," I told him. "Do you have any proof?" he asked. I didn't—so I spent that semester driving back and forth from Huntsville to Arkansas.

Our sighting launched the Big Woods Conservation Partnership and the largest, most extensive search for the ivory-billed woodpecker ever undertaken. The search that ensued resulted in fifteen more sightings and a videotape that would prove conclusively that the ivorybill had been rediscovered. I spent the next fourteen months in the bayous of the Cache River National Wildlife Refuge searching for and trying to get documentation of the ivorybill. I saw the Lord God bird four more times. Finally, on April 18, 2005, the existence of the ivorybill was made public worldwide.

• • •

Bobby Harrison, an award-winning nature photographer, is associate professor of art and photography at Oakwood College in Huntsville, Alabama. He is also the founder and president of the Ivory-Billed Woodpecker Foundation, which is dedicated to the location, recovery, protection, and conservation of the ivory-billed woodpecker and other endangered species populations. He is a charter member of the North American Nature Photography Association and a member of The Explorers Club.

Chapter 26

The Pass

DOC HERMALYN

It was the seventh week of the Mount McKinley expedition of the National Outdoor Leadership School (NOLS), and our members were ready to go home. By then we had placed five members on the summit, another ten were turned away at over twenty thousand feet by storms, and four members had come down with a high-altitude hacking cough. Yet here we were, now stuck at the fifty-eight-hundred-foot McGonagall Pass overlooking the Muldrow Glacier for days while Paul Petzoldt, founder of NOLS, ate oatmeal.

NOLS had agreed to a partial sponsorship of the expedition with the Quaker Oats Company. That was OK except that Quaker Oats needed to film the leader eating oatmeal on the pass with Denali over his shoulder. There was only one problem: Paul hated oatmeal. For the better part of three days the film company had tried to photograph him eating the stuff without much success.

Paul was a bear of a man in his late sixties who looked and acted like the mountaineer he was. He was always open to suggestions and new things, from equipment to food. His school helped create outdoor education in the United States and produced thousands of leaders. He was adored and trusted by the students, his knowledge was eclectic, and his stories were wonderful. He was the "great Paul." But for days the "great one" and our team were stuck playing cards for money, trying to get into the future commercial. Some wallowed and complained. Others ate the film crew's food. Some of us volunteered for every possible job, including ferrying supplies and equipment from the horse packers up and down the twenty-eight hundred feet to the pass. Even though I'd lost weight during the expedition, I was fitter than a racehorse. (In fact two weeks later, I ran a 4:20 mile, a never-to-be-repeated feat.) So, I was a perfect carrier mule.

As a wilderness leader, Paul trained his followers to eat well, to preserve the land, and walk lightly on it. In fact there are still many advocates of wearing wool hats, socks, pants, and shirts in layers who trace their lineage to Paul. To this day, even the hint of lanolin or perhaps seeing a picture of a flock of sheep brings forth a hearty laugh to any NOLS graduate from the era before clothes were made from old tires.

The problem was that Paul couldn't eat his oatmeal without grimacing. The filmmakers had him stand, sit, lay about; they placed soda, spirits, goulash, powdered eggs in the bowl—nothing worked—and finally the director gave up and the team was released from the pass.

We were two days' journey from Wonder Lake and the road head where a rented school bus awaited to take us to Denali National Park and Preserve headquarters, which was seven hours away. There we would have our first shower and real food and then board the train to Anchorage and finally the airport for our flights home.

On the last day I walked with Paul over the tundra along with a number of others and he talked to us about life—in the big way. We came to the McKinley Bar, which is a series of riverlets, streams, and gushing waters over a mile in diameter separated by gravel breaks. The water was barely more than thirty-two degrees and stepping into it gave one a severe headache. We moved onward following Paul as he led us through the watery maze.

Suddenly he started to sink very quickly into the bank and he turned and yelled out at the top of his lungs: "Save yourselves, boys, it's quicksand." But we were his boys and were trained to act and so it was that three of us jumped into the gravel bar and pulled and yanked the big man out of harm's way. Breathing heavily we looked at each other and started to laugh. "It's great here, isn't it?" asked the indomitable Paul.

Years later I telephoned Paul at his Maine home to work out the details of having him speak at The Explorers Club Millennium Awards Dinner. I recounted this story to him once again and his response was that he was proud to have trained so many to see the real world around them and to enjoy every moment. The NOLS was a grand success. But yes, after all the years, Paul still disliked that breakfast mush at the pass.

* * *

Doc Hermalyn is chief executive officer of the Bronx County Historical Society and president of the History of NYC Project Inc. Historian, educator, lecturer, and publisher, Hermalyn earned his doctorate from Columbia University. He is the publisher and editor of one hundred thirty-seven publications, and author of fifteen works including *Morris High School and the Establishment of the New York Secondary School System* (The Bronx County Historical Society Press, 1996), *The Study and Writing of History* (The Bronx County Historical Society Press, 2007), and *Time and the Calendar: A Book and Planetarium Show* (History of NYC Project Inc., 2007). He was the project editor of the ten-volume series *The History of the U.S. Supreme Court* (Grolier Education Corp., 1995) and the six-volume *Roots of the Republic* (Grolier Educational Corp., 1996). Hermalyn is a centennial historian of New York City and a fellow of The Explorers Club.

Chapter 27

Cloud Diving

JOHAN REINHARD

Near disasters are always unforgettable, but rarely are they sublime. In 1973 I experienced one that was both. I had returned to Austria the year before in order to finish my university studies in Vienna after spending three years in Nepal. I also started skydiving again.

The day started out simply enough. "Johan, can you come out to the airport now?" It was Hans, a friend of mine, and he called with an offer he knew an impecunious student couldn't refuse—getting something for free. "They are putting on a demonstration of Pilatus Porters, and we've been offered free jumps to help spice up the show."

Pilatus Porters are small, short take-off and landing planes, which at the time were something of a novelty in Vienna. The "we" was to be Hans, myself, and three other skydivers who had been training to form the core of the first Austrian ten-man star team. Stars are made by skydivers jumping out of a perfectly good airplane and joining up in a free fall to hold hands forming a circle. The first international ten-man star competition was to take place in Innsbruck the coming spring, and Austria was determined to field its own team.

Hans was an experienced skydiver with over two thousand jumps—a substantial number at any time, and especially so in the early 1970s. He had also won international accuracy competitions, where skydivers maneuver their parachutes to try to hit a small metal disk only inches wide. This was located at the center of a large, cleared circle called a "drop zone." Hans once landed on eight such disks in a row.

Within the hour we were all assembled at a regional airport some ten miles outside Vienna. (The international airport at Schwechat had too much flight traffic to allow jumpers to clutter up the sky.) We discovered to our glee that the authorities had given us permission to jump out from five thousand meters (over fifteen thousand feet)—the highest ever allowed. Oxygen would have been required to go higher, but even had it been available, such jumps were verboten in Vienna. Unfortunately, the weather was not as cooperative as the authorities had been. Thick, gray clouds filled the sky, but we were confident that we could find an opening once the plane was able to fly above them.

And if we couldn't find an opening? We would have no choice but to jump out beneath the cloud bank. If that happened, we wouldn't have time to form a star. The clouds began at about one thousand meters—only two hundred meters above the altitude we would have to open our parachutes.

Then again, we had to consider the possibility that if we did find an opening, we might not be able to form the star before we entered the clouds. We could lose sight of each other and have to pull our ripcords without any idea of where the other jumpers were. "If you don't see anyone, track away at two thousand meters," said Hans.

Tracking involved creating horizontal distance when skydivers put their hands along their sides and keep their legs straight—becoming human gliders, as it were. Of course, the higher this is started, the farther a skydiver can go. Hans reasoned that, with only five of us, we would have to be awfully unlucky to collide in free fall or open our chutes too close to each other.

On our first flight, we weren't able to put this to the test. The pilot wasn't happy flying in the clouds and insisted that we jump out below them. We were a discouraged bunch when we gathered back on the ground. If we couldn't do any real free fall, why bother going to the trouble of making another jump?

Hans walked over to the pilot and convinced him that he could find a break in the clouds for us to jump through—that is, if he would just take us up to five thousand meters. If not, we would just fly back with him. As soon as we had packed our chutes, we were climbing back into the plane.

We took off in the same unpromising weather conditions as before, but our spirits rose when the plane eventually emerged from the clouds into a brilliant, clear sky. You've probably observed similar sights from a jet, but it is unusual for skydivers to see a blazing sun shining on a billowing, white layer below. Unfortunately, we soon realized that the cloud bank was *too* white. If we couldn't find a break in it, we would have to abort the jump.

Hans leaned outside the open door. After a few seconds scanning below, he called out to the pilot, "Five left." Twice again Hans gave this order and each time the pilot aligned the plane by five degrees to enable us to reach the best exit point.

Hans is something else, I thought to myself as we looked out at the white mass. He must have spotted enough of an opening to figure out exactly where we were. Me, well, when I looked down I only saw clouds . . . or rather one huge cloud that covered the entire field of my vision.

On Hans's count of three, we were out the door and in only seconds had put together a star. It was so fast that we were still well above the clouds. I knew we would all feel foolish at not having planned something else to do during the jump. Several seconds passed by before whiteness enveloped us. We grinned across at each other as the air roared by, mixed with the sound made by the frantic flapping of our jumpsuits. We were, after all, falling at one hundred twenty miles an hour.

Suddenly, we emerged out of the clouds only to see another cloud bank below us. Two cloud jumps for one, I thought, and the others looked like they were equally pleased at this unexpected development. We held the star together and were soon engulfed in gray cloud vapor—not white this time. We let the two-thousand-meter break-off point go by since we were still together. Once we reached one thousand meters, each jumper would simply turn one hundred eighty degrees and briefly track away in order to cause separation. But still, I didn't like the idea of not seeing the ground that I knew we were fast approaching. Then, like magic, we left the clouds behind and looked down to see . . . Vienna!

I stared down toward the Ring Road, Saint Stephen's Cathedral, the Hapsburg Palace, and, hey, there was my university. For a few seconds, I marveled at the colorful scene spread out below. Then I felt a rush of adrenaline as the realization hit me that we were going to land in the city. I immediately let go of the star and started tracking for the suburbs. But it was a lost cause, as we were too low to make any horizontal progress.

Once I had opened the parachute and was hanging in my harness, I heard the characteristic *whooshes* and *whomps* as other chutes opened. This was immediately followed by shouts. "*Gotteswillen*!" (For God's sake!) was one of the milder exclamations that erupted from my companions. "The parking lot! Head for the parking lot!" someone shouted.

We guided our parachutes toward the only open space among the mass of high-rise buildings that rushed toward us. Fortunately, the parking lot was only about a quarter full, but I was still concerned that one of us could hit a car and be seriously injured. Worse, a jumper might get too close to the side of one of the nearby buildings. If even a small piece of his parachute caught on something, the air could be emptied from it, and he might plummet to his death.

It took about two minutes for us to descend under our parachutes, and there was plenty of time for thoughts to begin running through my mind—some a bit bizarre. If we wrecked a car, would the owner's insurance company cover the damage? How much of a fine would we have to pay for skydiving into the city? Would this, um, "diversion" get me booted out of the university? If so, I would have to leave my girlfriend and return to the United States—God, there goes my rent deposit!

But such musings ended as I got closer to the ground. I saw one jumper miss the cars. Then it was my turn. I laughed with relief as I landed amid a pair of them. Then, I watched as the remaining jumpers landed without even their parachutes touching a single vehicle. Someone exclaimed, "Volkswagens! It would have been terrible if I had hit anything less than a Mercedes!" Chuckling like the fools we had amply proven ourselves to be, we gathered our chutes and ran for a restaurant—the nearest cover. We wanted to be out of sight before the cops came.

Meanwhile, back at the airport, the realization gradually sank into the bystanders who were waiting for us that we were not going to materialize. It was as if we had vanished into some Bermuda Triangle in the sky.

As soon as Hans reached the restaurant, he called the airport to tell them where we were. While we assembled inside, the questions were flying, but one dominated: "What the hell happened?" Hans was clearly a bit embarrassed. How had a champion accuracy jumper not just missed a drop zone, but the entire airport? Gotteswillen, we had ended up in a city miles away.

"Well, I knew no one wanted to jump out below the clouds," he explained, "so I took a chance on seeing an opening once we were above them."

"Well, how did we end up here, if you saw an opening?" someone said.

"Well, I caught a glimpse of the Danube River, and I figured out our position using it as a reference." Then he grinned sheepishly and said, "Unfortunately, we happened to have been on the wrong side!"

To our surprise we managed to be picked up by bemused friends before the police arrived. While guiding our parachutes toward the parking lot, we had seen cars stop and people emerge to watch us land. Hadn't anyone notified the authorities? Did they think the whole thing had been planned, an exhibition put on for someone's benefit? Then the realization hit us: What other conclusion could they have reached? How could five skydivers land here *by mistake*?

Soon we were back at the airport. While we packed our chutes, I contemplated how the day's event had been mixed with such a unique blend of beauty, wonder, and peril. I turned to Hans and said, "No doubt about it. That was one experience I will never forget." He looked at me—the man who had leaped out from airplanes over two thousand times—and said, "You know, that was the best jump I ever made."

• • •

Johan Reinhard is currently an explorer in residence at the National Geographic Society. Born in Illinois, he received his PhD in anthropology from the University of Vienna in 1974. He is best known for his discovery of frozen Inca mummies on Andean mountain summits. In 2002 he was awarded the Explorers Medal from The Explorers Club for his explorations in the Andes and Himalayas.

Chapter 28

Sea to Sea

ANDREW SKURKA

My geology class ended at 1 p.m. and I had a few hours before I had to be at cross-country practice. I filed out of the lecture hall, walked across Duke University's gothic campus, and stopped at the student union to check my post office box. In it, I found the February 2003 issue of *Backpacker Magazine* and made a mental note to read the article "America's Newest Long Trail," which was about a vision for a coast-to-coast hike, then threw the magazine in my pack.

I read the article before practice and thought of almost nothing else during my ten-mile run that afternoon. When I showed the magazine to my girlfriend that evening, she said, with dread, "Oh, shit. This is it."

Already, the cogs in my brain were turning—fast.

At that time, the Sea-to-Sea Route was just an idea—the goal was to use a network of existing long-distance hiking trails that spanned between Quebec's Cape Gaspé and Washington's Cape Alava. The total route was estimated to be about seventy-eight hundred miles in length. It would pass through two Canadian provinces, Ohio, and the twelve U.S. states that border Canada, using six major long-distance trail corridors—the International Appalachian Trail, the Appalachian Trail, the Long Trail, the North Country Trail, the Continental Divide Trail, and the Pacific Northwest Trail.

No one had attempted it much less done it. There was no guidebook. There was no sea-to-sea association. There wasn't even any trail corridor for eighty miles across western North Dakota and eastern Montana. Until the article in *Backpacker,* no one had even thought of it. But I thought it was an awesome idea.

The Sea-to-Sea Route, also known as the "C2C," combines the best features of the two traditional types of walks. The first walk is romantic in nature. On these treks, walkers take to the country's backroads in order to see the diversity of the landscapes and people. The second is the long-distance wilderness walk, taken on one continuous footpath over several hundred or several thousand miles in order to experience the scenery and solitude of the wilderness. An example of the second type is the famed Appalachian Trail.

The person behind the idea for the C2C was Ronald Strickland, an Explorers Club member and lifelong advocate for long-distance trails. In 1996, Strickland recognized the opportunity for a coast-to-coast experience and had promoted it ever since. Strickland, who founded the Pacific Northwest Trail in the late 1970s, believed that the C2C had the potential to transform America's National Trails Systems from three north-south trails (the Appalachian, Continental, and Pacific Crest trails) into an interstate system for hikers.

From Strickland's perspective, the C2C was an electrifying opportunity, but from a hiker's perspective, the trail was a terrifying challenge. At seventy-eight hundred miles, the trail is the equivalent of three hundred marathons and more than 3.5 times the length of the Appalachian Trail. The length poses a logistical problem: even if a hiker travels fast, winter can not be avoided. Besides that, the C2C maintains a northern path—winter arrives early and leaves late, especially at both termini, where mountains pose additional problems. Finally, the trail is oriented horizontally. Since both termini are above the forty-eighth parallel, a hiker does not have the option of starting at the south in the spring and moving north with warmer weather—the traditional strategy for completing a long-distance trail. Essentially, the only way to complete the trail is to spend winter out on the trail.

Nonetheless, immediately after reading the magazine article, I started planning to make the hike. I told everyone I knew about it. I lined up sponsorships with GoLite, manufacturers of outdoor gear and apparel; Montrail, makers of outdoor footwear; and received a product and financial grant from the nutrition company Balance Bar.

Eighteen months later, I found myself at the very tip of Quebec's Gaspé Peninsula, the southern landmass along the Saint Lawrence Seaway, at Camp Gaspé. This was where the Appalachian Mountains end dramatically and abruptly at the Atlantic Ocean. It was also the northern terminus of the International Appalachian Trail, which I planned to take seven hundred miles southwest to its southern terminus on Maine's Mount Katahdin.

As I gazed at the Atlantic in preparation for this enormous endeavor, I felt overwhelmed. I was about to travel across the continent in the same manner that most people use to get from their car seats to their office seats and from their beds to their bathrooms—on foot. Was this endeavor even possible? Theoretically, I knew how to make the trip—one step, two steps, three steps, and if I took enough of those steps in the right direction, then I'd eventually get there. But practically speaking, I did not know if I could endure the physical challenge ahead. Yet, I began.

By the time I got to the International Appalachian Trail, I had a rude awakening. I'd expected the romance of hiking "from sea to shining sea" to fade quickly, but not as quickly as it did. The message was clear from the start: this hike would not be just another walk in the woods.

The Quebec section of the International Appalachian Trail, in particular, was brutal. For most of its length, the section is like a game trail, not a hiking trail. It features few bog logs, bridges, rock staircases, erosion controls, or switchbacks that might ease the sting of the rugged, rocky mountains that it traverses. For two straight weeks, my feet stayed soaking wet because of the combination of untamed overgrowth, perpetual rainstorms, and nightly dewfall.

In early September I reached the summit of Katahdin and was excited to begin a four-hundred-ninety-mile stretch southwest along the Appalachian Trail to Maine Junction. My plan was to then hike thirty miles north along the Long Trail to the Middlebury Gap, then shoot west across Lake Champlain into New York. However, my excitement was curbed by the scene on top of Katahdin. That day two dozen thru-hikers finally completed their walk from Georgia. They walked step by step, mile by mile, day by day, just as I would do. On average they had invested five to seven months of time and endured unfathomable amounts of hardship. On top of Katahdin they hooted, hollered, and cried in a well-earned celebration. I was both inspired and depressed. On the one hand, it was exhilarating to see that human beings are capable of walking such enormous distances. But I still had seventy-one hundred miles to go.

Throughout the fall, I put in miles, slowing chipping away at the task ahead of me. When I entered New York in late October I linked up with the forty-four-hundred-mile North Country Trail, which I planned to hike in its entirety to North Dakota. The terrain immediately mellowed beyond the Adirondacks. The Finger Lakes of upstate New York, the Alleghenies of Pennsylvania, and the Appalachian foothills and midwestern plains of Ohio were crossed mostly on the walking equivalent of cruise control. The summer crowds disappeared. Leaf season came and went. Temperatures steadily dropped. The days became shorter and shorter.

I prepared for what I knew would be the most difficult section of the hike—the long, hard winter. This was the crucible of the hike. I needed to find a way to stay alive, strong, and mobile through three of the coldest states in the country (Michigan, Wisconsin, and Minnesota) during their coldest months (January, February, and March).

When winter arrived, I really wasn't sure if I would make it. The challenge seemed impossible. During these months I endured temperatures as low as twenty below zero, with daytime highs between fifteen and twenty-five degrees Fahrenheit. I walked through four feet of trail-burying snow in the Upper Peninsula of Michigan, in Wisconsin, and in Minnesota. I snowboarded fourteen hundred miles, two-thirds of the length of the Appalachain Trail. I'd expected these conditions. I knew that this portion of the hike, which represented just 18 percent of the total miles and 20 percent of the total time, would be—in and of itself—a worthy undertaking that was unprecedented within hiking circles.

Winter ended around the time I reached Ely, Minnesota, in early April. During the months of winter, I had been humbled. Overcoming the inhospitable conditions and high stakes of the North Country winter was the most difficult thing I had ever done in my life. I *knew* that it would be, but actually *doing* it was another thing altogether.

In late April I finally reached the western terminus of the North Country Trail. That itself was an achievement: I was the first person to complete the trail in ten years, the first person to complete it end to end, and the first person to do it during the winter. I took a few moments to pat myself on the back, but I quickly shifted my focus to the next section of the hike—the trail-less gap across western North Dakota and eastern Montana.

I could have made it easier on myself by walking a paved highway (such as U.S. 2) for six hundred miles until I reached the Rockies. But I decided to scope out a route that would take me way off the beaten path, that would maximize the use of public land, and that would offer an incredible amount of scenic beauty. I hoped this route might one day become the basis for the C2C's official trail.

The route I put together was about eight hundred miles long, with just fifty miles on paved surfaces and three hundred miles on gravel roads. The remainder of it was on ranch roads or on cross-country or hiking trails. From the North Country Trail's western terminus at Lake Sakakawea State Park, I hiked southwest to the South Unit of Theodore Roosevelt National Park, where I took the one hundred-mile Maah Daah Hey Trail to the North Unit. From there, I went cross-country though the Little Missouri National Grasslands and into Montana. I crossed the Yellowstone River at Fairview, then moved north to the Missouri River, which I followed all the way to Great Falls. Along the Missouri, I went my longest stretch on the C2C without a resupply, a distance of two hundred and fifty miles. From Great Falls, I followed the Sun River due west to Benchmark Trailhead, where I then joined the Continental Divide Trail.

Based on my maps and guidebooks and everything I'd heard about the northern Rockies and mountainous Northwest, I knew that the last fourteen hundred miles of the hike would be the crown jewel of my C2C experience. While hiking on the Continental Divide Trail, I'd travel 225 miles north through the Bob Marshall Wilderness and Glacier National Park. At Waterton Lake, I'd pick up the Pacific Northwest Trail, which led me 1,150 miles through the Kootenais, Purcells, Selkirks, Kettles, Pasayten, Cascade, and Olympics and eventually to the westernmost point in the continental United States—Cape Alava.

The last fourteen hundred miles lived up to their expectations. The scenery was extraordinary. The remoteness gave me an opportunity to reflect fully upon the wilderness before reentering civilization. And the hike had enough challenges to keep me on my toes and sharpen my backcountry skills.

The last forty miles of my hike were spent cruising on the sandy beaches and over rocky headlands of the wild Olympic coastline. During these last few days, I had a tremendous sense of inner contentment. For once, I felt satisfied and pleased with something I had done. This was a strange feeling and it lasted for several weeks.

Like most ambitious people, I constantly push myself to do better and go bigger, without taking time to enjoy success. But not this time. I knew that hiking across the continent on difficult terrain in uncomfortable environmental conditions was an achievement. At the young age of twenty-four, I had done something remarkable.

• • •

Andrew Skurka became the first person to complete the 7,778-mile Sea-to-Sea Route in July 2005, a feat that helped him become *Backpacker Magazine*'s Person of the Year. Skurka has also completed the 1,692-mile California section of the Pacific Crest Trail, the 483-mile Colorado Trail (twice), and the 2,168-mile Appalachian Trail. He has logged many more miles in Montana, Wyoming, and Colorado. When not on the trail, Skurka is usually in his car driving all around the country to share his passion for and knowledge of backpacking.

Chapter 29

Seven Miles Down in the *Trieste*

DON WALSH

From 1958 to 1984, the U.S. Navy operated three manned bathyscaphes. A bathyscaphe is an innovative deep-diving, manned submersible developed in the 1930s by Swiss physicist Auguste Piccard. The first of the Navy's bathyscaphs was named *Trieste*. The second two were both named *Trieste II*. From 1962 to 1974, the French Navy also operated a bathyscaphe named *Archimède*. During a quarter century of naval service, these four submersibles were the only way to do manned work in the deep sea below fourteen thousand feet.

It was my good fortune to have been selected as the first commander of *Trieste* and designated as the navy's first submersible pilot. When I joined the program in 1959, there were only two manned submersibles in the world. My colleagues and I were truly deep-ocean pioneers.

The operating principle was simple: the bathyscaphe was an underwater balloon. Its thin-shell steel "balloon," or "float," was filled with gasoline for buoyancy. Suspended beneath the balloon was a thick-walled steel passenger cabin. While on the surface, two air-filled floodable ballast tanks in the float provided positive buoyancy. When vented, the tanks filled with seawater, making the bathyscaphe negatively buoyant so it could submerge. During the dive the submersible's descent was slowed or stopped by releasing weights in the form of steel pellets. If sufficient weights were dropped, then the vehicle came back to the surface.

Piccard's first bathyscaphe, *FNRS-2*, was tested in 1948 making a manned dive to ninety feet and an unmanned dive to forty-six hundred feet. While the dives proved the concept of the bathyscaphe, *FNRS-2* was not seaworthy on the surface. The submersible was taken to the French naval shipyard in Toulon for a complete reconstruction. In June 1953 it was launched by the French Navy as the *FNRS-3*.

About this time, Piccard and his son, Jacques, went to Italy to build a new bathyscaphe. Called *Trieste*, after the city where it was initially developed, it was launched on August 1, 1953. The design of *Trieste* incorporated lessons learned from *FNRS-2* and from *FNRS-3*. By the end of September 1953, father and son made a dive to 10,300 feet in the Tyrrhenian Sea, near the island of Ponza.

The Piccards discovered that maintenance and operational costs were too much for them to manage. In 1954 *Trieste* made only eight dives and in 1955 it did not operate at all. By 1956 the Piccards were looking for someone to charter their submersible on a long-term basis. Among others, the British and American navies were approached. It was the Americans, through the Office of Naval Research (ONR) in London, who showed the most positive interest. In 1957 ONR contracted for a special series of dives at Capri. From June to October a total of twenty-six dives were made. Most involved U.S. marine scientists from a wide variety of disciplines. At the end of the Capri program, meetings were held in Washington, DC, to decide if the U.S. Navy should acquire *Trieste*. Recommendations from the diving scientists were favorable, and *Trieste* was purchased from the Piccards in 1958. The ship carrying *Trieste* and its equipment arrived at San Diego in September of that year.

The sprawling Naval Electronics Laboratory (NEL) on Point Loma in San Diego was chosen to be the submersible's new home. And a good home it proved to be. The laboratory had several major oceanographic programs, an extensive waterfront area, and was located close to deep ocean waters. At NEL's waterfront area, *Trieste*'s newly designated chief scientist, Andreas B. Rechnitzer, put together the shoreside support infrastructure. A marine biologist and pioneering scuba diver, Rechnitzer had made three of the dives at Capri. He was familiar with the submersible's requirements ashore and afloat, and he was instrumental in getting the navy to assign it to NEL.

As delivered, *Trieste* could dive to a maximum depth of twenty thousand feet. This limit was imposed by the strength of the cabin and the amount of gasoline the float could carry. Nevertheless, this submersible's twenty-thousand-foot capability permitted access to 98 percent of the seafloor of the world's ocean. Already there were plans to reach that remaining 2 percent of greater depth.

In the summer of 1958, I was a lieutenant, qualified in submarines, and assigned to the submarine USS *Rasher* (SSR 269). The major submarine force command on the West Coast was Submarine Flotilla One at San Diego. A big organization, it consisted of twenty-four submarines, including *Rasher*; two tenders, and two submarine rescue ships. Captain Ralph E. Styles was the commodore. I was on a temporary assignment with his staff, but sitting behind a desk did not suit my nature. I wanted to get back to my seagoing home on *Rasher*. Never would I have guessed how, in just a few months' time, getting back to sea would prove to be such a bizarre adventure.

It was a warm fall afternoon when Rechnitzer entered my office on board the submarine tender. He was there to arrange a *Trieste* briefing for my boss. Commodore Styles suggested lunch in his cabin. I was invited to join the group. Rechnitzer brought along Jacques Piccard who had come to San Diego as a consultant on the *Trieste*. Over lunch they briefed us on the navy's plans for the submersible, explained how it worked, and outlined its future importance to exploration of the oceans.

Rechnitzer was very persuasive and the commodore politely asked how the submarine force could help. Rechnitzer didn't hesitate. "We need two submarine-qualified officers and about five enlisted men to maintain and operate *Trieste*, and we need them soon," he told Styles. "A military crew is needed to run and maintain it." My ears pricked up. Perhaps this was my way back to sea.

I was told to send a radio message to the flotilla submarines operating locally and ask for two officer volunteers. The response was surprising. Only one officer, Lieutentant Dick Davey, volunteered. Since the commodore had promised two officers, I asked if I could put my name on the list. Reluctantly he agreed.

Dick, the lone volunteer, went to NEL in December 1958 and became officer in charge of *Trieste*. In the navy, noncommissioned vessels do not have captains; the military commander is an officer in charge. On December 18, Dick was offshore with the newly assembled bathyscaphe when it made its first ocean dive as a U.S. Navy submersible, piloted by Piccard. But unfortunately Dick was not allowed to make that dive. For some reason, someone higher in authority mandated that a civilian photographer be allowed to make the dive instead.

I got to NEL in January 1959 and became assistant officer in charge. Shortly thereafter, Dick became ill and had to leave the *Trieste* program. By default, I became officer in charge. I needed another officer, and my Annapolis classmate Lieutenant Larry Shumaker, who had been a shipmate with me on *Rasher*, volunteered.

It was not until I got to NEL that I learned what Andy and others ultimately had in mind for the bathyscaphe. Their plan was to dive it into the deepest known place in the world's ocean. The site was called the Challenger Deep in the Mariana Trench, about two hundred miles from the U.S. Naval Station on the island of Guam. The depth was estimated to be about seven miles. That was exciting stuff. My experience to date had been with dives to *Rasher*'s maximum allowable depth of 312 feet. Now, with the bathyscaphe we were not even talking thousands of feet but miles—seven in all.

The proposed deep-diving project required a major upgrade of *Trieste*. Before the conversion began, we spent the first few months of 1959 making training and technical dives off San Diego. It was during this time I got my first ocean dive: forty-one hundred feet in the nearby San Diego Trough.

The upgrade work was done at NEL and the navy's ship repair facility in San Diego. There were three major improvements: a new cabin, an increase in the size of the float, and enlargement of the shot tubs. The Krupp-Werke company in Germany, built the cabin. A thing of beauty seven inches thick, it was made in three rings and glued together with epoxy at the joints. There were no mechanical fastenings of these pieces. Lengthening the size of the float increased its gasoline capacity from twenty-eight thousand to thirty-four thousand gallons, while bigger ballast tubs increased shot pellet capacity from eleven to sixteen tons.

While this work was in progress Andy, Larry, and I concurrently wrote out an operational plan for our Guam diving program. With so much at stake, it was agreed that I should hand carry the plan to Washington. Once there I found myself shuttling through various offices on what felt like a moving conveyor belt. No one wanted to make the decision to go ahead with the diving program. The commanders passed me to the captains, who in turn passed me to the admirals. Eventually, I found myself in front of the navy's most senior officer, Admiral Arleigh Burke, chief of naval operations.

Despite misgivings, Burke agreed to the project. He told me that the project was not to be publicized until after we were successful. I got the distinct impression that he believed a successful outcome was doubtful and did not want a high-visibility flop to embarrass the navy.

By mid-September 1959, the modified *Trieste* was reassembled and had made two test dives off San Diego. The bathyscaphe functioned as expected and was then loaded on a cargo ship for shipment to Guam. Two of our enlisted men were aboard to make sure everything stayed secure. The rest of the team of three military and seven NEL civilian workers flew to Guam where we set up our waterfront base at the navy's ship repair facility in Apra Harbor.

Working from dawn to dusk, seven days a week, we got *Trieste* assembled and tested. Beginning in early November, our team of military and civilian personnel—never more than fourteen people—began a series of increasingly deep test dives off Guam. We encountered many problems, but we were careful about how much detail we gave our bosses in San Diego, and in time we solved the problems.

On November 15, Andy and Jacques set a new world's depth record with a dive to 18,150 feet. The previous record was 13,284 feet made by the French Navy in 1954 with its bathyscaphe *FNRS-3*. Our dive was not flawless; the epoxy glue had failed in the cabin joints. *Trieste* was taken out of the water and our team fixed the problem in the field. On December 18, when Jacques and I made a 5,450 foot dive, *Trieste* worked just fine.

During the 1959 Christmas season Andy, Larry, and I made several solo dives in Apra Harbor to self-qualify as *Trieste* pilots. The water was not deep, but the procedures for making the submersible ready, maneuvering it underwater, and its postdive requirements were essentially independent of depth.

On January 8, 1960, Jacques and I dove to twenty-three thousand feet. This would be our last testing dive before trying for the deepest depth. While winter is not too severe in those latitudes, we were careful to keep an eye on the weather. With only a two-foot freeboard, *Trieste* was not the easiest ship to handle in any kind of sea. We were lucky.

Only fifteen days later, we made the nine-hour dive into Challenger Deep to a depth of 35,800 feet, nearly seven miles down. Finally our team had accomplished the goal that we had set a year earlier. Few in the navy understood what we were doing, but this worked to our advantage. Way out at Guam in the western Pacific we were truly out of sight and out of mind and had the freedom we needed.

A week after the deep dive, Andy, Jacques, Larry, and I went back to Washington to meet President Dwight D. Eisenhower and assorted senior officials. We had the chance to tell our story. Among them was a smiling Admiral Burke. We had not let him or the navy down.

Jacques left the program after the Washington trip. The rest of our team went back to Guam for a few more months for the new Project Nekton II. Our plan was to return to the Challenger Deep for one or more dives. However, for reasons not explained, the navy restricted *Trieste*'s depth capability to twenty thousand feet. Early that summer, Larry and Andy dove to that depth in the Nero Deep.

Guam operations were completed by the fall and *Trieste* was shipped back to NEL for an extensive overhaul. We were proud of setting records, but *Trieste* was primarily a research platform. Scientific measurements were made on every ocean dive at Guam. We proved the platform could dive to any depth in the world ocean. Once back in San Diego, we hoped the lessons learned during the nine months of Nekton operations would go into another upgrade of the bathyscaphe, including its scientific uses.

I spent three and a half years as officer in charge of *Trieste*. Lieutenant Commander Donald Keacher relieved me in July 1962. During his tenure, the major event was using the *Trieste* to investigate the wreck site of the nuclear submarine *Thresher* (SSN 598), which sank with all hands in April 1963 in eighty-five hundred feet of water. In late 1963 when Trieste returned to NEL from *Thresher* dives off Boston, the *Trieste* was retired at the age of ten.

At least two other versions of *Trieste*, all named *Trieste II* served with the navy until 1984. With the retirement of *Trieste II*, the world's last operating bathyscaphe was gone. An era had ended. Today *Trieste* is at the U.S. Navy Memorial Museum in Washington, DC, and the last *Trieste II* is at the Naval Undersea Museum in Keyport, Washington.

* * *

Captain Don Walsh, USN (Ret.), PhD, served twenty-four years in the navy, mostly in submarines. Educated at Annapolis, Texas A&M University, and San Diego State University, he has been involved for the past forty years with underwater technologies, operations, and exploration. Walsh has been awarded the Explorers Medal and the Lowell Thomas Medal by The Explorers Club as well as being elected an honorary member. In addition, he served six years as a member of the club's board of directors.

Chapter 30

A Crashing Bore

RALPH WHITE

During my career as a motion picture cameraman, some of my greatest adventures have involved a true giant of the sea—the California gray whale. This whale is unique in the annals of the animal world because of its yearly migration from the lush, plankton-filled feeding grounds of the Bering Sea to the warm-water lagoons of Baja California, where it breeds and bears calves.

The most famous of these is Scammon Lagoon, named after the Yankee whaling captain who discovered it during the 1800s. Located on the desolate west coast in the middle of the Baja, it is surrounded by the Vizcaíno Desert and is one of the largest land-locked lagoons in the world. The whales enter the lagoon by a narrow pass at the north end, known to be hazardous to navigation because of shifting sandbars and a tidal flow that can rise and fall up to seven feet. Within the lagoon the water is shallow—except for the natural channels that wind around the small islands, sandbars, and mudflats, enclosed by low-lying salt flats and sweeping sand dunes. Between November and February of every year, this is the ancient home for several thousand gray whales.

During one project, the producer wanted me to capture on film every activity of the gray whale, which he planned to use as background material for his actors. Cost was no object, but there were several restrictions. The lagoon was a wildlife preserve and filming permits were required. Brian Burton, the production manager, and I drove down the new Baja Highway to Guerrero Negro to obtain permission to bring a film crew into the lagoon. On our way down, we kept watch for another crew that we knew was filming. We found them all right, buried up to their axles in the soft sand of the newly paved road. After pulling them out with our four-wheel drive, we continued on down the road.

Later, Brian and I made camp on my favorite spot, a promontory that overlooked the nursery canal. Brian got his first close look at the gray whales that we'd be chasing for the next two months. As we walked along the beach back to camp, we spotted a man silhouetted against the evening sky. He greeted us with two perfectly chilled martinis and an invitation to join him for a steak and lobster dinner. This was my introduction to Mike McMahan, explorer of the Baja and well-known author.

Three weeks later, Brian and I returned with a full crew, including a scientific advisor—one of the requirements of our permit. He was a PhD in zoology but had never seen a whale close up before. The first time he did the whale came too close and Brian dove for cover and knocked himself unconscious on the deck of his Boston Whaler. After Brian did that several times, I made him wear a crash helmet and lined the deck with foam rubber.

Every week, we sent exposed film back to the studio and received critiques by radio. The crew particularly loved one scene of two whales mating. During the mating, the male's penis slipped out and whipped over and almost sank the Boston Whaler. We got it all in living color and in slow motion. It was a humbling experience for us, as the whale's penis was more than eight feet long.

We were looking for the chance to film the birth of a baby gray whale. Once off San Diego, we came very close. We noticed some unfamiliar behaviors through the binoculars, but sadly, by the time we got there all we found was the floating placenta. During our stay at the lagoon, we witnessed several births but never got close enough to film one. The whales put a barrier of flesh between us and the vulnerable female. As the female went through the agony of delivery, another whale stood by to nudge the newborn calf to the surface so that the calf could catch its first breath of air. The mother expelled the afterbirth and then supported the calf with her nose. When it came time to feed the calf, the mother rolled on her side, cradling the calf with her pectoral fin. She then gave the calf a blast of milk from her nipple, so large it looked like a fire hose. Meanwhile, a guard of several whales swam around mother and calf, offering protection.

One of the most fascinating behaviors we filmed was when we encountered four large whales traveling up the channel at an extremely high rate of speed making squeaking noises. The other whales in the area immediately stopped, swam into the group of travelers for several seconds, then broke off and continued their more leisurely activities. This baffling behavior has never been explained, but we got it on film.

While we were there, many tourists dropped by the lagoon for a first-hand look at the whales. Often they ventured into trouble. One day Brian's crew rescued one guy on his inner tube, shortly before the current swept him out to open sea. Another time we found a couple on Piedra Island who had spent an uncomfortable night after they beached their kayak. We lost count of how many people we pulled out of the soft sand. Out of desperation we finally put up signs directing the way to a safe vantage point for whale watching—far away from us.

Soon, we had troubles of our own. One day, Brian and Chuck Smith roared up in the Zodiac, jumped aboard the whaler, yelling they had just been attacked by a whale. As they talked, I looked aft and saw the whale coming for us at full speed. We started the engines, made some slow turns, but the whale followed us. We throttled to an idle and I got every camera ready. The whale stopped and spy hopped, raising half its body out of the water so that it could get a good look at us, and then slid gracefully back into the depths.

Suddenly, the whale appeared, swimming in a tight circle around our boat and glaring at us with its ice-cold eye. It disappeared for a few seconds and then resurfaced with a thundering crack, breaking our keel like a twig and sending us all sprawling on the deck. Brian had several broken toes. The incident left me with a few broken ribs. Chuck hit the throttles and we lurched forward. Just then, the whale breeched its entire body out of the water. When it fell back into the calm waters of the lagoon, the tremendous splash soaked everyone on board. Chuck ran the craft right up on the beach below our camp. Once on shore, a doctor taped Brian's foot and my ribs.

I recuperated for a few days before going back to filming. I spent most of my time watching the whales and the lagoon from this once-remote, peaceful spot. I felt sad for those people who don't appreciate the wonders of nature. They are missing one of life's best treasures. While there, I buried a note in the sand. It simply said: "On this beautiful spot, someday a hotel will stand." I signed my name. Such is my view of progress.

• • •

Ralph White has been an award-winning cinematographer, video cameraman, and editor for more than thirty years. In 1985, he documented the expedition that found the wreck of the RMS *Titanic* with Robert Ballard, and in 1987 and 2000 he codirected the salvage operation and photography during the recovery of more than five thousand artifacts from the *Titanic*. In 1995–96, he was the expedition leader and second unit cameraman for James Cameron's Academy Award-winning feature film, *Titanic*. He has served as a contract cameraman for the National Geographic Society and helped pioneer the development of remote cameras, 3D video, high-definition television, and deep-ocean imaging and lighting systems. A qualified helicopter and astrovision aerial specialist, White is a former member of the U.S. Parachute Team. A member of The Explorers Club, White was awarded the Lowell Thomas Medal in 2000 for his life achievements.

PART FIVE

South America

Chapter 31

Encountering Darwin

DANIEL A. BENNETT

My story begins on an island. By the time I came to sit on the crater rim of Volcano Alcedo, situated in the center of the Galapagos island Isabela between Volcano Darwin to the north and Sierra Negro to the south, reading Charles Darwin's *The Origin of Species by Means of Natural Selection*, I had devoted the better part of my fifty-two years to building my business. Now, I sat reading in the cool, misty higher elevations of the same islands that the young naturalist, Charles Darwin, tramped across when he gathered the plant and animal specimens that twenty-four years later became the basis of the very book I held in my hands.

During my seven-day stay at the top of Alcedo, doors opened in my brain. I got my first glimpse of the scientific way of thought, a vision that provoked a different conversation with myself. As I read Darwin's magnificent story of the evolution of life, I had an intense sense of my limited time here on Earth. Instead of feeling dispirited, however, I was absolutely thrilled to experience my own insignificance in the scheme of things that Darwin gently but methodically explained in his book. In a word, I was inspired to get a sense of my limited place in time and space. Yet, persistent but not quite concise thoughts began to creep into my mind—thoughts about what would I do with this last third of my life. I remembered simple sayings I'd heard back in Texas such as, "This ain't no dress rehearsal," and "I've never seen a U-Haul on the back of a hearse." On the crater, my own evolution seemed imminent.

Prior to my decision to shift my focus away from my business career to find different pursuits, I was invited by a friend and Explorers Club member, Catherine Nixon Cooke, to participate with her in the 2001 Nepal Upper Arun Valley Expedition. Shortly after that trek, I was invited on another Explorers Club project in Hawaii where I met my future wife, Colette. In The Explorers Club I found many new friends who shared my common interest in travel and exploration. Explorers Club member Suzi Zetkus sent me an e-mail about a trip to the Galapagos Islands on a forty-six-meter, ketch-rigged motor sailer, the *Alta*. Colette and I went on that trip, which included Frank Sulloway, our group leader and expert historian. Frank is one of the world's greatest living experts on Darwin. We spent eight days aboard ship with one of the few people who has dedicated most of his academic career to the study of Darwin. His work was infectious. During this trip Frank noticed my keen interest in history and science and asked if I would assist him in some of his future research by participating in one of his upcoming expeditions. I couldn't say yes fast enough.

Six days after leaving Ecuador I was back on Santa Cruz Island with Frank and his good friend Mark Moffett to begin three weeks of trekking in the rugged interior of Santiago Island. Frank was working on a multiyear study to document the ecological changes that have occurred on these islands over the past half century. I spent three weeks walking up and down the rugged slopes of Santiago with Frank and Mark, listening to their heated discussions about the history of science. I got a glimmer of just how much I did not know about life here on Earth. Then and there, I decided to play catch up.

I've always been an avid reader. With my interest in natural history renewed, I could not have found better mentors than Mark and Frank. They are both Harvard PhDs who studied under the great E. O. Wilson, professor emeritus at Harvard, who has been called Darwin's intellectual heir. I reread *The Voyage of the Beagle*, a book I had not touched since college, with a new fascination. When invited to participate in the project's next season in 2005, I accepted enthusiastically and vowed to read *Origin* in the right setting.

In January, Frank, Mark, and I left for the Galapagos, accompanied by Rob Smith, well known for his research on land snails. The trip was a physical as well as a mental challenge. In order to reach the crater rim with a week's supply of food and enough water to get to the top and back down again to our stash of *chimbuzos* (twenty-two-liter plastic jugs used in the Galapagos to store and carry water), we each had to make a relatively easy ascent, but with no less than thirty kilos on our backs. With midday temperatures reaching thirty-two degrees Celsius (ninety degrees Fahrenheit), and unsteady footholds on the dusty rhyolite pumice, it was not a trek for a daytripper. Volcano Alcedo is mantled by rhyolite, the light-colored volcanic rock that is produced by fractional crystallization. Fractional crystallization occurs as basaltic magma intrudes into the crust and cools. Alcedo is thought to be the oldest volcano on Isabela and now is in the final phase of its evolution.

We reached the rocky shore of Isabela and off-loaded our supplies of gear, food, and water from the diesel launch we had hired to make the run over from the inspection station at the Darwin Research Station in Puerto Ayora. Soon we were enveloped in a cacophony of seabird calls including many from the several species of boobies common in the Galapagos. Sea lions sought out the rare sources of shade provided by the highest globs of hardened lava. A huge colony of marine iguanas made their residence here as well. The marine iguanas, found only in the Galapagos, conserved their energy in the blazing equatorial sun and did not like being displaced from their basking spots as we dropped our heavy provisions on the few relatively flat surfaces.

None of the creatures we encountered seemed remotely interested in us. Indeed, they made no real effort to hide or hurry away when we approached them. I came across one fierce-looking, large black marine iguana busy chasing its inferior rivals from its personal piece of the beach. When I trespassed on its territory, it tried to chase me off as well. It stood tall, puffed out its chest, shook its head, and made short false charges, similar to behavior I had seen in male elephants in Botswana when the elephants protected their territory. This guy was much smaller. Even though I knew that these vegetarian reptiles live on a diet of seaweed from the intertidal zone, it still looked like a small version of a mythological fire-breathing dragon. I decided the beach was the iguana's and retreated.

After completing the hike to the top of Alcedo we arrived at the crater rim to look into a vast caldera. The sweaty, hot climb was worth it. I looked out at a magnificent panorama and contemplated how these islands must have looked in Darwin's time. When Darwin visited here, the bottom of the caldera was largely covered in water. Frank told me that when he first visited in 1970 the crater floor was home to the largest gathering of tortoises on these islands. Feral goats, with population estimates ranging as high as one hundred thousand, have taken a severe toll on the environment that supported life for the ancient species of tortoises. Now we found the crater dry and with no sign of living tortoises—just the haunting sight of their numerous sun-bleached carapaces strewn about in every direction in the areas that once held water. It was interesting to think about how the landscape had changed.

We'd hoped to find a park ranger hut to use as a base for our operations. Park service huts were not usually occupied, unless by goat hunters who were paid a bounty in a futile attempt to make a dent in the island's feral animal population. The huts were built with roofs that slope down into a cistern where we hoped to find enough water to sustain us for the remainder of the week. After a long hike around the crater rim, we found the hut.

One of the most amazing things I discovered on the rim of the crater was the relatively comfortable footpath that could be followed most of the way around. Unlike the rim on most craters I had been on, this one was not made up of sharp, broken lava with steep, dangerous outcroppings that you needed to climb over or find a way around. Here we found relatively broad, dusty boulevards. Occasionally, we saw one or more tortoises strolling casually in either direction. Frank explained that these paths, in fact the entire summit of the crater rim, had not been worn down merely by eons of the Pacific Ocean's wind and rain, but by the tortoises themselves, who'd used it for perhaps more than a million years. I was stunned. As Frank and I walked along, he told me that there are scientists who spend their lifetime studying the effects of animal life on the Earth's surfaces.

After the climb to the top, I decided to sit in the cooler upper elevation and read more of *Origin* while Frank, Mark, and Rob spent the day photographing the vegetation, collecting bugs, and searching for signs of extinct or living land snails. That night, Mark invited me to make a descent early the next morning to what appeared to be a wet area below us that we could see from our campsite. Mark thought it looked like a place where tortoises might congregate. Even though I dreaded the climb back up later in the day, I decided to head down with him to see what we could find. Actually, I was kind of curious to see what it would feel like to climb back up without a full thirty-kilo pack on my back.

In the morning, we moved down the slope through deep undergrowth. Even without a path, we were able to achieve in one hour what a few days before had taken four or five hours when we were coming up fully loaded. I felt carefree and light on my feet. Mark moved to one side of the mud puddles and ponds that were filled with tortoises slurping and wallowing in the slimy green water. I walked slowly to the other side to find a comfortable observation point. As the hours passed, I became immersed in a world that appeared timeless. I watched while tortoises drank. I observed them sticking their necks high into the air to signal to small ground finches that they would like the ticks removed from their necks now, please. The birds willingly obliged. Several times I intentionally parked myself on an ancient path, and once a large tortoise lumbered toward me, close enough for me to reach over and touch it. I realized that I was blocking its normal route, one that it might have taken for the past fifty or one hundred years. After a few minutes, I moved and the tortoise resumed its crawl, free to reach its objective and quench its thirst.

By early afternoon, the extreme heat, my own hunger, and my limited water supply forced me to begin my climb back to our campsite on the crater rim. Never before had I spent so many wondrous hours in the midst of nature. By this time, Mark was no longer anywhere to be seen. In the silence of the place, it did not feel appropriate to yell out to Mark and disturb all the inhabitants of the watering hole. So I headed back to the top alone. As the sun was setting later in the evening, I observed what I thought must be flashes of lightning coming up from down below. Frank told me that the lights were from Mark using his fill flash to photograph something as the sun was setting. By the time Mark struggled into camp, it was dark and his pockets bulged with plastic film canisters filled with insects he had captured during the day. I could see why E. O. Wilson, his former professor, would later tell me, "Oh yes, Mark was one of my students. You know he is the best insect photographer in the world." This was no small compliment. I'd spent my day in very good company.

When Darwin explored these islands, he wrote that he was "astonished by the number of their aboriginal beings, their confined range, and their distinct lava streams." He concluded: "Hence, both in space and time, we seem to be brought somewhat near to that great fact—that mystery of mysteries—the first appearance of new beings on this earth."

In the final passage of his great work, *Origin of Species*, Darwin wrote:

> *It is interesting to contemplate an entangled bank, clothed with many plants of many kinds, with birds singing on the bushes, with various insects flitting about, and with worms crawling through the damp earth, and to reflect that these elaborately constructed forms, so different from each other, and dependent on each other in so complex a manner, have all been produced by laws acting around us. . . . There is grandeur in this view of life, with its several powers, having been originally breathed into a few forms or into one; and that, whilst this planet has gone cycling on according to the fixed law of gravity, from so simple a beginning endless forms most beautiful and most wonderful have been, and are being, evolved.*

What Darwin saw—that mystery of mysteries—became the basis of modern biology. In Darwin's footsteps, I sensed the mystery as well, and it awakened in me a greater awareness of my place within our natural world. On the crater's rim, surrounded by the elegance and beauty of evolution, I shifted my focus from business to exploration, from a man who had no time for the things he loved to time for little else.

* * *

Daniel A. Bennett is the thirty-sixth president of The Explorers Club. As an explorer, he has participated in flag expeditions in Nepal, Hawaii, Madagascar, Tanzania, and Easter Island. In addition to his research work in the Galapagos, he has also participated in research projects in Greece and Peru. A native of San Antonio, Bennett was the founder of Sunbelt Sportswear, an international apparel design and manufacturing company.

Chapter 32

The Running of the Boundaries

WADE DAVIS

One afternoon not long ago, in the small Andean town of Chinchero just outside Cusco in Peru, I sat on a rock throne carved from granite. At my back was the sacred mountain Antakillqa, lost in dark clouds yet illuminated in a mysterious way by a rainbow that arched across its flank. Below me, the terraces of Chinchero fell away to an emerald plain, the floor of an ancient seabed, beyond which rose the ridges of the distant Vilcabamba, the last refuge of the Incas. Vilcabamba was a landscape of holy shrines and lost dreams where Túpac Amaru waged war, and the spirit of the Sun still ruled for fifty years after the Spanish Conquest. On this particular afternoon, two young boys played soccer on the village green, a plaza where once Túpac Inca Yupanqui, second of the great Inca rulers, reviewed his troops. On the very stone where I rested, he no doubt had stood, for this village of adobe and whitewashed homes, this warren of cobblestones, mud, and grass had been built upon the ruins of his summer palace.

For four hundred years, the Catholic Church, perched at the height of the ruins overlooking the market square, dominated the site. The sanctuary is beautiful and bears none of the scars of the conquest. It is a place of worship that belongs to the people, and there are no echoes of tyranny. Within its soaring vault, in a space illuminated by candles and the light of pale Andean skies, I once stood at the altar, a newborn child in my arms, a boy swaddled in white linen, as an itinerant priest dripped holy water onto his forehead and spoke words of blessing that brought the infant into the realm of the saved.

After the baptism, there was a celebration, and the child's parents, my new compadres, toasted every hopeful possibility. I, too, made promises, which in the ensuing years I attempted to fulfill. I had no illusions about the economic foundation of the bond. From me, my compadres hoped to secure support—in time, money for my godchild's education, perhaps the odd gift, a cow for the family, a measure of security in an uncertain nation. From them, I wanted nothing but the chance to know their world, an asset far more valuable than anything I could offer.

This pact, never spoken about and never forgotten, was, in its own way, a perfect reflection of the Andes where the foundation of all life, both today and in the time of the Incas, has always been reciprocity. One sees it in the fields, when men come together and work in teams, moving between rows of fava beans and potatoes, season to season, a day for a day, planting, hoeing, weeding, mounding, and harvesting. There is a spiritual exchange in the morning when the first of a family to awake salutes the sun, and again at night when a father whispers prayers of thanksgiving and lights a candle before greeting his family.

Every offering is a gift: blossoms scattered onto fertile fields, the blessing of the children and tools at the end of each day, coca leaves presented to the goddess Pachamama at any given moment. When people meet on a trail, they pause and exchange *k'intus* of coca, three perfect leaves aligned to form a cross. Turning to face the nearest *apu*, or mountain spirit, they bring the leaves to the mouth and blow softly, a ritual invocation that sends the essence of the plant back to the earth, the community, the sacred places, and the souls of the ancestors. The exchange of leaves is a social gesture, a way of acknowledging a human connection. But the blowing of the *phukuy*, as it is called, is an act of spiritual reciprocity, for in giving selflessly to the earth, the individual ensures that in time the energy of the coca will return full circle, as surely as rain falling on a field will inevitably be reborn as a cloud.

Almost twenty years after first visiting Chinchero, I returned to participate in an astonishing ritual, the *mujonomiento*, the annual running of the boundaries. Since the time of the Incas, the town has been divided into three *ayullus*, or communities, the most traditional of which is Cuper, the home of my compadres. To my mind, Cuper is the most beautiful, for its lands encompass Antakillqa and all the soaring ridges that separate Chinchero from the sacred valley of the Urubamba River. Within Cuper are four hamlets, and once each year at the height of the rainy season, the entire male population, save those elders physically incapable of the feat, run the boundaries of their respective communities. It is a race but also a pilgrimage, for the frontiers are marked by mounds of earth, holy sites where prayers are uttered and ritual gestures lay claim to the land. The distance traveled by the members of each hamlet varies. The track I was to follow, that of Pumamarca, covers some fifteen miles, but the route crosses two Andean ridges, dropping a thousand feet from the plaza of Chinchero to the base of Antakillqa, then ascending three thousand feet to a summit spur before descending to the valley on the far side, only to climb once more to reach the grasslands of the high puna and the long trail home.

At the head of each contingent would dart the *waylaka*, the strongest and fleetest of the youths, transformed for the day from male to female. Dressed in heavy woolen skirts and a cloak of indigo, wearing a woman's hat and delicate lace, the waylaka would fly up the ridges, white banner in hand. At every boundary marker, the transvestite must dance, a rhythmic turn that, like a vortex, draws to the peaks the energy of the women left behind in the villages far below.

Each of the four hamlets of Cuper has its own trajectory, just as each of the three ayullus has its own land to traverse. By the end of the day, all of Chinchero would be reclaimed: the rich plains and verdant fields of Ayullupunqu; the lakes, waterfalls, mountains, and cliffs of Cuper; the gorges of Yanacona, where wild things thrive and rushing streams carry away the rains to the Urubamba. Adversaries would have been fought, spirits invoked, a landscape defined, and the future secured.

This much I knew as I approached the plaza on the morning of the event. Before dawn, the blowing of the conch shells had awoken the town. The waylakas, once dressed, had walked from house to house saluting the various authorities: the *curaca* and *alcalde*, the officers of the church; as well as the *embarrados*, those charged with the preservation of tradition. At each threshold, coca had been exchanged, fermented maize *chicha* imbibed, and a cross of flowers hung in reverence above the doorway.

For two hours, the procession moved from door to door, musicians in tow, until it encompassed all of the community. Everyone was drawn in celebration to the plaza where women waited, food in hand: baskets of potatoes and spicy *piquante*, flasks of chicha, and steaming plates of vegetables. There I lingered, with gifts of coca for all. At my side was my godson, Armando. A grown man now, father of an infant girl, Armando had been a tailor but worked now in the markets of Cusco, delivering sacks of potatoes on a tricycle rented from a cousin. He had returned to Chinchero to be with me for the day.

What I could never have anticipated was the excitement and the rush of adrenaline, the sensation of imminent flight as the entire assembly of men, prompted by some unspoken signal, began to surge toward the end of the plaza. With a shout, the waylaka sprang down through the ruins, carrying with him more than a hundred runners and dozens of young boys who scattered across the slopes that funneled downward toward a narrow dirt track. The trail fell away through a copse of eucalyptus and passed along the banks of a creek that dropped to the valley floor. A mile or two on, the waylaka paused for an instant, took measure of the men, caught his breath, and was off, dashing through thickets of buddleia and polylepis. The rest of us scrambled to keep sight of his white banner. Crossing the creek draw, we moved up the face of Antakillqa. Here at last the pace slowed to something less than a full run. Still, the men leaned into the slope with an intensity and determination unlike anything I had ever known. Less than two hours after leaving the village, we reached the summit ridge, a climb of several thousand feet.

There we paused, as the waylaka planted his banner atop a *mujon*, a tall mound of dirt, the first of the border markers. The authorities added their ceremonial staffs, and as the men piled on dirt to augment the size of the mujon, Don Jeronimo, the curaca, sang rich invocations that broke into a cheer for the well-being of the entire community. By this point, the runners were as restless as racehorses, frantic to move. A salutation, a prayer, a generous farewell to those of Cuper Pueblo, another of the hamlets, who would track north, and we of Pumamarca were off, heading east across the backside of the mountain to a second mujon located on a dramatic promontory overlooking all of the Urubamba. Beyond the hamlets and farms of the sacred valley, clouds swirled across the flanks of even higher mountains, as great shafts of sunlight fell upon the river and the fields far below.

We pounded on across the backside of the mountain and then straight down at a full run through dense tufts of ichu grass and meadows of lupine and rue. Another mujon, more prayers, handfuls of coca all around, blessings and shouts, and a mad dash off the mountain to the valley floor where, mercifully, we older men rested for a few minutes in the courtyard of a farmstead owned by a beautiful elderly woman who greeted us with a great ceramic urn of frothy chicha. One of the authorities withdrew from his pocket a sheet of paper listing the names of the men and began to take attendance. Participation in the mujonomiento is obligatory. Those who fail to appear must pay a fine to the community. As the names were called, I glanced up and was stunned to see the waylaka, silhouetted on the skyline hundreds of feet above us, banner in hand, moving on.

So the day went. The rains began in early afternoon and the winds blew fiercely by four. By then nothing mattered but the energy of the group, the trail at our feet, and the distant slope of yet another ridge to climb. Warmed by alcohol and coca leaves, the runners fell into reverie, a curious state of joy and release, almost like a trance.

Darkness was upon us as we rushed down the final canyon on a broad muddy track where the water ran together like mercury and disappeared beneath the stones. Approaching the valley floor and the hamlet of Cuper Alto, where women and children waited, the rain-soaked runners closed ranks behind the waylaka. Then the group emerged from the mountains as a single force, an entire community that had affirmed through ritual its sense of place and belonging. In making the sacrifice, the men had reclaimed a birthright and rendered sacred a homeland. Once reunited with their families, they drank and sang, toasting their good fortune as the women served great steaming bowls of soup from iron cauldrons. And, of course, late into night, the waylakas danced.

• • •

Wade Davis is an anthropologist, botanical explorer, and author who received his PhD in ethnobotany from Harvard University. He spent more than three years in the Amazon and Andes as a plant explorer, living among fifteen indigenous groups in eight Latin American nations. His book *The Serpent and the Rainbow* (Simon and Schuster, 1985), based on his experiences in Haiti, was an international best seller. He is the author of five other books.

Chapter 33

The Flying Giant of the Andes

JIM FOWLER

During the summer of 1969, Explorer's Club member George Wallace, founder of the Explorers Research Corporation, agreed to fund my expedition to the coastal deserts of Peru in order to conduct the first studies of the Andean condor, the largest soaring bird in the world. At that time, no scientist had found the nest of the condor in Peru. About the same time Jerry McGahan, a student of John Emlen, a well-known professor of wildlife behavior at the University of Wisconsin, traveled to Columbia to describe a condor's nest that had been found high in the mountains not far from the city of Cali. These two studies were the first ever undertaken of this flying giant of the Andes.

My goal was to trap some of these condors and attach radio transmitters to their backs so that their movements and habits could be studied. Scientists had begun to study animal behavior with the use of transmitters, but no one had tried to apply this new technology to large birds. Recently, transmitters have been miniaturized so successfully that they can be attached to even the smallest of birds.

After having trapped and tagged a few condors under beach cliffs on the mainland with a large forty-by-sixty-foot net trap that was fired over their heads by two mortars while they were feeding, I decided to try to take my traps to a small, strange-looking island about a mile offshore called Zárate. It was there that I was in for a surprise.

Zárate is devoid of vegetation, as is most of the southern coast of Peru. I discovered that very few people had ever gone there, even fishermen. It looked mysterious, covered with fog and mist from the cold water and crashing waves. There was a cobblestone beach on one side, but the rest of the island was rocky with volcanic columns of basalt rising several hundred feet straight up to form a plateau in the center. One in particular had the shape of a giant tree stump. With my binoculars, I spotted a small cave on the far side of the beach that might be useful. I hoped that I could find shelter there, away from the constant fifty-mile-per-hour winds. Even better, I could see that Zárate's beach was home to a large colony of fur seals. Condors soared over the beach each day to try to make a meal of the dead or dying.

My plan was to hire a boat, land on the cobblestone beach, store my equipment in the cave, set the trap at night, and trap condors the next day. But it didn't quite work out that way. First, even though there was a small, accessible, protected cove on the mainland where a dozen fishing boats were at anchor, the waves were high and no one would take me there. In fact, the fishermen I asked seemed nervous. Every time I mentioned the word "Zárate," they walked away.

Finally, a man with a small skiff agreed to take me and give me a few fish for bait if I paid him a large fee. He spoke very little English and I spoke lousy Spanish. On the way, the motor seemed underpowered and unreliable. Even worse, until we reached the island, I didn't realize he planned for me to jump off the boat with my equipment well out into the surf and swim to shore. The waves were so high there was no way he could land the boat.

Suddenly I realized that something big and black and longer than the boat was alongside us. At first I thought that it might be a small submarine surfacing. As the waves moved us up and down, the back of a giant turtle surfaced. It was a leatherback sea turtle at least six or seven feet across. Earlier on the beach, I'd seen a dead one on its back being butchered by a dozen fisherwomen. This one was big enough to feed an entire village and probably could have capsized our boat.

As the fisherman carefully backed us to the top of a large wave about to crash onto the beach at Zárate, I threw my equipment wrapped in plastic bags into the surf and jumped off just as the wave broke. The boat moved away as I was swept toward shore then pulled back to sea. All at once, the fur seals on the beach came right at me. As I struggled to keep track of my equipment and my head above water, two large bulls, barking and baring their teeth, looked as if they were about to attack. But fortunately they were deterred by the equipment bags. Later, I realized my dumb mistake: I'd approached the rocky beach from the seals' only exit point. After they were gone, the fisherman backed in again and threw off the rest of my bags. He gave me a "loco" gesture and then he left, saying that he'd come back in three days. I realized that I had no way of contacting him if he decided not to come back for the rest of his money.

Once ashore, I ferried my equipment up to the base of the cliff and looked for the cave so that I could escape the wind. It would not be good if a condor saw me from a cliff or when the birds came over to scout for dead seals. As I rounded the cliff I saw the cave I had spotted from the mainland—not as large as I thought but big enough to hide in.

Just as I began to feel more secure, I got a whiff of air and noticed a smell that caught my attention. They say that smell is one of our most powerful senses and I'd smelled this particular odor before. Against the sound of pounding waves and the wind that kept me against the rocks, I crept around, looked into the cave and instantly saw its source—vampire bats! They were hanging from the ceiling in scattered bunches about six feet above the floor. The floor was covered with reddish-brown defecation. It was the fresh blood in their droppings that created the unforgettable odor, the same kind of a sickly sweet smell that I had detected coming from the hollow trunk of a tree one day in the Amazon after my camp cook was bitten by a vampire bat three times the night before.

The vampire bat is one of the few dangerous animals that Hollywood has not overexaggerated. It is equipped with two sharp, spatulalike front teeth that stick out and are perfect for lifting a piece of skin enough to cause bleeding. Vampires are also equipped with an anesthetic in their saliva that numbs the cut so that it can't be felt. With the aid of these very special adaptations, the victim usually feels nothing. Although indigenous people in the Amazon say that the bat flaps its wings while it is drinking blood so you can't feel it. More often, the blood from the wound drips onto a leaf or on the ground and the bat flies down and then laps it up with its tongue, like a dog laps water from a bowl.

Vampires seem to be less afraid than other bats, and they seem to be able to think. When I peered in the cave, the bats didn't panic. Several dropped off the rocky ceiling to the floor like apples falling from a tree. One tried to get past me by running on the tip of its wing one way and then the other. Another flew right at me and tried to take a bite.

I knew I had to find another place for shelter. In many South and Central American countries, vampire bats carry rabies without showing the effects themselves, and they can infect other animals. If you are bitten you can't take any chances. I now had to figure out, as quickly as possible, where to build a place to sleep that would block the wind and ensure that I wouldn't be fed on by the bats. Their cave was only a few feet away from the only other site I could find that was protected. Even though I had frightened all of the other living things off the island when I came ashore, I was pretty sure the bats wouldn't feed on me. They were supposed to be "host specific," and were not likely to change their routine to feed on an unfamiliar species. Just in case I built a rock shelter.

Luckily the rubble at the base of the cliff was volcanic and columnar in shape. It was stackable, and by dark I had constructed a fairly tight fortress. Just at the moment when I finally bedded down with my sleeping bags, the fur seal colony suddenly returned. I was barely able to see their shapes in the moonlight, but above the howl of the wind I could hear their barks and calls. The rocks that I had to lie on reeked of bird droppings. I had to wait until it was dark before I could go out to set up the trap.

Earlier, on the way back from the beach, I had noticed that a couple of condors were roosting on the cliff not far from the cave. Below them was a large bull seal, so sick or weak he was barely able to reach the water with the others. He was probably the object of the condor's interest. The wounded bull was of interest to me also. As soon as it was dark but still light enough to see his silhouette, I planned to leave my shelter, shoot him with my .30-06 rifle, and use his carcass as bait for the trap instead of the few fish I had brought.

With binoculars, I could see he had been badly cut. The wounded bull may have been in a fight or attacked by a shark. A few minutes later as I crept out into the open and lifted the rifle to my eye, thinking the seals wouldn't spot me, suddenly and with a lot of noise, they all headed for the water. I misjudged their ability to see in the dark. Later, when I thought more about it I realized that their eyesight is well adapted for seeing in dim light underwater. It's no wonder that they left the beach as soon as I stood up. Only the old bull was still there. He didn't seem to move.

Then the fun began. As I approached the bull in the darkness, I realized that he was dead and much larger than I thought. He probably weighed over five hundred pounds and would be hard to move to the trap site. Then, above the noise of the wind I heard a strange *swishing* sound. In the dim light of the flashlight that was hanging from my belt, I saw movement. A vampire bat fed from a vein on the seal's flipper; another licked blood from around the wound. The noise was the flapping wings of a dozen other bats that either hovered over the carcass or landed on cobblestones. All were after blood.

For a while I hesitated, but I knew that I had to somehow move the dead seal a distance of at least a hundred feet to the trap site or my mission would fail. He was too heavy to drag so I rolled him over, using his flipper as a lever. It was dark and the work was slow going. I noticed one bat tried to stay on for the ride. The bat showed no fear of me. It was halfway through the night before I finished setting up the cannon-net trap. I armed the two cannons with shotgun shells and ran the electrical detonator wire to the blind. Then, I crawled into my sleeping bag cover, zipped everything up except a hole for my nose and hoped for the best.

The next morning at daybreak, after little sleep, I awoke to what I thought was another world. Mist, fog, and spray obscured the island and the trap. For a few seconds I didn't know where I was. Then I realized that I was in the middle of the Pacific Ocean's Humboldt Current on an island that had not changed in thousands of years. Its unique ecosystem with vampire bats, seals, and condors flying around was a scene out of the Pleistocene epoch. For a while I was transported back in time and a little spooked, until I realized that I was there to trap and tag condors.

Two condors were perched on the cliff above me. A few others soared over the island from the direction of the mainland. The bats were in their cave, but the wind had blown the net out of position over the seal carcass so the condors were suspicious. Only a turkey vulture landed near the net but couldn't rip open the seal's skin. That was a job for the condor.

The next day, after much effort, I finally trapped a condor, put on a tag, released it, and documented the operation on film. Part of my mission was done.

At the time, no one knew that vampire bats lived on islands off the coast of Peru. They're normally found in forests or the adjacent savannas where livestock is prevalent, not in high mountains or deserts. The Zárate vampires were probably a remnant population that followed the movements of the seal colonies after human activity destroyed the vegetation growing along the coast and turned the land into a desert.

I wasn't able to film the vampires feeding on the flippers of the seals, but a film crew heard about my discovery and visited Zárate later with a bigger boat. They brought lights and sophisticated cameras. The vampires were still there and probably still are there today. The flippers of the fur seals provided a sustainable source of food for the bats.

Much later, the vampires, the fur seals, and condors were featured in a spectacular segment for a PBS documentary called *Land of the Condor*. No one mentioned that I and the Explorers Research Corporation had been there first.

One more thing: the fisherman left me on Zárate for five days.

• • •

Jim Fowler is one of the world's best-known naturalists. For more than thirty-five years, he appeared on the television show *Mutual of Omaha's Wild Kingdom*. In addition, Fowler was the official wildlife correspondent for NBC's *The Today Show* and was regularly seen on *The Tonight Show* with Johnny Carson. He is an honorary president of The Explorers Club and in 2003 was the recipient of the Charles Lindbergh Award for his dedication to wildlife preservation and educating the public on the importance of wildlife.

Chapter 34

A Treetop Walk

EDWARD BURGESS

I walked quickly down the dark trail, anxious to see what the Peruvian jungle had to offer that day. Not long after setting out from the nearby field station, I almost slipped off the narrow log bridge as my thoughts drifted to Blue Morpho butterflies and rare hoatzins. These were just a few of the stunning creatures spotted on yesterday afternoon's boat journey up the Amazon River. The air around me was moist and the ground saturated after a newly fallen rain. Leaf-cutter ants paraded up and down the trunk of a nearby tree. Finally, I reached my destination: platform number one. Fourteen of these canopy research platforms were in place at the Amazon Conservatory for Tropical Studies, connecting the treetops via a series of swaying walkways. The mile-long structure served not only as a research tool for scientists wishing to study the forest canopy, but also as a stop for ecotourists looking for a new way to view the jungle. Though I had been helping out with the scientific research for most of the expedition, this afternoon I took some time off to take in the sights and sounds of the majestic tropical rain forest.

As I climbed into the canopy, my surroundings brightened. On the ground, foliage blocks most of the light, and activity is subdued, but up high in the treetops, objects are illuminated and active. In a sense, two forests exist. The cool, damp understory is home to an entirely different set of species as compared to the hot, windswept desert of the canopy one hundred fifty feet above the ground. This layered structure of the rain forest adds levels of complexity not seen in temperate regions and leads to a vast abundance of ecological mysteries in the tropics. In truth I could have spent years studying the intricacies present in those few trees.

Despite the urge to linger for a while, I kept moving so that I could enjoy the rest of the canopy walkway alone before a tour group arrived. Solitary observation always yields better results than observation with a noisy group. I was hoping to add a few more tropical birds to my life list but had not yet seen any ornithological activity. Rain forest birds are normally shy during the lull of the late afternoon, as their peak of activity occurs in early morning. Suddenly a peculiar brown shape glided over my head and landed on a mossy branch. The bird itself was not so extraordinary—its average size and drab coat were not uncommon—but it had the longest bill I had ever seen! The narrow bill curved so sharply that the bird could have easily scratched its belly. I fumbled for my field guide as the curious animal crept along the limb. Unfortunately, the bird noticed my commotion. When I looked up, the creature had taken flight and left me once again alone. I thought hard to remember exactly what it looked like for identification. Finally, I settled on the Red-billed Scythebill, a new discovery for my life list and perhaps even for the field station.

After that sighting, I noticed more activity as the crepuscular animals emerged to take advantage of the day's last light. Parakeets of all colors chattered in another tree. Myriad insect shapes darted past my face. The clicking of castanet frogs resonated through the understory beneath me. Hummingbirds sipped nectar while suspended by their ghostlike wings. I saw a variety of exotic species that afternoon, but for some reason the Scythebill amazed me the most. I could not stop thinking about its bill. What purpose did that unique apparatus serve and how had it evolved to be that way? As the bridge swayed slightly in the breeze, I contemplated how lucky I was to be in the canopy at that moment. Indeed the most rewarding moments in exploration come from unexpected discoveries like this one. If I had not been there at that exact instant, I never would have spotted the bird. How many other remarkable birds was I missing? What rare and wonderful new species existed in the fragile green sea of treetops along the horizon? Sadly I never got a chance to answer these questions as I soon heard shouts from a tour group on the trail below. The abundance of life dissipated as the crowd drew nearer. Probably the noisy group would not experience the same excitement I had felt during my quiet observations. I felt sad for any people who can't take the time to carefully appreciate the wonders of nature. They are missing one of life's best treasures.

* * *

Edward Burgess was born on a sheep station in the outback of Australia. He has had his ears bitten by rosellas in the jungles of Australia and slept with tarantulas in the tropical forests of South America. He is a student member of The Explorers Club and attends Princeton University, majoring in environmental chemistry. He hopes to undertake research on climate change someday in graduate school, as well as continue to explore the world's extreme environments, including the treetops.

Chapter 35

Elixir of the Spirit

ROBERT "RIO" HAHN

When the research vessel *Heraclitus* entered the mouth of the Amazon River in early 1980, it took its first step onto the stage of world-historical expeditions. The largest freshwater river in the world, the Amazon enters the South Atlantic Ocean at Belém, Brazil. Home to the largest rain forest on the planet, the Amazon has given humanity a wide variety of useful plants, ranging from rubber for our automobile tires to medicines that save our lives. Any excursion into this unparalleled world of biodiversity offers endless opportunities for exploration. In addition, the Amazon offers tools to those interested in pursuing their own inner exploration in tandem with their investigation of a world filled with a still unknown array of life-forms.

Our expedition sailed halfway around the world. We motored twenty-two hundred miles up the Amazon River and then found ourselves at an impasse. Our ship required immediate repair and the crew was exhausted from the relentless push upriver. However, even after repairing our ship and basking in the lugubrious effect of powerful Amazonian drinks containing some of the plants and herbs we were sent to research, which aided our rest, we still found ourselves psychologically and spiritually aground. How we recovered and achieved our aim heralded our entry into this magical world.

As scientific chief, principal organizer, and the person responsible for the Institute of Ecotechnics Amazon Expedition, I was to lead the expedition toward its ultimate goal of contacting and working with the Amazonian shamans who hold the keys to the secrets of the rain forest. Richard Evans Schultes, director of the Harvard Botanical Museum and revered as the father of modern ethnobotany, inspired our expedition in 1979 during a speech at the Institute of Ecotechnics Jungle Conference in Penang, Malaysia. Schultes viewed the Amazon as an emporium of chemicals, most of which will probably remain unknown to humanity. During his fourteen years in the Amazon, which yielded an unparalleled body of research, he became not only the world's expert on rubber but also an initiate shaman with knowledge of a wide range of psychoactive plants. He had recently led a laboratory-based expedition to the Peruvian Amazon aboard the research vessel *Alpha Helix*. Looking at our vessel anchored outside the conference hall, he challenged us to carry on where his expedition had stopped.

We accepted his challenge and the following year we sailed *Heraclitus*, an eighty-two-foot, one-hundred-twenty-ton, ferro-cement, junk-rigged, motor-auxiliary sailing vessel from Penang, Malaysia, to the mouth of the Amazon River. The ship was built in 1975. It was designed for both ocean and river cruising. Now, five years after its launch, the *Heraclitus* faced its first test as a river vessel with the king of rivers.

En route to the Amazon we paused in France. With the assistance of Bo Holmstedt, of the Karolinska Institute in Sweden, and Laurent Rivier, of the University of Lausanne, we installed a photochemical laboratory on board that would enable us to make extractions of fresh plant material for later analysis. Lacking field laboratory facilities, most field researchers are forced to bring home dried plant specimens for analysis, which often lose potency or undergo chemical alteration. Following Schultes's work with the *Alpha Helix* from Scripps Institution of Oceanography, we were reputed to be only the third laboratory-equipped ship to venture up the Amazon—another research ship had sunk in the river.

In 1980 botanical research permits were almost impossible to obtain for sanctioned work in the Amazon. After months of advance work and traveling to Brazil, Peru, Colombia, and Ecuador, I managed to negotiate research *convenios* (permits) with the Universidad de Lima, which would allow us to make plant collections in Peru and take botanical voucher specimens and laboratory plant extracts out of the country. We later shared our plant collections with herbaria in Peru, the Missouri Botanical Garden, the New York Botanical Garden, and the Royal Botanic Gardens, Kew.

After the long ocean voyage from Penang, we were anxious to get into the field. Rather than spend additional time waiting for permits from Brazil, we decided to make our way upriver to Peru, where we could immediately begin work. Regardless, we faced a long voyage through the Brazilian section of the Amazon. The Brazilian Navy placed an officer on board to assist us in our passage. He helped us navigate around the constantly changing and nearly invisible sandbars that threatened to ground the *Heraclitus*, and also ensured that we went ashore only long enough to obtain fresh food, water, and fuel, lest we be tempted to do fieldwork along the way.

During our transit of the lower Amazon, we were beset by dust storms that resulted from the clear-cutting of the forest. The cutting was in full swing at that time and made way for cattle farming and the accompanying ecologically disastrous effects. Efforts to turn the Amazon rain forests into agricultural land were doomed to failure. Once the forest is cut down, the lateritic soils lose their fertility and are washed into the Amazon where they are lost forever in the ocean.

Without permits for research work in Brazil, we had to push our way upriver. The voyage was not the *tranquillo* river trip the crew expected. For nearly a month, we fought the constant downstream current, a dawn-to-dusk effort that put both crew and ship under constant stress. In our first encounter with Amazonian river water, which unlike the clear blue water of the deep ocean is laden with silt and fine sand, we learned to deal with new mechanical problems. The impeller in our engine room bilge pump had to be replaced several times during the journey upriver. We now faced a problem of much greater proportions.

The propeller shaft bearing, which had a hard rubber inner surface pressed against the stainless steel propeller shaft that kept water out of the ship, was damaged during the voyage upriver. It was scoured smooth by the silt and sand in the cloudy river water and no longer prevented water from entering the engine room. To replace the bearing, we had to lift the ship out of the water, high enough for the bearing to clear the surface of the water, so it could be safely replaced. Finding a dry dock in the Amazon, let alone one capable of lifting a one-hundred-twenty-ton ship was not going to be easy. Our only possibility was to continue upriver to Iquitos, Peru.

We left Brazil behind at the small border town of Tabatinga, where the Brazilian Navy officer bid us a bittersweet farewell. Despite the stress of the voyage, we had all enjoyed a most adventurous passage and became friends. Our location was at the point in the Amazon where Brazil, Columbia, and Peru converge. The town of Tabatinga is separated from the city of Leticia, Columbia, by a line in the road, and the outpost of Ramón Castilla, the port of entry for Peru, lay across the river.

It was now late 1980, before political upheavals created a threat to travel in the region, before tourist agencies booked visits to Indian shamans, even before Jacques Cousteau ventured up the river. It was a time of genuine hospitality along the Amazon. The cocaine trade had generated new wealth. Instant global communication did not yet exist. For good or ill, local officials wielded their power largely without oversight. In the Amazon, how the officials exercised their power depended on how effective one was at making friends with them.

Once we convinced the Leticia cocaine chiefs that our laboratory-equipped vessel, which had a black hull and red deck and looked like a pirate ship, presented no threat to their business, we were able to rest and enjoy the hospitality of the local people. Once rested, we continued our push upriver to Iquitos against the strong head currents of the Amazon. Iquitos is the largest city on the upper Amazon. We planned to use it as our base to repair the *Heraclitus* and to begin our ethnobotanical fieldwork.

We located a floating dry dock on the Rio Nanay, a small tributary near Iquitos. The dry dock belonged to the Peruvian Navy. The head of the base was sympathetic to our plight and permitted us to use the navy facility, the only dry dock on the upper Amazon capable of lifting the *Heraclitus*. During the course of our repair, we became friends. One beautiful Amazonian evening, on my way to give a slide show to the members of the base, disaster struck. A twin-engine pontoon plane belonging to Grupo 42 of the Peruvian Air Force sank after landing. The passengers safely escaped, but the plane and its valuable observational gear lay at the bottom of a tributary about an hour by speedboat from the base. Besides the value of the plane, the Peruvians needed their observational equipment to monitor their border with Ecuador, which was the scene of ongoing conflicts at the time.

I canceled the slide show. Our captain, Jason Baer, and I fitted the navy's boat with a battery and spotlight and we departed by speedboat to inspect the scene. The aircrew had cleverly tied a line with a buoy to the plane before it sank, and we had a marker on the surface to locate the wreck. The squadron tried to keep the plane from sinking by holding it up with a Russian helicopter and dragging it to more shallow water, but the attempt failed.

We had the only scuba diving equipment in this part of the Amazon and offered to dive down to the plane the following day. The plan was to take the wing covers off in order to expose the plane's lifting eyes and attach wire ropes to them so that a floating crane could lift the plane out of the water. Our ship's repairs were also in full swing at the time. In order to accommodate my need to be in both places on the same day, the Peruvian Air Force provided a two-person single-propeller plane to fly me between its base and the navy dry dock.

Jason and I suited up, strapped on our air tanks, and descended into the murky water using the marker buoy and line as a guide. We had not anticipated the lack of visibility created by the river water. At times we could hardly see our hands against our face masks. The shifting current helped clear the water, and eventually we accomplished our task of exposing the lifting eyes and attaching the wire ropes. The plane was safely lifted out of the river and deposited on dry land. The mechanics and engineers at the base fully repaired the plane in a matter of weeks, in time for their commander's birthday party, which took place on the runway.

For our efforts, the commander treated our entire ship's crew to a celebratory dinner at the Chinese restaurant in Iquitos, the place of choice for special events. He also offered us air transport to any part of the region serviced by his group. We were considering an expedition to the Putumayo River in Columbia, infamous from the days of the rubber boom when rubber traders would cut off the hands of Indians who failed to gather their daily quota of rubber. I accepted the commander's offer to make a reconnaissance mission to the river.

When we began to board the pontoon plane, I realized this was not going to be a conventional flight. The copilot climbed into his seat, followed by his girlfriend who strapped in on his lap. The pilot, instead of putting on radio headphones as he prepared to take off, put on headphones connected to his Walkman. Luckily, we cleared the treetops, unlike the plane that had sunk in the river, and landed safely on the Putumayo.

I didn't have the time to spend a week on the Putumayo waiting for the return flight, so I made my expedition evaluation while the crew took a break. I had several hours to explore the local area. It quickly became clear that the logistical difficulties of mounting an expedition to the Putumayo by ship were impossible because there was no water passage from the Amazon to the Putumayo capable of handling a ship the size of ours.

About a month later, having completed the ship's repairs, we returned to the main Amazon waterway, just ahead of the falling river. The rains had come to their seasonal end, and the Nanay tributary dropped some twenty feet in the space of a few days. The lack of rain did not present a problem for us. Unlike many ships on the Amazon, including oceangoing cruise vessels as far upriver as Iquitos, we did not lack for freshwater. When we first entered the Amazon, we stored most of our sails and rigging in Belém at the mouth of the river. From the remainder of the sail equipment, we fabricated a rain catchment system that fed freshwater directly into our tanks, which were now full.

We were in better physical condition to carry on the expedition, but we had not yet managed to revive our spirits and reinvigorate our expedition's objective of contacting and working with local shamans. Our expedition adviser and Institute of Ecotechnics total systems consultant, John Allen, recalled that when Alexander the Great and his troops reached a similar hiatus in their campaigns, they got rip-roaring drunk, slept it off, and then decided which direction they would next march in.

I decided to try Alexander's technique. A bottle of Captain Morgan Rum was secured from the captain's locker, and with John by my side, I planted myself in the center of the large central room of the *Heralcitus*. All the crew members had to pass by me as they moved around the ship. I started drinking in the late morning. By lunchtime, I had emptied the entire bottle of rum. Needless to say, the fine rum put me in an uninhibited state of consciousness. The poor souls who entered the room found themselves subject to my comments, including unedited personal observations. By late afternoon I collapsed in my bunk, to which the crew, thankfully, had secured a bucket. I only had to move a few inches to safely empty my stomach. By dinnertime I was up and eating, having survived an experience that I have since allocated to those singular experiences of life.

The next morning, fully recovered physically, I also recovered my resolve to resume the expedition. We returned to the river town of Pevas, the location where Schultes had been forced to abandon his fieldwork with the Bora and Witoto Indians. In contrast to Schultes's crew, who after a stay of several weeks in Pevas, having consumed the available beer and partied with the available women, insisted that his expedition move on, the *Heraclitus* crew both sailed and carried out fieldwork. But it was not all work. Upon our arrival, we attended a feast and dance in our honor given by our new friends in Pevas.

Then we were faced with a new obstacle. The Indian shamans and the people who inhabit the rain forest—and the forest itself—had not given us permission to enter their sacred world and partake of their secrets. The shamans served as the gatekeepers to this region, inhabited not just by the Amazonian Indians but by their spirit allies, powerful fauna, some largely unknown, ranging from the fantastic to the deadly. To test the purity of our motives and see the substance of our subconscious, our expedition botanist, Robyn Tredwell, and I were taken to an *ayahuascero* (shaman) by the director of the neighboring herbarium, Franklin Ayala, who had local jurisdiction over our research *convenios*.

Early one evening, Franklin led us through a remote part of Iquitos, to a tin shack whose front door opened onto a dirt back street. Soon we found ourselves in an Amazonian-style doctor's waiting room. Illuminated by a single bare lightbulb hung from the ceiling by its electric wire, the small room had simple wooden benches and a dirt floor. Women with babies, seated on wooden benches, waited to be seen by the shaman, who could treat ills of the body and spirit, which were considered to be interconnected and therefore required simultaneous treatment.

The shaman, an older, slightly stooped man, dressed simply in old pants, a plain T-shirt, and baseball cap, took an old wine bottle from a rickety wooden wall shelf. It was filled with the extraordinary brown liquid known as ayahuasca, variously called *caapi* or *yaje*. Each shaman has his own special recipe for the substance that is made from the hallucinogenic liana *Banisteriopsis caapi*, considered the most important of the many sacred plants used by the shamans of the northwest Amazon, and a variety of other plants.

In their book, *Vine of the Soul* (Synergetic Press, 2004), Schultes and phytochemist Robert Raffauf, with whom I later developed a plant field-test kit based on our Amazon work, translated the Ketchwa word ayahuasca, the most commonly used name for this hallucinogenic brew, as "vine of the soul." Schultes and Raffauf chose the word "soul" even though the Indians do not themselves use a concept of soul. The authors considered that ethnologists and anthropologists might find terms such as *vine of vision, vine of insight, vine of wisdom,* or *vine of enlightenment* more appropriate, but they felt, as they wrote in their book,

> *none of these, in our opinion, convey to the general reader the importance of this vine to Indian culture. They do not so effectively describe the other-worldly experiences in which these Indians believe they can communicate through visual and auditory hallucinations with the*

> *supernatural world, the spirits of the ancestors, the plants, animals and the mythological beings of this vast region as does* vine of the soul.

My own experience of ayahuasca supports this interpretation. I shared first-hand with the Indians their otherworldly experience induced by ayahuasca, in which communication with the supernatural world is possible. Indeed, ancestral spirits, plant and animal spirits, and mythological beings of the region come to life during an ayahuasca journey. Through contact with them during my journey, I gained an understanding of the rain forest world that a lifetime of academic study could not match.

The shaman poured a large, full glass of ayahuasca and gave it to me to drink. When I later recounted this story to the writer William S. Burroughs, who also partook of ayahuasca in the Amazon, he told me the dose was large enough to have killed me. Clearly, the protectors of the forest intended to test my subconscious, if not every fiber of my being, before permitting our expedition to proceed.

I forced myself to drink the entire glass of a vile-tasting liquid. After consuming the drink, Robyn, who was given less than a quarter of the dose I received, and I were directed to an open-air enclosed yard behind the shed, with benches partially covered by a thatched roof. Several men who had just consumed ayahuasca were seated on the benches. Periodically, the shaman attended to the men.

Soon my body felt as if a two-hundred-twenty-volt current was pulsating through my nervous system. In my mind's eye, I was in the center of a large blinding light. Like most initiates, I couldn't keep the liquid down and began to regurgitate on the ground. Instead of seeing green liquid pouring out of my mouth, what I saw was liquid fire. The liquid fire flowed freely out of my mouth and continued in an unbroken stream to the ground where it spread and formed a puddle of fire.

The experience did not feel illusory or hallucinatory. Indeed, it felt more real than anything I had ever experienced. The fire of my soul spread out before me, illuminating everything and everyone around me. The forest became alive, spoke to me, and in an instant I understood its plight. A jaguar, calling to me, crossed the back of the yard, calling me to follow it on a journey through the Amazon rain forest.

The shaman directed me to lie on the bench before him. He blew smoke over me and chanted in order to remove spirits from my stomach that had recently caused me abdominal pain. His melodious chants helped my spirit adjust to this new world. The chants sounded like the Tibetan language to a Tibetan friend of mine, who later listened to my recording of the session.

After I survived the shaman's medicine and the investigation of my subconscious, Ayala was convinced our research intentions were genuine. We were free to proceed. The effect of this experience was transformative. It changed my life in ways I am still discovering.

One lasting change was that I became known by the sobriquet "Rio." A sobriquet is different from a nickname; a sobriquet is bestowed upon a person in recognition of some accomplishment. After the ayahuasca, I proved my new connection with the rain forest by navigating the main course of the Amazon at night in a small wooden boat. I found the *Heraclitus* in an unknown location and arrived just before a tremendous storm turned the river into a deadly turmoil of wind and wave. Traveling on the river at night is an extremely dangerous undertaking because of the submerged floating logs that threaten to sink any watercraft, especially a wood-bottomed boat. Had we hit a log, in all likelihood my companion, whom I was bringing to the ship, and I would have drowned.

A phrase borrowed from participants of the annual Burning Man arts festival that started in 1986 at Baker Beach in San Francisco best describes the effect of ayahuasca on my life. "Build a man a fire, and you keep him warm for the night," goes the saying. "Light a man on fire, and you keep him warm for the rest of his life." The fire of ayahuasca that flowed from my mouth has kept me warm ever since. My ayahuasca experience restructured my values and elevated the importance of my inner life over consuming external demands. As a result of this qualitative change, I strive to transform external reality, to bring reality nearer to the heart's desire.

Physically and spiritually renewed, we moved the *Heraclitus* downriver and moored next to the town of Pevas on the Rio Ampiyacu, a small tributary off the main course of the Amazon River. We continued Schultes's work there and made contact with a number of local shamans, including Pablo, a shaman whose name had been given to us by Schultes. Pablo, still relatively young at the time, had already gained a deep knowledge of medicinal plants from his father, who had recently passed away.

With Pablo as our guide, Robyn; her assistant, Jeannie; and I motored our small boat up the shallow Rio Ampiyacu. We penetrated deep into the rain forest to the pristine village of Brionuevo, the home of Pablo's second family. Pablo opened the forest to us. We collected medicinal plants. Robyn and Jeannie pressed the plants into botanical specimens. I made field-laboratory extractions of fresh plant material to be analyzed later using advanced laboratory techniques.

The village chief, after observing us for a number of days, invited us to participate in one of the village's three annual dances that celebrate different agricultural periods of the year. The dances serve as a means of transmitting tribal knowledge and history. The men helped me gather and carve a dancing stick. Each of us was given a mouthful of coca, which helped provide energy for the twenty-four-hour dance. It was exhilarating.

After the festival, we made our way back downriver. As we motored back toward the modern world, Pablo told us about his experience as an apprentice in plant lore, an experience that had all but ceased to exist. When I first set sail for the Amazon, I considered the extinction of plant species as the most pressing danger threatening the rain forest. However, Pablo's story made it clear that while plant extinction was real and immediate, the death of a single shaman who had no apprentice was a catastrophic loss. With each shaman's death, a lifetime's knowledge of the rain forest's beauty and power was lost forever.

* * *

Robert "Rio" Hahn is a director of The Explorers Club, a fellow of the Royal Geographical Society, president of Tropic Seas Research, Inc., and a founding director of the Institute of Ecotechnics. The recipient of five Explorers Clubs flags, Hahn is a licensed sea captain, an open-water diver, and a titled high chief of Western Samoa. In addition to his research in the Amazon, his expeditions include a three-year circumnavigation and a shamanic initiation in Nepal. A photographer, filmmaker, entrepreneur, and real estate investor, he coinitiated the Biosphere 2 project and operates OrganicAvos.com, an organic avocado farm in Bonsall, California, where he resides.

Chapter 36

Exploring Easter Island with Thor Heyerdahl

JOHN LORET

It was the fall of 1954 and I was a graduate student at the University of Oslo, Norway. I wanted to escape the cold, dark rain season in Norway so I asked to be sent to the Canary Islands to collect algae specimens while skin-diving into undersea caves along the coast. I flew from Oslo to the city of Las Palmas on the island of Grand Canary. Outside the city I set up camp on the beach at a beautiful site. On the second day, while diving in the sea, children stole my tent, money, stove, and equipment. All that I had left were the clothes, sneakers, and skin-diving equipment I'd used for the dive. Before I left Oslo, a professor mentioned to me that Thor Heyerdahl, the famed Norwegian ethnographer and explorer, was staying at the Hotel Santa Catalina in Las Palmas with his wife, Yvonne, and new baby girl, Annette.

Since his remarkable expedition on the Kon-Tiki raft in 1947, Heyerdahl and his crew were my heroes. His 101-day, forty-three-hundred-mile journey across the Pacific Ocean on small rafts made of balsa wood and other native materials showed that prehistoric peoples could have traveled from South America. Not having any friends or contacts in Las Palmas, I decided to seek help from Heyerdahl. As I approached the lobby of the hotel, I felt apprehensive. I called the great explorer's room and was told to wait in the lobby. Soon, he came downstairs. He was a tall, gentle, and soft-spoken man, with the bluest eyes I had ever seen. He listened quietly to all I had to say. He was interested in my work with the university and asked if he could go out with me to dive. After lunch he provided me with sufficient funds to rent a small room in town.

When we went out to make our dive, the boatman was careful not to come too close to the breaking waves. The lava caves along the wall of land extended into the sea. Thor and I put on our snorkel gear. I had my net bag with collecting vials as well as my Leica camera mounted in a waterproof metal housing. I dove down about thirty-five feet into a cave and scraped the algae off the cave ceiling. I labeled the vial with a wax pencil and placed it in my net bag. When we surfaced, a seven-foot whitetip shark came up close to us. The boatman was worried and started speaking frantically in Spanish. Thor and I dove underwater, swam up close to the shark that then turned and swam away. I managed to take its picture while it was still in view. Later Thor told me that this was the first encounter he had had with a shark underwater.

The following summer, I was working in Austria for the U.S. occupation forces. My assignment was to set up a camp in the mountains for the children of U.S. troops stationed there. However, a week before camp was to open, Austria received its independence. All U.S. troops were evacuated. Suddenly, I was out of a job.

One evening I read in the newspaper that Thor was planning a new archaeological expedition for Easter Island. The expedition was scheduled to start in September and to last ten months. This was my chance! My work at the university could wait. I telephoned Thor in Oslo to ask if there was a position for me. He told me there was an opening for a seaman and diver. He said that with my biology background I could also assist the expedition surgeon in emergencies.

The ship selected for the expedition was a one-hundred-fifty-foot trawler, a strong, well-equipped, seaworthy-enough vessel for anything the ocean could muster. It was named the *Christian Bjeland*, and was built to work in the seas off Greenland. His Royal Highness Crown Prince Olav (later King Olav) of Norway agreed to be the patron of the expedition. On a rainy day in September, the future king came aboard to meet the crew and wish us all well. We soon set sail across the Atlantic and into the Caribbean to Cristóbal,

Panama. While en route, we sailed directly into Hurricane Carol. For days the crew sat on their heels. No meals were cooked and many men were seasick, but the *Christian Bjeland* rode the storm without difficulty.

At Cristóbal we took aboard new supplies and mail. With the mail came a package from my mother containing a set of blue-and-white-striped pajamas. I'd never worn pajamas in my life, but I held on to them, thinking that perhaps I could trade them with the islanders. In Cristóbal, Thor; his wife, Yvonne; and daughter, Annette, joined us; along with scientists William Mulloy, Carlyle Smith, Edwin Ferdon from the United States, Anne Skjolsvald from Norway, and Gonzalo Figueroa from Chile.

Soon, we passed through the Panama Canal and set our course for the Galapagos Islands. Finally, I had the opportunity to try our new diving gear, the Scott Hydro Pack with two seventy-two-cubic-foot tanks. I used the Norwegian Viking dry suit. The sea was full of life everywhere—groupers, snappers, jacks, sea lions, marine iguanas, even the giant manta ray. The dive was interesting, almost like diving in an enormous aquarium.

After Galapagos, we then set our course for the uninhabited island of Sala y Gómez, located six hundred miles east of Easter Island. The island's rocky coastline and heavy seas made it difficult to land a boat. The captain and first mate lashed a raft together with two aluminum pontoons and timbers. The raft was put overboard. With a sextant and chronometer, the captain and I went aboard and began rowing toward shore. Our raft was secured with a long line to the ship. As we came close to shore, I jumped overboard with snorkel gear to guide the raft between rocks and coral heads. The water was alive with fish. I swam alongside the raft and saw sharks, rays, butterfly fish, tangs, and many other forms of life. The captain took his bearings and we returned to the ship.

It was late afternoon in October 1955 as we quietly sailed into Hotuiti, a small cove located on the southeastern corner of Easter Island. The massive Poike Peninsula was off to starboard. We anchored, but the captain was not happy with the bottom. Unfortunately, there are very few good anchorages off Easter Island where most of the surrounding sea bottom is rocky. Where there is sand and a clear bottom, there are coral heads. If a captain anchors in clear sand, the ship moves and the anchor chain snags around the coral heads. In addition, the constantly changing wind makes it difficult for a vessel to find a safe anchorage under a lee shore. As the diver for the expedition, I anticipated that my work for the future would be to untangle anchor chain in order to free anchors. This we had to do on several occasions.

From the deck of the ship we could see the giant statues that are famous the world over standing along the slopes of the volcanic crater of Rano Raraku. That evening native male visitors came aboard to trade. They hid wood carvings under their clothing. After some trading, one of our visitors played the guitar. He played music while other men sang along. Then we all began to dance.

In the morning we weighed anchor and sailed around the island. The north side of the island was the calmest while the southern shore had the heaviest surf. The southern coast of Easter Island is the most exposed to the Antarctic Ocean. There were no trees except for a few scattered eucalyptus as we approached the village of Hanga Roa. Eucalyptus trees were probably imported from Australia because of their fast growth. Unfortunately, the eucalyptus drains the soil of all moisture, leaving the soil barren. Today there are large stands of these trees in many locations on the island. In the 1960s a large grove of coconut palms were also planted at Anakena beach.

We selected Easter Island's only beach to establish a campsite. It was a beautiful sandy area on the north side of the island. Small two-man tents for the crew and scientists were set up. The tents had cots and were quite comfortable. A large dining tent was used for eating and recreation. In our off hours, we read, listened to music, and had lively conversations.

Soon, we met Father Sebastian, a Catholic priest from Austria who was a Capuchin, a branch of the Franciscans that adheres strictly to the order's rule. Father Sebastian had been on Easter Island for twenty-five years and planned to remain there until his death. He had written a book on Easter Island, as well as a dictionary of the native Rapa Nui language. He could speak to the natives in their own language and was fluent in English, Spanish, French, and German. Easily the most powerful man on the island, Father Sebastian loved the native people. One day Father Sebastian came up to me and said, "Loret. That's a Christian name." We talked for a while. Then, he asked if I would be interested in helping him serve Mass. I told him that I had forgotten most of my Latin. "We will take care of that," he said. "I'll talk to Heyerdahl." And then the priest was gone.

Later that evening, Thor approached me and said it would help the expedition if I worked with Father Sebastian. I was assigned to work during the week at Te Pito Kura in La Pérouse Bay. But Thor asked me to ride into Hanga Roa and stay with Father Sebastian on Saturday and Sunday. He gave me a bottle of Johnny Walker scotch for Father Sebastian, who liked Scottish whiskey.

On our first evening together, after a wonderful dinner of chicken, Father Sebastian brought out two glasses and poured out the scotch. Until the bottle was empty, we talked about many things: conditions in Europe, as well as life on Easter Island. According to the rules of his order, the priest had to fast after midnight so we went to bed shortly before then. About 6:00 a.m. the roosters crowed and Father Sebastian woke me up.

"We must say Mass first at the leper colony," he said. I had no idea there were lepers on Easter Island. I quickly dressed and followed Father Sebastian and three nuns to a neighborhood outside of town. There we met twenty or more lepers in various stages of the disease. Father Sebastian set up his altar on a table outdoors and began. I fumbled through the Latin. All of the lepers received Communion.

Then, we returned to town for the main Mass. The church was small but beautiful. The altar stood at the far end beneath a thatched roof. The sides and front of the church were completely open except for a small stone wall. Father Sebastian said Mass in Rapa Nui. The natives sang Rapa Nui songs. Birds, also singing, flew in and out of the church. It was one of the most beautiful scenes I can ever remember. Of all the negative things I've heard and read about missionaries, Father Sebastian was the exception. He loved the people and the people of the island selected him to negotiate terms for diggers who were to work with our expedition. Obviously, they trusted him.

We spent many months on Easter Island, exploring *moais*, monolithic statues along the coast believed to be ceremonial sites erected between 1400 and 1600. We crawled into caves, speared fish in the sea, scuba dived to recover anchors and sunken shipwrecks. I realized that I was learning so much from my work with the scientists that I did not regret postponing graduate school. In fact, the work on Thor's expedition made me briefly consider changing my chosen field of marine biology to archaeology. Eventually, however, I returned to complete my work at the University of Oslo and finished my PhD in environmental science.

Thor wanted to document the history of the natives and indeed there was a lot of mystery surrounding Easter Island. I found the most interesting part of my stay to be the interaction with the natives—making friends and exploring with them. The island population at that time was a bit over nine hundred. We traveled over the entire island on horseback. The locals had little of anything valuable except their wood carvings. When expedition members first set up camp, a native came to trade carvings. I traded my blue-striped pajamas—the ones my mother had sent to me—for a horse. Later, on a Sunday, I was shocked to see a native friend of mine walking to church dressed in my colorful pajamas. He thought they made a fine suit.

Many times while I was there I wondered what would happen to the aboriginal people of the island. In 1955 only one ship visited the island that year. With the exception of a few Europeans and Chileans, including the small naval garrison, the entire population was Easter Islanders. All spoke Rapa Nui, which was the native language; Spanish was the second language. The natives had a deep respect for their island and demonstrated great pride when we discovered a petroglyph, cave, or any artifact made by their ancestors.

At that time, most of the island was a sheep farm, pastoral and calm. But by 1963, the population had grown to over twenty-five hundred people, including many immigrants, mostly from Chile, Germany, and Scandinavia. In 1968 NASA, looking for an alternate landing field for the space shuttle in the South Pacific, constructed a huge landing field on Easter Island. The island now has hotels, restaurants, a bank, hospital, schools, bars, supermarkets, discotheques, an automobile service station, car rental agencies, and other vestiges of a modern economy. Tourism is now the island's main source of income. Tourists fly to the South American mainland or go on to the islands to the east such as Tahiti and Samoa. Small cargo vessels now visit the island four times a year and cruise ships come in several times a year. All of this growth had negatively affected the Easter Island people. Today Spanish and English are taught in schools; consequently less than 10 percent of the children can speak Rapa Nui. The friendly natives of 1955 are now too busy to take time to show visitors the island except for money.

The impact of increased tourism is one of the most critical problems affecting Easter Island today. The present boundaries of Easter Island National Park, a UNESCO World Heritage Site, covers about 40 percent of the island's surface area. These limits were established in 1976 and were fixed to encompass most of the monuments including moais, caves, quarries, ceremonial centers, rock paintings, and most of the estimated five thousand petroglyphs. But visitors indiscriminately climb over statues and walk on petroglyphs.

Still, there are reminders of our expedition. All these years later, the new, much larger church in town stands where Father Sebastian and I said Mass years before. It has walls, a metal roof. Today, no birds fly in and out of the sanctuary. The Mass is in Spanish, but the older natives still sing their Rapa Nui songs. Father Sebastian is buried in a grave on the south side of the new church, a powerful symbol of the island's legendary past.

• • •

John Loret is an oceanographer and past president of The Explorers Club. In 1947–48, aboard the icebreaker *East Wind* he set two Arctic records for circumnavigating Baffin Island and achieving the farthest north any boat had reached at that time. Loret has published in the fields of archaeology, aquaculture, maritime history, and the environment. This chapter is excerpted from *Easter Island*, edited by John Loret and John T. Tanacredi (Kluwer Academic/Plenum Publishers, 2003, pages 1–15), with kind permission of Springer Science and Business Media.

Chapter 37

Escape from Darién

CAMERON McPHERSON SMITH

Another big Pacific swell came up fast and silent, moonlight flashing on its face. Hurrying east, it lifted and then dropped our sixty-foot raft with the smooth motions of an elevator. I caught my stomach and adjusted a steering plank. The glowing compass revolved slowly as the raft pointed back on course. I marveled at how quickly the vessel responded, and in perfect measure.

But I didn't marvel for long. My mind was following that eastward-driving swell, thinking on where it would end up. I knew exactly where it would end up, but I didn't want to believe it. I knew that eight miles east the swell would rise and then curl and crash as luminescent foam on a dark, stony beach that cowered beneath thick jungle vegetation. I sensed the Darién out there, to my right, like the open jaws of a medieval hellmouth.

Darién. I said it softly aloud. "Darién." How many conquistadores' tales ended there? How many human disasters had that monstrous jungle hosted, like a grinning specter? How many old explorers' tales of the Darién had I read throughout my life, and had the jungle—like an enormous net—finally drawn me in?

I took a breath and told myself that none of that mattered. All that mattered now was the wind. If it gave up completely our raft would follow that swell and run aground on that beach. Nobody could help us. Our sailing raft, a replica of a native vessel encountered by Spaniards in 1526, was built of logs, rope, and canvas. We had no engine. Our radio took an hour to set up, and contact was intermittent. We were halfway up a two-hundred-mile stretch of primordial jungle that for five centuries had shrugged off every bloody club and every subtle wedge of civilization.

Manila rope creaked and clicked as the raft wallowed ahead. I looked up at the mainsail, a three-story-high triangle of dirty canvas glowing yellow from a kerosene lamp. The sail fluttered, barely tugging us along. If the wind died we'd have just a few hours before the swells drove us aground. I imagined six men scrambling in the dark to get clear of a heaving raft that weighed as much as a Sherman tank. The breakers would destroy the little bamboo deckhouse containing our supplies and the radio. And then what?

As another swell swiftly elevated the raft I focused on the turning compass like a warlock hunched over his seeing stone.

Hours later the stars winked out as the Earth rolled sunward. Dowar Medina, a fit Ecuadorian fisherman, was slipping on a T-shirt as he came out of the deckhouse. He inhaled deeply, smelling the jungle, and glanced at the scraps of vegetation floating in the water. He knew we were too close to shore, but he calmly put a hand on my shoulder.

"Todos OK?" he asked.

"No," I said, too quickly for grace and pointing at the barely inflated mainsail. All was not OK. "The wind is dying and we're too close to land." Dowar nodded absently and stepped back inside.

He returned with John Haslett, the mastermind of the expedition. John and Dowar had sailed this route three years before on a raft that was eventually devoured by shipworms. They'd landed in Panama after thirty-five days at sea. Now it was reassuring to see them coldly assessing the conditions together. John stood with his arms folded and his legs spread wide against the swells. He sucked his teeth and said, "This is no good," punching out the words as cold as ticker tape. "We've got to get offshore. If the wind gives up," he said, jabbing his thumb eastward, "we're done."

By noon all stood on deck, facing east. The wind had given up and the swells had driven us in. We were only three miles offshore. The entire eastern horizon was a billowing chaos of vegetation that roiled skyward, tier upon tier, like oil smoke. Here and there the greens were blurred gray by pockets of clinging mist.

Through my binoculars individual trees sharpened before swinging wildly away as the raft rolled. I looked up at the sails. They hung like great curtains. We were going in. Our charts weren't good enough to tell us where to drop our anchor. The desperate idea of letting it drag as we approached shore—in the hope of snagging rocks, sea grass, anything—rattled around my mind.

I imagined the pieces of a horrible puzzle sliding into position: the raft would run aground, spinning and heaving against a nameless, cobbled shore; we would escape with minimal gear and perhaps a quick SOS; we would be stranded in southern Darién where FARC guerrillas held dominion; nobody could risk a rescue attempt; we'd try to hack our way out, alone. Maybe some of us would make it.

It was an old story. Darién had a bad reputation. Since the conquistadors arrived in Panama in the early 1500s, expeditions had been swallowed up time and again. I imagined a legion of ghosts out there, rags of mist in the treetops.

Perhaps some of those mists were all that remained of a handful of Columbus's men; in 1502, on the Caribbean side of the jungle, they'd paddled up a river for wood and freshwater. They returned as arrow-pierced corpses floating downstream. Later, Balboa lost men by the score, forcing himself across the Isthmus of Panama for the first European glimpse of the Pacific. A little after that, seven hundred Spaniards died in a year out there, enfeebled by disease as their colony failed. It was the same gruesome dysentery fate that finally buckled a thousand Scots in their disastrous 1599 colonization effort. Even into the 1800s, Darién's appetite was sharp. In 1854 it took less than two months to reduce a disciplined American expedition crew to maggot-infested, crazed, and near cannibalistic survivors. And the jungle produced weird tales, like prospector Thaddeus O'Shea's ravings about having shot a ten-foot ape in the interior. Darién remained so impenetrable that a 1970 plan for a new Panama Canal seriously considered "nuclear excavation." The final solution to this entangling forest, it was said, was to blast it with civilization's most devastating weapons. The idea sounded less like an engineering plan than deep human frustration with Nature in the same days that men walked on the moon.

Not much has changed. In the late 1990s, the able adventurer Alvah Simon took on Darién against all advice. Clawing his way up a mere hill through grasping vegetation, he babbled into his video camera: "This has become something more than crazy, something that not anyone could call safe, or even prudent." He retreated not long after. More recently the Briton Karl Bushby successfully threaded the jungle from south to north, avoiding Colombian guerillas by disguising himself as a transient and clinging to a log that floated him, like Gollum, down the sluggish rivers.

Part of the Darién is a Panamanian national park now, but it's often closed. Panama doesn't have an army, so there's nobody to confront the FARC guerillas who wander freely across the border from Colombia. A party or two makes it through the jungle each year, and some researchers return year after year without incident. But still others go in and never come out.

As I recalled this history, my mind crafted an image of Darién as a diabolical mirror house; a place of quarter truths where you might look at your watch and see time running backward; a dark, quiet, glistening place where water might flow uphill and only the Cuna Indians and the FARC could expect to survive, the former because they'd been there for thousands of years, the latter because they were madmen. We couldn't survive—I was sure of it.

"OK," John said, breaking us from the spell. "We're closing in on the two-mile mark. If we land here, any survivors are going to have to walk fifty miles south to that last settlement."

Fifty miles overland, wrestling through mangrove swamps! The buccaneer Henry Morgan tried the same thing in 1670, and within a week his crew was eating leather. I thought of my friend, Evan Davies, who'd spent months in the Congo and years later was still taking dog heartworm pills to combat the parasites he'd picked up. I looked at John's left leg. It was already swollen from a massive infection that had started from a scratch. I'd always been drawn to snowy mountains, expansive glaciers, or open savannas, and now I felt sick.

Nobody liked the overland trek idea, least of all John. In 1995 he narrowly avoided landing on an island that turned out to be an unstaffed prison colony, an event that understandably soured him on uncontrolled landings in strange places.

"So," he said, coolly peeling a half-rotten pineapple, "We're going to turn south and try to sail down and make a controlled landing in that last settlement." We all knew that the settlement, a simple black dot on our chart, might be abandoned or a drug-runner's lair or a pirate's cove or a FARC base. "Anything," John said, tossing a rind into the water with a quiet plop, "is better than landing here."

We set to work, adjusting the steering planks and the sails to hook a gust that wheeled the bow south against the northward-flowing Humboldt Current. We coaxed the sails into position by tugging their sheets as gently as horse reins. By nightfall we were still just under two miles from shore. I smelled the wet, crawling soil, and heard breakers crashing ashore. By midnight we'd slowed our eastward drift, but we hadn't moved a mile south. Pointed south against the current, and shoved from the west by wind and swell, we were on the wrong side of just holding our position. We were edging in. Soon we were just a mile offshore.

In the morning we didn't need binoculars to make out the huge, twisted limbs of ancient trees netted with enormous vines. Someone spotted a white, boxlike shape on the beach. It was a small house, almost overgrown. There was no sign of life, but we doubled our watch for pirates.

Early in the voyage, Ecuadorean fishermen had warned us to stay at least thirty miles offshore, particularly off Colombia where pirates approached their victims in boats painted like those of the Colombian Coast Guard. We checked out our only armament, a rusty double-barreled shotgun purchased in a back alley in Ecuador. Even if it worked, what good would it be against half a dozen automatic rifles? We all knew we couldn't survive an attack. *Bloody hell,* I thought, *if I ever come back here, I'm going to be armed to the teeth.*

After midnight I was on watch again. Now I could hear the soft crash of every wave on the shore. The sails hung limp. The rest of the crew slept, or pretended to sleep, saving their strength for the disaster. Scott, my watch partner, produced a bottle of red wine. At least we would go down in style.

Just as he poured, a wind crept up and fully inflated the mainsail for the first time in forty-eight hours. The bottle clattered away underfoot as we jumped up and yelled for the crew and set to work. By dawn we were seven miles offshore. The relief was enormous. But we still had to land safely in a friendly place.

At noon we were just five miles out from the bay and the little settlement dot on our chart. We'd successfully navigated the lumbering raft against the current, and with poor winds, to precisely where we needed to be. We sailed through a narrow passage between enormous rocks. Soon the little harbor appeared, an ear carved neatly out of the coastline. Several vessels were anchored in the flat water. Come what may, we were headed in, completely exposed now, and we would meet the owners of those vessels in less than an hour.

Peering through binoculars, John told us he saw a sophisticated vessel, possibly a warship. If it was FARC guerillas, we were finished. We'd be captured for ransom and probably killed even if the money was paid; that had happened to the brother of our Colombian crewmates.

Through binoculars I could see that the ship bore the insignia of the Colombian Coast Guard. I saw figures standing at the ship's railing, watching us as we came in. I couldn't tell if they wore uniforms.

When we were closer in it was clear that the vessel was armed with heavy machine guns. We were all very quiet as we let off the sail a little and slowed our approach. A launch was lowered from the ship and motored out toward us. Again we saw the Colombian Coast Guard insignia. This was it. We could only wait; we were at their mercy.

Reprieve! It was the *real* Colombian armada, anchored here while on patrol for pirates. The executive officer inspected our passports and invited us to dine with the captain that night. Laughing with disbelief at our luck, we anchored right next to the one-hundred-foot *Sebastian del Benalcázar*, the greatest concentration of firepower on the entire Colombian coast. Even the FARC would steer clear of it.

Early the next evening we paddled our inflatable dinghy toward the Darién and waded to shore, setting our feet on land for the first time in seventeen days. The jungle was silent. We explored the weedy ruins of an abandoned settlement, a cluster of leaning houses.

I was overawed by our connection with a bloody history. Over four hundred years ago Francisco Pizarro had landed exactly here and fought a battle on this very beach. As we looked into the muddy house frames, where filthy mattresses lay abandoned in bare rooms and blackening magazines rotted like leaves, I imagined Pizarro grunting as he poked through Indian huts, looking for food or gold. In the end, despite capturing the wealth of the Aztecs and the Incas, Spain declined as a European power. *All that effort*, I thought, *for what?*

In the end, all that remained here was the Darién—leering, stoic, unassailable as ever. Its greenery would crawl up and engulf whatever was built here. Only a rain of hydrogen bombs could annihilate this forest. And when that happened, nobody would be left to care.

* * *

Cameron McPherson Smith, a fellow of The Explorers Club and a life fellow of the Royal Geographical Society, is an archaeologist at Portland State University. The 1998 Manteño Voyage—an attempt to retrace a pre-Columbian trade route between Ecuador and west Mexico on a replica of a native balsa sailing raft—was John Haslett's second balsa raft expedition. Smith and Haslett are currently planning another attempt, documented at www.balsaraft.com. Haslett's account of his expeditions to date can be found in *Voyage of the Manteño* (St. Martin's Press, 2006).

PART SIX

Chapter 38

Ah, Open Space

LEROY CHIAO

Finally, it is time. We are on board the International Space Station, the final destination of our tenth expedition. We launched from Kazakhstan on October 13, 2004, and docked with the station two days later. I'm the commander in charge of our six-and-a-half-month stay aboard. We are dressed in our Russian Orlan space suits and presently the ground crew calls us from Moscow and gives me the go to open the outer hatch for the first space walk of the mission.

I reach down and turn the hatch tool and confront my first problem. The space suit arms are too long. All of my fingers are about half an inch—the width of a finger—from the fingertips of my gloves. It's difficult to work since the gloves are too long. The Russian space suit known as *Orlan*, which in English means "eagle," stretched out during the last hour and a half while under pressure. There's nothing I can do about it now and I continue to work.

I unlatch the hatch and grasp the handle, which will crack open the seal. At this point, my Russian partner, Salizhan, has vented the airlock down to less than 15 mm Hg of pressure. It still takes a minute or so of holding this handle to get the remaining pressure out of the airlock so that I can physically open the hatch. I watch little pieces of dust and paint flecks get pulled out through the hatch seals as the last bit of pressure leaks out into open space. I release the handle and pull on the hatch. As the hatch pops open, I am greeted by the sunrise. I open the hatch completely and in Russian say out loud, "Ah, open space! Hello, my old and real friend. May I come in?" In the mission control center, the NASA interpreter edits my comment to "Hello space, my old friend" in his translation that later appears in English-language stories around the world. (I thought my version carried more emotional weight, but no matter.)

I affix my tether to the ladderlike porch outside and pull myself out into space. It is just past sunrise. As daybreak greets those below, I look down and watch the black velvet curtain of space crawl across the seams of white clouds and see beneath me the ocean's vivid pools of blue. Behind me, Salizhan is moments away from peering out of the yawning airlock hatch and "stepping" out into open space. This is his first EVA, or extravehicular activity.

It's my fifth time outside in a space suit, but my first time in a Russian one. During my four previous EVAs, I wore a NASA space suit called the extravehicular mobility unit (EMU). The Russian suit is stiff and has limited visibility. In the past, while walking in space in the EMU, I was affixed to the spacecraft structure with a retractable steel cable. The cable reeled itself out as I moved. I didn't have to open and close tether hooks while moving from work site to work site in the EMU. In addition, I wore an emergency jet pack. In the event of the unthinkable, I knew that I could fly back to safety. If all failed, the space shuttle itself provided me with a certain level of comfort. I knew that the shuttle could have quickly undocked and at least attempted to rescue me if I came loose from the station or the shuttle.

Now, none of those comforts exist during this Russian EVA. The Russian technique is to use two local tethers for restraint. As Salizhan and I move we unhook the first tether, move it down the path, reattach it, and then repeat the process with the second hook. This sounds easy, and in principle it is. However, the hooks are cumbersome to handle in the pressurized glove and are frequently dropped; during these moments, the astronaut is attached to the spacecraft by only one tether, as he or she fumbles to recover the dropped hook to attach the second tether to the spacecraft.

In the environment I am now in, a mistake like that could be fatal. If I fall off, there is nothing anyone could do. I would drift like a free-flying satellite in space and watch the station get smaller and smaller. The view of the Earth would be incredible, but as my oxygen tanks emptied and the carbon dioxide absorbers became saturated, I would die a slow death. The Russian radios are quite good, so I would be in voice contact with both Salizhan and the ground for a long time. This is not a pleasant thought because if the worst happened, Salizhan and I would have a long time to talk about it and the crew would hear me suffocating as I used the last of the oxygen in the tanks. I shake myself to the present moment and focus on the timeline of 6.5 hours of planned tasks.

The hooks are difficult to operate, especially since my hands are partially out of the gloves, but I manage. Salizhan tells me that his fingers are out of his gloves as well. This is a problem that will have to be worked out before the next EVA. For now, we'll have to make do. I turn around and receive the first large package from Salizhan. It is a European/Russian robotics experiment called "Rokviss," which is mounted on a platform called "URM-D," which is designed for a robotics experiment. We start our work. As we move down the side of the station, one of the hooks slips out of my hand. My heart jumps. I am tethered to the station only by the second hook. I grip the handrail tighter with my left hand and use my right hand to grapple for the first. Finally, I get hold of the lost hook and reattach it.

Inside the cocoon of the suit, I hear the reassuring whirs of the fan and pump package. The common belief that space is silent except for the sound of one's breathing is not true. If things get quiet inside my suit, that means trouble. Earlier, while still inside the airlock, I amused myself by whistling inside my suit. This is interesting, because in the lower-pressure NASA EMU space suit I was unable to whistle. Moreover, my voice in the EMU changed because so few molecules were moving past my vocal chords. The Russian suit operates at a higher pressure than NASA's suit and the added pressure makes my limbs stiffer. Consequently, I tire faster.

Our first task is to attach the large URM-D package (about half the size of a man and about two hundred pounds) to the hull of the ship. Although weightless in space, the package still has mass and inertia and is difficult to control. To install it, we must remove covers off the hull, expose threaded holes, and attach matching bolts on the URM-D. The problem is that there are no handrails in this area, and the URM-D has no soft-dock mechanism, which is designed to hold objects temporarily in place. We will have to attach a tether between two distant handrails across the work site. The tether will serve as a strap, or "soft" handrail. Using this strap to restrain ourselves, we must wrestle the URM-D into position and try to engage the first threads of the first of four bolts.

I affix two tethers to each other and attach my end. Then, I hand Salizhan the other end. He moves to his side and makes the connection. I pull up the slack and we move out onto the strap. I attach one hook to the strap in order to get the reach to the work site. I remove a cover made of fabric and throw it into space, something I've never done before. This is the Russian way. At NASA, we are trained to never let anything get away into open space, much less throw it away intentionally. Everything must be tethered. Now I smile and let the cover fly, feeling like a guilty schoolboy.

We are ready to mount the URM-D. During our preparations, I worried that this would be a major obstacle. Sure enough, the URM-D is difficult to handle. We hold on to the soft strap as we struggle to move this large, bulky mass into position. We almost get it in position, when both of our bodies react to the motion of the package. I feel my legs swing away from the module. The URM-D comes up, and then as we struggle with it while restraining our bodies with only one hand on a strap, the URM-D slams down against the hull on its side. We wrestle it upright again and I manage to get one of my bolts aligned with the hole.

"Hold on," I tell Salizhan, as I press the bolt down into the hole. Suddenly, the package pivots. I try to turn the bolt, but it is obvious that unless we get the other bolts lined up, I will cross-thread it. I tell Salizhan to move the rear of the URM-D toward my side. I can only hold the bolt down so long. My body is reacting against this force. I am slowly moving up and swinging away again, so we must hurry.

"Too much," I say to him. "Back off a little. . . . Stop there!" I start turning the handle on the first bolt and am gratified to feel the threads catch, just as my body swings out of position. "I've gotten the first one started!" I tell Salizhan, then use that anchor point to pivot my body around. My left hand reaches for the second bolt. I feel it engage and I start to turn both bolts with both hands. Thankfully, Salizhan has engaged a bolt on his side. We tighten the package to the hull.

Near the end of the EVA, Salizhan talks to Moscow. He is tired and tells them that his space suit's arms and legs have lengthened and that his fingers are about a centimeter shorter than the tips of his gloves. I have the same problem. With the fingers out of the tips of the gloves, every squeeze of the hooks, every movement of the wrist takes a lot of effort. I am not only tired, but also hungry and looking forward to getting back inside.

Salizhan still needs to mount the Biorisk experiment package. My job is to follow and photograph the installation. During training, we practiced these sorts of tasks in a pool using full-size models of the space station components, but there are limitations to training. Now, it is unclear how best to get to the work site, but Salizhan ventures forward. He squeezes underneath the Strella, a crane used to move objects or astronauts around, and bumps his backpack against it. This way is not going to work.

"San," I said, calling him by his nickname. "Come back around and go over the other side, like we trained in the hydrolab." It is the long way around the module, but at least it will be familiar to him. I see that he does not want to retreat. His hands are tired. I tell him again that there is no way to go forward where he is. I don't want to say out loud that he is bumping the Strella because I don't want to alarm the ground team. There's no need to alarm them unnecessarily. Finally, he returns to the airlock porch and starts up the long way around.

There, Salizhan encounters another roadblock. The mock-up we used during training did not accurately replicate the locations of gap spanners and installed equipment. Now he sees that he can't go around on the training route either. I suggest he make his way around the base of the Strella. I can tell from his voice that he's physically exhausted. He talks to Moscow again about his hands. After several minutes, Sergei, the Russian specialist who is directing our activities, suggests that he rest for a moment and that I continue with the Biorisk package.

Although I have not trained for this task, it seems straightforward. I unclip the tether from Salizhan and take the package. I make my way up to the base of the Strella. I am now literally hanging off the station, which is pointing directly down toward Earth. It feels as if I am hanging off a balcony on the tallest building in the world. I watch the clouds and the ocean move past my visor at five miles a second. I notice that my breathing is rapid and shallow now and my stomach churns. To break the spell of this momentary terror, I bring my eyes back to the handrails in front of me and continue on. I click the package into the magnetic soft dock and rotate the locking collar. My hands are tired, but I feel the relief of getting the task done.

One task remains. We must return to the antenna work site. The ground team has determined that somewhere in the cables that we have connected, there is no electrical continuity. We have to find the bad connection and correct it. I lead the way out. Though Salizhan's voice is a little stronger than mine, he still sounds pretty tired. I think I have enough strength left to mate the connectors. In training, these connectors required a ninety-degree twist. That twist was difficult because the connectors had spent a lot of time in the water and were sticky and corroded. I assumed that the flight connectors would be much easier, but I was wrong. They too are sticky. Now, with our hand strength waning, I must make these connections again. I start out to the work site, aware of every compression that I have to make of the safety tether hooks. Finally, I arrive at the antenna work site. I peel back the Velcro cover and immediately find what I'm looking for—the first connector has not been fully engaged. The second set of connectors is not even partially mated. I report this and Salizhan insists that he fully mated them before. No matter, the connections must be made, otherwise the robotics experiment will not function and the main objective of this EVA would be lost.

With some difficulty, I make the first connection, sliding the lock into place. I then turn my attention to the second. It doesn't want to turn at all. My forearms ache and my wrists writhe with pain. I stop and pull the connectors apart and look inside again. All clean, no debris. I align the arrow with the stripe and push them together again. To mate them, I must keep them pushed together while twisting. The problem is that the markings are not clear. I try one way, then the other. Neither way works. I examine the markings again and decide that I must twist my right hand away from me. I'm only good for one more try. Mustering all of my remaining hand strength, I twist with all I have left, grunting involuntarily. Miraculously, the arrow moves! A little more . . . There! The arrow is aligned with the white mark. I slide the lock into position.

I ask Moscow to check for continuity. They will have telemetry in a few minutes. Sergei tells us to take a rest. No kidding. I have only a few fingers barely curled around the handrails of the work site, letting my hands rest as much as possible. Finally, good news! Sergei reports good continuity. Both Salizhan and I say in unison, "Thank God."

Sergei asks if I have engaged the slide locks. "Yes, yes," I tell him, with relief. "OK, thank you for your hard work, guys. Head on home," he replies. Slowly and carefully, we start back toward the airlock.

This is no time to relax. I tell myself, "OK, we're heroes right now, but if you make a mistake, fall off the station and die, then all that good stuff will be forgotten."

On the pool deck during training, the hooks had made a clickety-clack sound when opened and closed. We now clickety-clack our way back to the waiting airlock of the space station. It looks so inviting. We've been outside now for almost five and a half hours. I thought it would take only three. Finally, Salizhan is inside. He moves into his position, making room for me. I reverse directions, putting my feet in first. Clickety-clack, my long tether hook is inside, securely on a handrail. I release the short one. Turning to face the hatch, I remove the protective ring and fold it up. We report to Moscow that we are ready to close the hatch.

Sergei tells us to first inspect the O-rings. To our dismay, the O-rings seem to have some lint on them. Where did this come from? Was it always there? Was it on the inside of the protective ring? No matter, it should be removed. We have nothing to wipe them with and improvise by trying to remove the lint with the tips of our gloves. I motion to Salizhan and neither of us explains what we're doing to the listening ground control team; our gloves are covered with white paint dust from the exterior of the station. I decide that we are contaminating the O-rings even more by our actions and motion to Salizhan to stop. We tell the ground team we're finished and soon receive the go to close the hatch.

Salizhan releases the restraining tether and I swing the hatch through its arc. It closes and I reach down and turn the hand crank. I watch the rollers engage. "The hatch is sealed," I announce. Moscow gives Salizhan the go-ahead to begin re-pressurization. However, only after the pressure checks showed that we had a perfect seal, did the two of us breathe easy. I feel a wave of exhaustion and exhilaration roll over me.

* * *

Leroy Chiao was selected by NASA as an astronaut in January 1990. He is a veteran of four space flights and has logged more than 229 days in space, including thirty-six hours and seven minutes of time in six space walks. He was the first Asian and ethnic Chinese to perform a space walk, and he became the first Asian and ethnic Chinese mission commander in 2004 when he served as the commander and NASA science officer of the tenth mission to the International Space Station. During that mission, he completed almost thirty-one hundred orbits of Earth. Currently, he works as a consultant and public speaker and is involved in entrepreneurial business ventures. He is an executive vice president and a director of Excalibur Almaz Ltd., a private manned space mission, and also holds a distinguished chair mechanical engineering professorship at Louisiana State University.

Chapter 39

Race to the Moon

JAMES A. LOVELL

On December 21, 1968, while the Soviet Union temporarily vacillated about whether to launch a manned flight to the moon, Frank Borman, Bill Anders, and myself—all three NASA astronauts aboard Apollo 8—lifted off on man's first visit to another heavenly body. I had trained for this mission for what seemed like my whole life. The night before, I was so keyed up that I hardly slept at all. Our mission was to test the navigations and communications systems in deep space and look for suitable landing sites during Apollo 8's ten orbits around the moon.

It was the highlight of my space career to be one of the first three men to see the moon's far side—a side never seen from Earth as the moon orbits our planet. With our noses pressed against the glass, the three of us were like three schoolboys looking into a celestial candy store. Ancient craters slowly slipped past. And then, as we approached the near side of the lunar horizon, I saw the most unforgettable sight—Earth suspended in an absolutely black sky, like a beautiful blue Christmas tree ornament. At the time, I described this vision of Earth as "a grand oasis in the vastness of space."

When I put my thumb to the window, it completely hid the Earth. That's how small Earth looked from deep space. It dawned on me how from this perspective, everything seemed insignificant. Looking at Earth, everything I knew—my friends, family, colleagues, my home—seemed as if it had been erased. Earth is a small planet orbiting a rather normal star. And that star—our sun—is tucked away in the outer edge of the Milky Way, a galaxy made up of millions of stars. The Milky Way is one of millions of galaxies in our known universe.

From the moon, we could see the oceans and continents on the Earth. The cloud patterns were prominent. I could even see the ice caps of the Arctic and the Antarctic. What we could not distinguish were cities or people. From that vantage point, there were no whites or blacks, no Soviets or Americans, no Italians or French, no Christians, Muslims, or Jews. The Earth looked uninhabited. And yet I knew that on that fragile, spinning ball lived five billion people, all striving for basically the same things in life.

We orbited the moon on Christmas Eve 1968. To symbolize the significance of our journey, we took turns reading to the people on Earth the first ten verses of Genesis, the story of the origins of creation that is the basis of many of the world's religions. Our words were broadcast worldwide over the NASA communications network. From where we sat in deep space, the opening words carried a special weight. "In the beginning God created the heavens and the earth," we read. "The Earth was without form and void, and the darkness was upon the face of the deep, and the Spirit of God moved over the face of the waters."

At such a moment, it was impossible not to feel a sense of religious awe. After we landed on the moon, without making a big announcement about it, I served Communion because I was an elder in the Protestant church.

Each of us on board Apollo 8 knew that we were at both the end and beginning of separate phases of the space race between the United States and the Soviet Union. With Apollo 8, we had beat the Russians to the moon. But a new race—to become the first to land on the moon—had begun.

The space race started out on friendly terms. In 1957, the official International Geophysical Year, leaders of our two countries agreed to cooperate in space. The United Space planned to put a small satellite in orbit; the satellite weighed only eleven pounds and was shaped like a grapefruit. The idea was that it would be sent up by a pencil-thin rocket called the Vanguard. But in October 1957, the Soviets surprised us by launching their own satellite called "Sputnik." Determined to keep up, we rushed the Vanguard out to the launch pad, only to watch it blow up in flames, its wreckage piling on the pad, a mocking symbol of the failure of American technology.

After that, cooperation between the two nations was over, and the space race had begun. For the next few years, the United States was left at the starting gate, watching as the Russians accomplished one spectacular space feat after another.

Then, in the summer of 1961, President John F. Kennedy announced that the United States would place a man on the surface of the moon and bring him back safely before the end of the decade. Kennedy's vision was bold. Some thought it was lunacy. Whatever his motivation—boldness or madness—his goal triggered the start of the Apollo moon program and America's ascendancy in space.

If Kennedy believed he took the Soviets by surprise, he was wrong. They too had plans to send a man to the moon. By 1961, they developed a huge booster rocket called the N-1. It was more powerful than NASA's planned Saturn V. The plan was for the N-1 to have twenty rocket engines in its first stages. But only ten were built. Unlike the Soviet's other missions, the N-1 failed. The failure caused the Soviet Union to fall behind NASA's timetable of accomplishing a lunar landing. Still, the Soviets persisted. By the fall of 1968, they planned to put two cosmonauts on a circumlunar flight.

Meanwhile, NASA had its own trouble. A launch pad fire in 1967 set the Apollo 8 program back more than a year. By the end of 1968, NASA's plan was to fly an Earth orbital flight—Apollo 8—to test the space vehicles before attempting the lunar mission. But Grumman Aircraft, the manufacturer of the lunar module, announced that it was impossible to have a flyable vehicle ready before 1969.

In the United States, rumors flew about an upcoming Soviet circumlunar flight. In 1968, a test flight containing small animals was made using a Proton rocket and a Zone spacecraft. The high deceleration and heat buildup caused by reentry into the atmosphere killed the animals. A second Proton rocket was launched with small animals with a modified reentry path. This time, the animals lived. Then the Soviets made a critical mistake: They hesitated to put a man in space and decided to do one more test with animals.

No such hesitation existed at NASA. Based on Apollo 7's prior orbit mission, NASA officials quickly decided to send Apollo 8 to the moon. And that set the stage for the first leg of the race. When our mission was over, the question for America was: would we meet President Kennedy's goal and successfully land on the moon?

The answer, as history knows, is yes. On July 20, 1969, Neil Armstrong, the thirty-eight-year-old American astronaut, landed Apollo 11's lunar module on the Sea of Tranquility. It was tranquil, but the moon is also a desolate place. Temperature changes are extreme and radiation is always present. Put yourself in Armstrong's space suit. Feel the excitement as you open the hatch, move gently out on the platform, and then slowly down the ladder. Your foot strikes the lunar surface and sinks a fraction of an inch into the graphitelike sand. You realize you are standing on the surface of the moon. You have accomplished what the greatest explorers in history only dreamed about. As you scan the horizon, your eyes take in the craters, hills, rocks, and boulders of another planet. No other man has seen what you now see.

The sights on the moon are in stark contrast. It's a colorless black-and-white world with many shades of gray. The brilliant reflection of the sun on the lunar surface clashes with the velvet black sky and meets the horizon, as well as the black shadows inside the craters. The only sound you hear is your reflected breathing inside your helmet. The moon is void of any atmosphere. Therefore, moon dust kicks up with every step and falls back to the surface with mathematical precision. Because there is no atmosphere, the temperature climbs to over 200 degrees Celsius (392 degrees Fahrenheit) in the sun to minus 200 degrees Celsius (or minus 328 degrees Fahrenheit) in the shadows. Because of the low gravity, when you walk you feel as if you're hopping around like a rabbit.

The sight before you is beautiful but short. Your time is limited and you have the feeling that you are trespassing on the sanctity of a world that is not your own. As you look up into the blackness of space, you see that blue ball—Earth.

The incredible decade that began in 1957 first with the cooperation of, followed by competition with the Soviet Union, is now history. We've come full circle: cooperation drives our space activities. A consortium of countries, including the former Soviet Union, now works together to place in orbit the International Space Station. This facility is manned by star sailors from many countries.

We aren't reaching for the moon anymore. We won that race. But as a person who has seen the moon's far side, I wonder if we will one day revisit the moon. My guess is yes—and that is also my hope. As a society, we need to be thinking twenty or thirty years into the future, not just for today. I'd also like to see us send a manned mission to Mars, a considerable challenge but one worth taking. The United States needs a space imperative because the exploration of space is a human imperative. The real significance of Apollo was simple: we came in peace for all humankind. That should be the purpose of the next voyage—and all the others that will follow.

• • •

Captain James A. Lovell was selected as an astronaut by NASA in September 1962. In 1970, as spacecraft commander of the Apollo 13 flight, Lovell became the first man to journey twice to the moon. Previously, he served as backup commander to Neil Armstrong for the Apollo 11 lunar-landing mission. He was a pioneer on several Gemini missions. On December 4, 1965, he and Frank Borman were launched into space on the history-making Gemini 7 mission. The Gemini 12 mission, commanded by Lovell with Pilot Edwin "Buzz" Aldrin, began on November 11, 1966. In 1973, Lovell retired from the navy and the space program to join Bay-Houston Towing Company in Houston, Texas.

PART SEVEN

Horizons

Chapter 40

On Exploration

STEFANIE POWERS

To be an explorer is not to be confused with being a traveler, although traveling, when not peripatetic, can be in itself a form of exploration. Since mass tourism has invaded the formerly distant places, long gone is the world of Gertrude Bell, Wilfred Thesiger, and Freya Stark who lived in an era where there was still enough wilderness in the world for solo adventures.

I remember flying up to Maralal from my home on the slopes of Mount Kenya a few years ago to visit Wilfred Thesiger. I was accompanied by Sandy Field, an old chum of Thesiger's from his school days. Wilfred had recently returned from a visit to what we now call Saudi Arabia, the scene of some of his greatest exploits, long before oil changed its complexion forever. He was there for an exhibit of his photographs enlarged to gigantic dimensions. During one of his outings, he saw in the distance a part of the Empty Quarter, the vast desert he had crossed on foot in 1946 and 1947, which this time he viewed from an air-conditioned car on a smartly paved highway.

Indeed, Field himself, as the district commissioner of Karamoja Valley in Uganda, ventured solo into a land of tribal conflict whose combatants physically towered over him. He attempted to administrate a wild and unruly region, in the twilight of the British Empire. Field was charged with the important task of aligning the complex and remote borders of Uganda, Kenya, and Sudan. He accomplished his mission on foot. The daring of that generation in a world with more corners left untouched was adventurous to say the least, and certainly qualify as exploration.

My own travels always had purpose and were never confined to the comfortable. Perhaps there are two kinds of people in the world: those who fear being out of their element and those who are addicted to it, or, to put it another way, those who stay home and those compelled to venture forth.

In the early days, when the People's Republic of China (PRC), as we called it then, opened to passports from the United States, I seized an opportunity to gain the privilege of entry. I traveled as and when I wished, within reason, in that formerly forbidden country. All through the late 1970s and in the 1980s, when my work as an actor was finished, I literally walked off the set and onto an airplane usually bound for the PRC. The Chinese weren't used to outsiders and the demeanor of the people vacillated day by day. They were open and friendly some days and other days, many stared blankly, as if the windows of their souls were shut tight and the curtains drawn.

One of the satisfying purposes of exploration can involve getting to know people. On one of my trips, I met a woman who was the longest expatriate resident in the history of China. Muriel Hoopes Tu was, of all things, an American who met and married a Chinese national in 1919, followed him to China in 1920, and never left. I spent the next ten years listening to her story and recording her experiences for posterity.

I have always been amazed by the virtuosity of the people tucked away in isolated places. Once, I was six days up the Sepik River in Papua New Guinea, when I came across an Australian who operated a sort of all-purpose trading center and upcountry guest house. In his case, trading mostly meant crocodile skins, a contraband item that is now banned worldwide. Even then, business was not booming. The guest house was a last-ditch effort to keep his center financially afloat. The man's library was well used and the worn patina of his books reflected how often the books had been read. I realized that if I dared to venture into any one of the myriad subjects covered by his collection, the debate would be lively and I'd better have a working knowledge of the subject. The man knew his books.

To these parts of New Guinea came Margaret Mead, the great American anthropologist. While pursuing her treatise on the garden of humanity, Mead walked among some of the most diverse and treacherous peoples, which included eight hundred tribes speaking a thousand different languages. I followed in some of her footsteps in pursuit of art for an exhibit and sale in New York City at the request of New Guinea's first prime minister, Michael Sumari. The prime minister wanted to help improve his country's flagging economy, to build cottage industries out of handicrafts, such as traditional carving.

The face of poverty is everywhere in New Guinea; it has afflicted many noble tribalists, reducing them to beetlenut-chewing vagrants. Today, I would not be advised to take, nor would I probably survive treading, the same paths as I did then, which seems like only a few years ago in my memory.

If indefatigable curiosity is a prime ingredient to inspire exploration, then I have that in abundance and am grateful for whatever throwback gene pool gave me the privilege. Indeed, most important discoveries are made by leaving the known world to seek out the unknown. That's how we evolve as human beings.

• • •

Stefanie Powers, actress and conservationist, created the William Holden Wildlife Foundation to carry on the conservation activities in Kenya of the late actor William Holden. She is a frequent keynote speaker for humane treatment for farm animals and the effects of overexploitation of forests in Africa. In 2003, the maker of the Jaguar automobile named her its conservation consultant, in charge of the company's conservation program for the jaguar cat. She is a past recipient of The Explorers Club's Lowell Thomas Medal.

Chapter 41

Out on a Limb

MARGARET LOWMAN

During the 1970s, a tropical rain forest was scientifically considered a "black box." Translation: a big, dark region full of the unknown. How many species exist on our planet? What lives in the tops of tall forests? Why don't those millions of beetles eat up all the foliage? How do tropical forests control the climate and lifestyle we enjoy in the temperate zones?

As a young graduate student—armed with a tolerance for leeches, mud, and smelly socks—I wanted to solve the mysteries of tropical jungles. In order to study tropical trees, I needed to climb to reach their foliage. So I packed some ropes, a harness, climbing hardware, camera, and notebooks into a rucksack and set off for the jungles of Australia.

My career has been unconventional. I climb trees for a living. My children were extraordinary in their patience to accompany me on forays into the jungle, where they in turn became explorers in their own right, discovering new species. I feel fortunate that I was never knocked unconscious by a falling cannonball tree fruit nor bitten by an Australian brown snake, and I never fell from a tall tree. I voyaged to Australia some thirty years ago because a graduate school scholarship in botany seduced me. Upon arrival, I decided to study the tropical forests in part because no graduate students at Sydney University had previously studied rain forests in Australia. Only an estimated 5 percent of the original Australian rain forest had escaped the chain saws by 1978. I had to hurry. In trying to find something important to study, I realized that almost 95 percent of every tropical tree was both out of sight and of reach. In essence, these jungle canopies were never seen, much less studied. I sewed my first harness and carved my first slingshot to rig my ropes, and set my sights on exploring at the top. I have never looked back—or down.

E. O. Wilson of Harvard University characterized forest canopies as the last biotic frontier on earth. Tree crowns escaped scientific exploration over the past one hundred years for the simple reason that the logistics of overcoming gravity were never solved. Charles Darwin was allegedly hoisted in a chair by South American natives to view the canopy, just as a novelty. Some one hundred and fifty years later, I was fortunate to become one of the first explorers into this uncharted frontier, and remain awestruck by each and every return voyage out on the limb. The canopy is home to the greatest number of species, including plants and animals, on Earth and is now considered a hotspot for biodiversity. Current scientific literature estimates that our planet houses up to one hundred million species, of which almost half live in the treetops. Forest canopies are centers for photosynthesis, for foods and medicines, for flowering and fruiting, and for growth, so it is logical that animals will tend to live up there in the sunlight and among the foliage.

Initially, my biggest challenge was to design safe methods to reach the treetops. I spent long hours becoming adept with a slingshot and propelling my fish line through a safe passage up and over a strong branch. On the back of a napkin in an Australian pub, I sketched the first walkway for ecotourism. With another colleague, I adapted a nautical bosun's chair to hoist kids into the treetops. Back at Williams College as a professor several years later, I helped build the first research canopy walkway in North America. More recently, the first walkways for public visitation and another accessible for wheelchairs were completed outside Sarasota, Florida. While I was busy perfecting rope techniques and walkways, other colleagues created additional methods. Cherry pickers, hot-air balloons, inflatable rafts, canopy bubbles, zip lines, and construction cranes complete the toolkit for treetop exploration. Once the methods were designed and tested, the stage was set to solve the biological mysteries of these aerial ecosystems hidden just above Earth: the treetop inhabitants and their interactions and the dynamics of growth, death, productivity, and diversity. In essence, what makes these complex systems function, and how can we ensure their stability for future generations?

As a relatively new type of planetary exploration, canopy research has been 95 percent sweat equity and 5 percent intellect, or at least sometimes it feels that way. Having solved the rudiments of access, I now focus on teasing apart the ecology of these forests in order to understand their complex interactions. Like a doctor diagnosing human health, an ecologist measures and diagnoses change in ecosystems. Ecologists consider it critical to collect baseline ecological data to understand the health of our planet and predict change. Throughout years of canopy research, I have been assisted by hundreds, if not thousands, of explorers in training. Earthwatch volunteers, college students, high school students and their teachers, elementary and middle school students, fellow scientists, and citizen scientists have donned harnesses, lassoed a branch with my slingshot, and measured thousands of leaves and insects as part of the process to learn about life above the forest floor. Specifically, my long-term research involves plant-insect interactions. It is a *beetle-eat-leaf* world up there, oftentimes noisy at night with millions of foliage-feeding insects (termed herbivores) chomping on millions of leaves, vines, and air plants. This process of herbivory can lead to pest outbreaks, an important applied outcome of this research. Since plants can not run away from enemies, leaves have evolved different strategies to defend themselves: thorns, hairs, poisonous chemicals, and toughness. The interaction of insects eating plants actually stimulates the production of chemicals in leaves and serves as a plant's major defense tactic. This response creates a veritable apothecary in the sky. The samples that scientists extract from plants may someday be used to treat human ailments, as they have been used for thousands of years by many indigenous cultures. Over many years, I have measured more than two hundred fifty thousand leaves as part of my canopy exploration—finding out that some tropical leaves live more than twenty years, and that insects defoliate approximately 20 percent to 25 percent of the treetops per year. That is a much higher level than previously measured from ground-level observations. The removal of approximately one quarter of the foliage from a forest has obvious consequences to its health. Continued "pest pressure" can ultimately lead to declining tree health and ultimate dieback of entire forests.

One of my favorite expeditions was an international balloon survey of the lowland tropical rain forests in Cameroon, Africa. To travel across two oceans among different cultures, immersed in totally new plant families via hot-air balloons and inflatable rafts represented the ultimate in challenge and adventure for my aerial botanical career.

This venture into an unknown Africa was beyond comprehension. How can a vast landmass remain so unknown, so unexplored, so void of scientific discovery? During our four months of preparation, we had unearthed relatively little literature on the Biafran Congo rain forest basin. The Campo Faunal Reserve in southern Cameroon was nothing but a dot on the map representing our destination, yet this region was considered one of the most colorful and diverse in the tropical world.

We finally arrived at base camp. Opération Canopée was aglow with lights, but noisy generators, not quiet candles, were the source of power. The scene was reminiscent of a jungle movie, with thatched huts in a forest clearing. The camp was in its second month of operation when we arrived. That night almost fifty people were in residence, ten of whom would depart the next day. So we literally bumped bottoms, setting up our hammocks in a long line under the roof of the sleeping hut. A dashing, muscular Frenchman looked aghast when I slung my hammock next to his. He was obviously less than enthusiastic about a female intruding on his monastic tree-climbing adventure, but fortunately I could not understand his dismayed comments in rapid French. It was a strange sensation to hear people speaking so many languages in the middle of the African equatorial jungle—French, German, Japanese, and English. The only common thread was a sense of adventure in canopy science.

As the only female in an otherwise male camp, I found showering to be a real challenge, not only because of insects but also because of staff intrusions. I probably became a prime educator of the local pygmy assistants on the subjects of American female anatomy and ablutions. My Western colleagues were amused that whenever I headed for the shower cubicles with my towel, an attentive group of ground staff would follow. Their most common ploy was to clamber up on the hot tin roof, as if to check the water hoses, and then peer over the edge into my stall. Once they brought machetes and proceeded to cut the grass just outside the shower stall—all ten or so blades that had resisted our continual trampling. Getting dressed in the morning was another challenge, in the open hut with fifty men in hammocks, but just another liability of fieldwork.

The dirigible was launched daily at 6:00 a.m., weather and health of crew permitting. A launchpad had been carved out in the forest and was covered with a plastic tarpaulin to cushion the huge balloon. Entry onto the tarp was permitted only with bare feet. The French have a wonderfully casual sense of organization; everything got done with nothing like the fuss or stress that might occur if Americans were shouting orders and organizational advice to one another. Two Africans held the ropes in front while Danny, the pilot, fired up a small flame just under the dirigible. A tiny balloon was always released first to test wind conditions: a lovely combination of high and low technology. Finally, liftoff! The colorful balloon sailed quietly over the tips of the umbrella trees (*Musanga cecropioides*, family Cecropiaceae) that edged the clearing, and then ventured out over the vast sea of green.

Our canopy expedition was the first collaborative project in this region of equatorial Africa. A large majority of our findings will doubtless embody new records for science. This pioneering sense kept the morale of the scientists very high, despite minor setbacks such as diarrhea, the absence of amenities (electric lights, fans, and ice), equipment failures, and sheer exhaustion from vertical rope climbing in the tropical heat and humidity.

The transition between field expeditions to the tropics and my temperate-based abode is always awkward. Those back home can never quite envision my life in the bush, nor understand what new dimensions have been added to my perspective by being temporarily without Western trappings. It took several months to fully comprehend my reentry after this trip to Cameroon—after all, I had flown across an ocean, spanned three continents, traveled between tropical and temperate zones, and—most significant—adapted to two vastly different cultures, each with its own marvelous, but not easily interchangeable, mores and attributes.

The living conditions of tropical expeditions are usually worthy of tall tales upon return. Africa was no exception, and I affectionately called our base camp the "Cameroon Hilton." A rudimentary open-air, thatched long hut housed fifty scientists who managed to string their hammocks in a long line. As the only female present during this part of the expedition, I was thoughtfully offered the end position to provide some (questionable) privacy for dressing in the morning. The sleeping quarters provided almost as many tales of biodiversity as the treetops. Imagine fifty pairs of muddy, sweat-soaked boots with fifty pairs of dirty, smelly socks, some of which were unwashed for many weeks, all cramped in a hot, humid shed with relatively little air circulation. The smells were almost as diverse as the sounds. Forty-nine men plus one lone female sleeping on their backs with knees inclined backward (which is the only possible posture in hammocks) provided some wonderful snoring concerts, not to speak of the somnambulation, sleep talking, and wild dreams triggered by hard, sweat-and-toil climbing days in the jungle.

Another special feature of the Cameroon Hilton was the challenge of using the outhouse in the middle of the night. God did not endow women with the precision to aim off the edge of a sleeping platform, so I was the only one to regularly clamber down and walk to the outhouse nestled in the forest interior. On several occasions, millions of army ants had discovered the outhouse, creating a broiling carpet of tiny, fierce bodies swarming around the hut's perimeter, rendering it unapproachable and downright dangerous. But on most nights, my biggest concern was the Gaboon viper that lived in a hole just under the sleeping platform at my edge of the structure. According to the resident herpetologist, Gaboon vipers were deadly poisonous with no known antivenom. They were also beautiful to behold. Whenever a visitor came to camp, someone enthusiastically hauled our resident viper out of its hole using a red noose attached to a snake stick. This viper was likely to be downright cranky from the frequent disturbances. With a potential combination of poisonous and angry, I stepped very cautiously during my nighttime descents.

Despite its rough exterior, our sleeping quarters featured night sounds that far exceeded Carnegie Hall. Laughing tree frogs, a chorus of crickets and cicadas, intermittent sonar sounds of bats, the chewing noises of beetles and stick insects, titillating screeches by troops of monkeys, plus occasional growls of mammals on the forest floor provided a backdrop for sleeping unsurpassed throughout the planet. The night symphony of the forest easily outcompeted the snoring concert on the platform.

During almost thirty years of treetop exploration, I have whittled away at relatively small goals—one tree at a time. I can only hope that my scientific research will strengthen conservation and education about our planet's last remaining wild places for the next generation. As a scientist and explorer, I managed to discover a few new species, and I pioneered some new methods of canopy access that opened some new frontiers in forest ecology and left a modest legacy of treetop walks encircling the globe to encourage ecotourism instead of chain saws. Moreover, I shared my exploration with kids through the wonders of distance learning. In my other role as a parent and explorer, I used my canopy exploration as an opportunity to connect my children to nature, and to remind them that human health links directly to the environment, not to computer screens or cell phones. Children need to get muddy, explore the outdoors, and to understand that we are all part of our ecosystem, not outside of it. By advocating this ethic, both parents and scientists alike can impart environmental ethics to the next generation.

The greatest exploration remaining in the tropical treetops is perhaps not to map the last remaining remote jungles or climb the tallest trees. The most urgent exploration, with rewards far exceeding the discovery of a new beetle or a lost city, is to discover the secrets of how these complex ecological machines called rain forests function. It is a race against time. Our children and grandchildren depend upon the success of our exploration to unravel the ecological mysteries in our home, planet Earth. Many challenges remain in our exploration of the world's tropical jungles. We do not yet know the commonest tree in South America, nor do we have any idea how many creatures live in a cubic meter of foliage. Yet we know the chemicals that compose Mars, the structure of an electron, and the genetic makeup of a mosquito. Science has advanced in many arenas, but the ability to understand the machinery of our "home" is still lacking. The exploration and scientific advances in canopy biology over the next twenty years are critical to understanding the health of forests that regulate the quality of life on our planet. For my children's sake, I hope we can expand planetary explorations "out on a limb," and use our scientific results to generate sound conservation policies.

* * *

Margaret Lowman has explored the world's major forests from the top down. As both mom and scientist, she pioneered canopy exploration, bringing her sons into the treetops instead of to day care. She is the author of *Life in the Treetops* (Yale University Press, 1999), and she has coauthored more than one hundred peer-reviewed scientific publications, and inspired more than fifteen million children through her science outreach programs for the Jason Project, the National Geographic Channel, and *Reading Rainbow*. Lowman serves as professor of biology and environmental studies at New College of Florida, is on the board of directors of The Explorers Club, and was a recipient of the Lowell Thomas Medal in 2006.

Epilogue
Presidential Roundtable: The Face of Exploration Today

The following interview, conducted by editor Jan Jarboe Russell, took place at The Explorers Club with Daniel A. Bennett, the thirty-sixth president of the club; well-known naturalist, lecturer, and television host Jim Fowler, who is an honorary president of the club; and Alfred Scott McLaren, a deep-sea explorer who was president of the club from 1996 to 2000.

JJR: *How has technology changed the nature of exploration?*

McLaren: It has changed dramatically since I first started serious exploration as a submarine commander, surveying the Siberian continental shelf in a nuclear submarine some thirty-six years ago. Right now, I'm a senior pilot on a technically advanced and revolutionary new submersible that is flown like an airplane to depths of five hundred meters, or sixteen hundred feet. This vehicle will allow marine scientists and archaeologists to search and survey, with precise navigational accuracy, as much as two hundred nautical miles in a single day.

What evolving new technology requires, however, is that the explorer must remain as current as possible in his or her field. Explorers would also be wise to remain in close contact with and learn from younger colleagues who are often more knowledgeable about such new developments, and at the same time work with them to use the new technology to the best advantage. This is an ideal time to use teamwork in order to make the best use of a particular new technology.

Bennett: Technology is changing the face of exploration in many ways. You see few compasses anymore on expeditions—they are antiques—because today's explorers carry GPS [global positioning system] devices. These devices have sometimes saved lives.

In addition, everyone is dragging laptop computers up and down the mountains and carrying satellite telephones. One of the things that The Explorers Club is trying to do is make sure that scientists doing important research in forest canopies around the world have access to computers that can help them.

However, technology has its shortcomings. What happens when the technology breaks down—you forget your batteries or there is a blackout in some remote part of the world? If all you know how to do as an explorer is turn on a computer and push a button, then you can become a hostage to technology and get in real trouble.

McLaren: I agree. I still like to use the sextant and other tried-and-true methods, such as basic dead reckoning at sea. Too much technology can be a distraction. You can get too involved with it and, as a result, not see or observe what you had come for. Even worse, I've had people get a cell phone call at a critical moment with an immediate adverse impact on the data collection or research in progress. It can be maddening!

Let me give you an example from the past when overdependency on the latest technology can let one down. During the summer of 1970, my crew and I conducted an underwater survey of all twenty-six hundred miles of a totally uncharted Siberian continental shelf for the first time in history. We had absolutely state-of-the-art everything on board a multimillion-dollar nuclear attack submarine. When we completed the voyage two months later off Nome, Alaska, we found that we were unable to report our safe emergence from under the Arctic pack via radio because of electromagnetic disturbance in the atmosphere, which was no match for our state-of-the-art equipment. We ended up rowing ashore in a life raft in order to find a pay phone from which to make a collect call to inform our superiors that we had successfully and safely completed our mission.

Fowler: One of the missions of exploration is education and that's changed drastically with the access to worldwide television. We can really teach people what we learn on expeditions.

The other thing is that the study of the movement of animals has been revolutionized by technology. I was in on the ground floor when they first start using the M99, a reliable sniper rifle, as an immobilizer to tranquilize elephants. In the late 1960s, I went on some of the early expeditions in what was then Rhodesia. In those days when we knocked an elephant out with an M99, we didn't know how much antidote to give it to wake the animal up.

The technology has gone from fairly crude immobilization drug techniques to very sophisticated systems. The new drug levels are more appropriate in terms of sedating the animal, and the delivery systems are now based on dart guns or crossbows, which are more accurate than the older rifles. We can also inject a dart that has a radio device attached to it so you don't have to stay with the animal, which might overstress it. You can stay back and give the animal time to go under with the drug and then track it with the radio device. One more thing, I can't say enough about the importance of satellite tracking. Even in the 1960s we were tracking polar bears with satellites, but now satellite tracking has become much more common. It's easier and more accurate than tracking animals on the ground.

The documentation of exploration has always been an important challenge. We can now take small digital cameras with us into the field and document much more than we could in the past.

JJR: *In a world with fewer unexplored places, what do you think is the future of exploration?*

Bennett: There are still many areas of our world that are largely unexplored—places like the hidden landscape beneath the sea, the canopies of our shrouded forests where explorers are solving mysteries about insect outbreaks that may just help us save our rain forests, to the exciting frontiers of deep space.

McLaren: That's right. The deep sea, for example, represents 97 percent of the world's habitable space. There are estimated to be some two million species of life in the deep sea, yet only about three hundred thousand have been identified to date. Humans have seen a small fraction—less that 1 percent—of this vast undersea region. Every dive made to a deep depth is certain to result in the discovery of a new species of marine life. Also the tremendous abundance of microorganisms discovered to be emerging from hydrothermal vents along seafloor spreading areas has resulted in Russian scientists, with whom I have gone to sea, now saying that petroleum may be a renewable resource beneath the deep seabed. This is just one example of the exploration and field science that remains to be done in order to better understand and environmentally protect our planet and all its inhabitants (not just humankind!).

Fowler: As explorers, we are constantly uncovering new knowledge. Every minute that goes by explorers are discovering new information that gives us new perspectives about life on our planet and beyond.

What has been lacking is that those of us who are discoverers and researchers have not always paid attention to our mission of communication. Without communication, finding out all these new things doesn't affect human welfare. The intent of exploration should be to create a better quality of life here on Earth.

JJR: *How does The Explorers Club, which was founded in 1904, stay relevant in the twenty-first century?*

Bennett: Our purpose in 1904 was "to unite explorers in the bonds of good fellowship and to promote the work of exploration by every means in its power." Our purpose is as universally relevant today as it was in 1904, maybe more so.

We can use the tools of the twenty-first century to serve that purpose—we can print, videotape, podcast, and publish the information our members bring back from their fieldwork on the Internet. In other words, we can use the technology that the modern world has available.

As a club, we are adding to the body of the world's knowledge. Our members are discovering places, ideas, and species that will help us fix problems. You don't get more relevant than that.

Fowler: We stay relevant by offering the world increased awareness. We have to put new discoveries into perspective. For instance, it wasn't that long ago—only three hundred or four hundred years ago—that in Central America they were cutting people's throats and giving human flesh to the gods. From our perspective today, that sort of thing seems unimaginable.

Yet, I remember it wasn't that long ago that there was a bounty for killing hawks. But because we had people out in the field studying birds of prey, it became evident that this was a stupid thing to do. Explorers expand our knowledge, which changes accepted perception, especially when they communicate their findings. It's not enough to discover new things without telling the stories of our adventures. That's one of the things that technology can help us do—instead of black-and-white photos, explorers can use all the bells and whistles on their laptops to bring their adventures to life.

McLaren: We have to increase our outreach efforts. It always goes back to education and the sharing of new knowledge! From time to time, our club has gone through periods when we've turned inward and ceased to do this. We need to not only reach young people, but also older fellow citizens, particularly those involved in policy making as it relates to our environment.

We're doing some innovative programs right now. For instance, we have an ongoing partnership with Reach the World, a nonprofit education organization, whose mission is to link students and teachers in low-income communities with real-world expeditions. Recently, we've helped conduct a BioBlitz, which is a 24-hour inventory of species in New York City's Central Park. Each year, the club supports annual grants for field research to graduate, college, and high school students. More and more, our members are launching their own Web sites, which gives everyone access to ongoing expeditions. All of these are steps in the right direction.

Fowler: Our members can go on television and talk about what they've seen on expeditions all over the world. Television is a big part of how we convey this knowledge, but there are other ways—books, lectures, podcasts, Web sites, documentaries, and films. The general public is likely to trust the opinions of field researchers and scientists more than politicians and policy makers. That's why we need to get our message out, especially when it comes to issues such as the overcrowding of our Earth and the extinction of certain species.

Exploration has to do with the future welfare of humanity. I'd like us to be communicating with our fellow citizens about what will happen in the next twenty to fifty years—to say nothing of the year 4000—if we stay on our present course in terms of energy use and population.

JJR: *If time, money, health, and age weren't a factor, what would be your next dream expedition and for what purpose?*

Fowler: Number one, I'd like to see the Earth from outer space. I've always been haunted by our fragile planet. If I want to be an effective spokesman for our world, there would be nothing greater than to see the fragility of our world from outer space. I can't imagine what I would see, but in this day and age, it would no doubt be disturbing images of melting ice caps and other visible threats to our environment.

Here at home, I always like to look at what hasn't been done. There needs to be an expedition to find the spectacled bear and the mountain tapir in the mountains of Peru for the purpose of documenting these two endangered species.

McLaren: I have several in mind! I would like to be the first to dive to the bottom of the sea along the extension of the Mid-Atlantic Ridge into the Arctic Ocean. If ecosystems living on chemosynthesis—the biological conversion of certain carbon molecules into organic matter—such as those in similar seafloor spreading areas in the open Atlantic, Pacific, and Indian oceans, were found in these remote, ice-covered areas, it would increase the probability of finding the same sort of life beneath the sea-ice-covered moons of Jupiter, Europa and Ganymede, and other planets.

I would also like to be the first to reach the bottom of the sea at the North Pole, which lies within one of two very deep basins in the Arctic Ocean, the bottoms of which have been isolated from the rest of the world's ocean for two million years. Heaven knows what sort of marine life is there!

Finally, I would like to use the *SAS Aviator* submersible, of which I am presently senior pilot, to look for evidence of pre-Columbian exploration by ancient sailors on ships on the continental shelves of the Americas.

Bennett: As president of The Explorers Club, I hear all these fascinating plans for expeditions. The latest one I hear about is the one I want to go on.

I'd like to go with Fred here and park myself actually at the bottom of the North Pole. Think about that: 3,172 meters.

If I had to pick only one, it would be every explorer's dream: to fly around the moon—just once—and see what it looks like on the back side.

Final Thoughts

The forty-one explorers who lived to tell these particular tales come from a long list of adventurous storytellers, dating from Christopher Columbus and Vasco da Gama. While the tools used to convey the stories of explorers may have changed since antiquity, the demand for such stories has not diminished.

As surely as a few individuals are driven to tempt injury and even death in order to blaze a trail into the future, the demand for stories about setbacks overcome and the lessons about overcoming adversity along the way has, if anything, increased. Even though there are fewer places on the world's map left to explore, the stakes of exploration have never been higher. Today's explorers, whose far-flung exploits can be documented on digital maps and animated PowerPoint displays and books such as this one, aren't just living to tell their own individual tales; they're tackling issues of planetary survival important to us all.

The Explorers Club

History and Mission Statement

Founded in 1904, The Explorers Club is a multidisciplinary, professional society dedicated to the advancement of field research, scientific exploration, and the ideal that it is vital to preserve the instinct to explore. The overall mission of the club is the encouragement of scientific exploration of land, sea, air, and space, with particular emphasis on the physical and biological sciences. The headquarters for the worldwide activities of The Explorers Club and its chapters is the landmark Lowell Thomas Building on East 70th Street in New York City.

The club is international in scope, with thirty-five hundred members representing every continent and more than sixty countries. Over the years, membership has included polar explorers Roald Amundsen, Robert E. Peary, Matthew Henson, Ernest Shackleton, and Richard C. Byrd; aviators James Doolittle, Charles Lindbergh, and Chuck Yeager; underwater pioneers Sylvia Earle, Jacques Piccard, Don Walsh, and Robert Ballard; astronauts John Glenn, Buzz Aldrin, Neil Armstrong, Sally Ride, and Kathryn Sullivan, and cosmonaut Viktor Savinykh; anthropologists Louis Leakey, Richard Leakey, and Jane Goodall; mountaineers Sir Edmund Hillary and Tenzing Norgay; former U.S. Presidents Theodore Roosevelt and Herbert Hoover; and other notables, including journalist Lowell Thomas, explorer/anthropologist Thor Heyerdahl, and biologist James Watson.

The Explorers Club is a gathering place and unifying force for explorers and field scientists the world over, serving as a base for expedition planning, presentations, meetings, and events. The club's library and archives hold an unparalleled collection of exploration-related literature, documents, and artifacts. Its unique grants programs provide funding to undergraduate and graduate students who are pursuing field research around the globe.

Today, the importance of The Explorers Club's mission remains as powerful as ever: to be a wellspring for the impulse to explore and to serve as a stimulus for the enduring spirit of exploration and scientific inquiry in human life.

For more information on The Explorers Club, go to www.explorers.org